A Short
Dictionary of Simplified
Chinese Characters

BY

E. W. JAMESON, JR.

PROFESSOR OF ZOOLOGY, UNIVERSITY OF CALIFORNIA

DAVIS, CALIFORNIA

Second Edition (Revised), 1967   Sambi Printing Co., Ltd., TOKYO

Preface

This little dictionary was assembled to satisfy my personal need. Although there are numerous tables in which the newly simplified form is correlated with the original, these are very cumbersome and time-consuming to use. As a consequence of the difficulty of reading modern scientific publications from the Chinese mainland, I arranged the simplified characters under the conventional system of radicals, and added the corresponding original form, the pronunciation (according to the Wade-Giles System), and the meaning. I have made no attempt to include either the numerous combined forms or grammatical notes as these are already available in several popular dictionaries.

The desire for such a dictionary of simplified characters surely must not be mine alone. Because these forms are widely used today in popular and technical literature, many students must have experienced the same frustration that has plagued me. I hope that this slender volume will assist others in their studies of modern Chinese publications.

It has occasionally been difficult to place a simplified character under any given radical, and some of my decisions may disturb the bona fide scholar of Chinese. Whenever the original radical has been retained, I have, of course, made no change.

In many cases the simplified form has in it a different and readily apparent radical, and these also offer no difficulty. In a few cases the radical I have selected is certainly not readily apparent, and I have assigned such forms to radicals which seemed most appropriate.

Suggestions and corrections will be greatly appreciated. A greatly expanded revision, including many more characters, is now in preparation.

12 April 1966   E. W. Jameson, Jr.

Preface to Second Edition

This edition is approximately three times as large as the first, and includes more than two thousand simplified characters used in current publications in mainland China. No doubt the list is incomplete, for the proliferation of simplifications seems to continue at a constant rate. The meanings are sometimes vague, especially with regard to names of biological entities, and I have tried to follow usage of modern technical publications.

The organization is essentially as in the first edition. Pronunciation is given in Wade-Giles and in National Phonetic.

I am indebted to Mrs. Irene Liu for the execution of the characters and to Mrs. Ann Carlson for the typing.

14 March 1967   E. W. Jameson, Jr.

Table of Contents

Pattern of Simplification of Characters

Any given simplified character has been created by one of several methods. The result is a reduced number of strokes. This economy occurs most often in the phonetic, but the radical may be altered so that it becomes another radical, the altered radical may no longer represent a radical, or the radical may be dropped completely so that the simplified character may consist of the phonetic of the original one, which itself may be simplified. In a few cases the phonetic is omitted.

A great many of these simplified forms are known to students of Japanese; but the shorter characters are not always those in use in Japan. Many simplifications are the cursory form and well familiar to one who has used them for many years. Unfortunately, most western students are not so experienced, and these simplified forms simply constitute a new character to be learned. These changes may involve either the radical or the phonetic but most often the latter. In 愛 (ài), for example, the radical 心 is replaced by 一 to form 爱. Also, in 黨 (tǎng), the radical 黑 is replaced by 八 to produce 党. The phonetic is simplified in 隊 (tuì), with the resulting 队. By the same token 這 (chè) becomes 这, and 對 (tuì) is changed to 对. There are many such cases in the "writing reform" undertaking by the mainland Chinese government. The new phonetic has lost its phonetic significance; and, except as pointed out below, the change is simply in the direction of orthographic simplicity.

Frequently, however, the simplified character has employed a different phonetic of few strokes, but a well-known phonetic of the same or similar pronunciation. Thus in 達 (tá) 幸 is replaced by 大 with the resulting 达. In 蝦 (hsiā) and 嚇 (hsià) the phonetic is replaced by 下, and the simplified forms are 虾 and 吓. In another case 用 is used as a simplified phonetic for 庸 to make the simplified 佣, 雕 to produce 庸, and 雍 to make 拥; and in each case the pronunciation is yūng. In the above paragraph 人 (jén) replaced 豕 in 隊, the pronunciation of which is tùi: the simplification lacks phonetic significance; but in 認 (jèn) the phonetic is again replaced by 人 to make 訒, in which case the simplified phonetic has an obvious phonetic value. The radical may also be simplified from 言 to 讠 with the resulting 认. The character 几 (chǐ), the simplified form of 幾, can replace this form wherever it occurs. As a phonetic 中 replaces 重, as in 肿 (from 腫, chǔng) and 种 (from 種, chǔng), or 童 in 钟 (from 鐘). But when the phonetic occurs in a character pronounced tung (as in 動, tùng), then 重 is replaced by 云. In a number of characters the phonetic 雚 is replaced by 又: see 劝 (ch'üan), 权 (ch'üan), 观 (kūan), and 欢 (huān). There are many examples of such substitutions.

Simplification by reduplicated substitution often uses the convenient and ubiquitous 又. In 雙 (shuāng), the simplified form is 双, a character well known to a native writer. Another two-stroke substitute is 厶 as in 厸 for 晶 in 壘 (lěi). For the phonetic 聶 there is the substitution 聂 in 摄 (shè) and 鑷 (niè). Another example is the duplicated replacement of 又 for 車 in 轟 (hūng) to make 轰. One wonders how 姦 has been simplified.

Certainly the easiest and most obvious method of simplification is the omission of part of the original form; in most cases in which the simplification is achieved by omission, the radical is dropped. It has been done in cases in which the phonetic by itself is intelligible and unambiguous. Although the simplified character (sans radical) may be identical to an original (unsimplified) character, the meaning should be clear from the context in which each occurs. As an example the radical 麥 (no. 199) may be dropped: 麵 (mièn), wheat flour, then is 面, with the same pronunciation as the radical 面 (no. 176), face or side. Similarly 麯 (chū or ch'ǘ), yeast is 曲, orthographically identical to 曲 (ch'ǖ), meaning crooked or perverse; but there should be no confusion there. In certain cases the radical may be either simplified or omitted. Generally 見 (no. 147) may be written

3

見 , but it is now sometimes omitted: 親 when simplified is written without the radical, or 亲 . Another case is the radical 頁 (no. 181): it may be written 页 , but in some cases (願 or 類) it is dropped. In many cases the radical is omitted: important are the following: 扌 (no. 64), 癶 (no. 79), 門 (no. 169), and 隹 (no. 172). Again, the reader should realize that some radicals may be either omitted or simplified, depending upon the phonetic. 門 (no. 169) is either omitted or written as 门 .

Less commonly a phonetic is omitted. Simplified, 氣 (ch'i) is written 气 , but both the meaning and pronunciation are clear. Simplified, 廣 (kuāng) becomes 广 , the phonetic being lost.

The Simplified Forms and the Standard Equivalents,

Arranged According to Radicals

一 1

2. 与 與 yǔ ㄩ To give; and.

yù To participate.

3. 车 車 ch'ē ㄔㄜ A vehicle (This is radical 159).

乌 烏 wū ㄨ A crow or raven; black.

4. 丛 叢 ts'úng ㄘㄨㄥ Thicket, a grove; crowded.

业 業 yèh ㄝ Profession, occupation.

5. 长 長 ch'áng ㄔㄤ Long, good; excelling. (Radical 168).

6. 丽 麗 lì ㄌㄧ Beautiful, elegant.

丨 2

3. 丰 豐 fēng ㄈㄥ Rich, abundant.

书 書 shū ㄕㄨ A book; to write.

韦 韋 wéi ㄨㄟ Leather, hide (This is radical 178).

丶 3

1. 讠 言 yén ㄧㄢ Speech, language (This is radical 149).

丿 4

2. 乡 鄉 hsiāng ㄒㄧㄤ Rural, rustic.

6

2. 义 義 ì ˉ Right (correct), meaning; - ism.

3. 収 取 chīen ㄐㄧㄢ Firm, strong.

8. 临 臨 lín ㄌㄧㄣ To approach, draw near; just before, about to; provisional.

乙 5

6. 乱 亂 lùan ㄌㄨㄢ Disorderly, reckless, rebellion, anarchy; to confuse.

㇓ 6

1. 了 瞭 .liáo ㄌㄧㄠ Clear; to understand; to clarify.

二 7

1. 亏 虧 k'ūei ㄎㄨㄟ Deficiency, loss.

2. 专 專 chūan ㄓㄨㄢ Only, specially; alone, unassisted; to assume responsibility.

   开 開 k'āi ㄎㄞ To open; to explain; to operate.

3. 兰 蘭 lán ㄌㄢ Orchid.

4. 亚 亞 yǎ ㄧㄚ Transliteration for a; 亞洲

亠 8

4. 产 產 ch'ǎn ㄔㄢ To produce; reproduce (biol.).

   齐 齊 ch'í ㄑㄧ Even, equal, uniform; to arrange (This is radical 210).

   亦 䜌 lùan ㄌㄨㄢ To tie together.

7. 亲 親 ch'īn ㄑㄧㄣ Related, near to; parent; intimate, to love, to kiss.

8。 离 離 lí ㄌㄧˊ Distant from.

亻 人 9

1. 亿 億 ì ㄧˋ — A hundred thousand.

   个 個 kò ㄍㄜˋ (Classifier for persons or things)。

2. 仅 僅 chǐn ㄐㄧㄣˇ Merely, barely; barely enough.

   仑 侖 lún ㄌㄨㄣˊ To think; to arrange.

   仆 僕 p'ú ㄆㄨˊ Servant.

   什 甚 shén ㄕㄣˊ What? (e.g., 什 么)。

   仓 倉 ts'āng ㄘㄤ Granary; surname.

   仓 艙 ts'āng ㄘㄤ Cabin, hold of a ship.

   从 從 ts'úng ㄘㄨㄥˊ From; to follow.

3. 仪 儀 ì ㄧ — To discuss, talk over; to consult.

   们 們 mén ㄇㄣ Plural suffix, applied to pronouns,
   or personal nouns.

4。 价 價 chià ㄐㄧㄚˋ Value。

   传 傳 ch'úan ㄔㄨㄢˊ To preach, promulgate, perpetuate;
   to interpret; to spread, as a rumor
   or conduct electricity.

   众 衆 chùng ㄓㄨㄥˋ Great number, crowd; all, entirety.

   会 會 huǐ ㄏㄨㄟˇ A moment.

       huì   To meet。

   伙 夥 hǔo ㄏㄨㄛˇ A band, group of companions; buddies.

   伦 倫 lún ㄌㄨㄣˊ Constant, ordinary, regular; natural
   relationships; degrees (in comparison).

   伞 傘 sǎn ㄙㄢˇ Umbrella.

伤	傷	shāng ㄕㄤ	To hurt, wound; distressed.
伧	傖	ts'āng ㄘㄤ	Confused, disorderly.
伪	偽	wèi ㄨㄟ	False.
伟	偉	wěi ㄨㄟ	Admirable, powerful; fine-looking.
优	優	yū ㄧㄡ	Superior.
伛	傴	yǔ ㄩ	Hunchbacked.

5.
伥	倀	ch'āng ㄔㄤ	Rash, wildly.
佥	僉	ch'īen ㄑㄧㄢ	All, unanimous.
体	體	t'ǐ ㄊㄧ	Body, form, substance.
佣	傭	yūng ㄩㄥ	To employ, hire.
余	餘	yǘ ㄩ	The rest, remainder.

6.
侪	儕	ch'ái ㄔㄞ	A class, company.
侦	偵	chēn ㄓㄣ	A scout, spy.
侥	僥	chǐao ㄐㄧㄠ	By luck or chance.
侨	僑	ch'iáo ㄑㄧㄠ	An inn; to sojourn; tall.
侠	俠	hsía ㄒㄧㄚ	Generous, heroic, bold; a knight-errant.
侩	儈	k'uai ㄎㄨㄞ	A broker, middleman; to hint.
舍	捨	shě ㄕㄜ	To give up, part with, relinquish.
侧	側	ts'è ㄘㄜ	The side; prejudiced; mean; to incline to.

7.
俭	儉	chiěn ㄐㄧㄢ	Frugal, economical.
俦	儔	ch'óu ㄔㄡ	A group of four people; friends.
俪	儷	lì ㄌㄧ	A pair, couple.
俩	倆	lǐa ㄌㄧㄚ	Two.
侬	儂	núng ㄋㄨㄥ	First personal pronoun (archaic).
俨	儼	yěn ㄧㄢ	Majestic, stern; like, as.

8. 债 債 chai 㞷 To be in debt.

借 藉 chièh 㐭 By means of, to borrow.

倾 傾 chǐng 㿟 To upset; to be overthrown; to collapse; to fall flat.

9. 偿 償 cháng 㿜 To recompense; indemnity.

偻 僂 lóu 㐭 Hunchback; bent, deformed.

lǚ 㐭 To bend.

10. 储 儲 ch'ú 㐭 To collect, store; savings.

偾 僨 fèn 㐭 To ruin.

龛 龕 k'ān 㐭 A shrine or recess for an idol; to contain.

傩 儺 nó 㐭 To exorcise the devil.

傥 儻 t'ǎng 㐭 If, supposing.

儿 10

儿 兒 érh 㐭 Diminutive suffix.

4. 尧 堯 yáo 㐭 Lofty; Emperor Yao.

5. 克 剋 k'ò 㐭 To subdue, control, overcome.

八 12

4. 乔 喬 ch'iáo Tall, lofty; a surname.

兴 興 hsìng 㐭 Interest.

hsīng To flourish.

6. 凭 憑 p'íng 㐭 Proof, evidence; rely upon; according to.

7. 舉 舉 chǔ ㄐㄩˇ To lift, raise; to elect.

8. 养 養 yǎng ㄧㄤˇ To give birth to; to rear, care for, support.

冂　13

2. 见 見 chìen ㄐㄧㄢˋ To see, meet (This is radical 147).

　 冈 岡 kāng ㄍㄤ Ridge, hill; a mound.

　 贝 具 pèi ㄅㄟˋ Shell, clamshell; precious (This is radical 154).

4. 网 網 wǎng ㄨㄤˇ A net; to fish (with a net).

　 页 頁 yèh ㄧㄝˋ A page, leaf (This is radical 181).

5. 两 兩 lǐang ㄌㄧㄤˇ Two (used with 個).

　 肃 肅 sù ㄙㄨˋ Stern, respectful; to write; Kansu.

6. 丽 麗 lí ㄌㄧˊ Hsien and river in Yunnan.

　 　 lì Beautiful, glamorous, elegant.

冖　14

3. 尔 爾 ěrh ㄦˇ You; just so.

4. 写 寫 hsǐeh ㄒㄧㄝˇ To write.

冫　15

2. 习 習 hsí ㄒㄧˊ To practice; habit.

11

4. 冲 衝　ch'ūng ㄔㄨㄥ　To rush to; collide.

　　　　　　ch'ùng　Facing.

5. 冻 凍　tùng ㄉㄨㄥ　To freeze, jell; very cold.

8. 准 準　chŭn ㄓㄨㄣ　Exact, tone; to measure; to adjust, equalize; to allow.

几　16

几 幾　chī ㄐㄧ　Very nearly.

　　　　chĭ　How much; how many?

2. 风 風　fēng ㄈㄥ　Wind　(This is radical 182).

风 鳳　fèng ㄈㄥ　Phoenix, symbol of joy.

6. 凯 凱　k'ăi ㄎㄞ　Victory; victorious return.

凭 憑　p'íng ㄆㄥ　According to, as.

凵　17

3. 出 齣　ch'ū ㄔㄨ　A stanza, couple; classifier for plays.

10. 凿 鑿　tsò ㄗㄨㄛ　A chisel; to chisel.

刀 刂　18

4. 划 劃　hùa ㄏㄨㄚ　To designate; to mark off.

创 創　ch'ùang　To create, invent; to begin.

刚 剛　kāng ㄍㄤ　Hard; constant, enduring.

刘 劉　liú ㄌㄧㄡ　Surname; to slay, destroy.

则 則　tsé ㄗㄜ　A rule, standard, patterns, a particle denoting responses in accordance with.

12

5. 划 劃 ch'ǎn ㄔㄢˇ To level off, trim.

　 刭 剄 chǐng ㄐㄧㄥˇ To cut the throat.

　 別 彆 piěh ㄅㄧㄝˋ Difficult, contrary; awkward.

6. 刘 劑 chì ㄗ To trim; to adjust; to compound medicine.

　 制 製 chìh ㄓ To cut and make clothes; to construct, build.

　 剀 剴 kāi ㄍㄞ To sharpen a knife; carefully; to influence.

　 刮 颳 kūa ㄍㄨㄚ To blow (wind); to be blown.

　 刿 劌 kùei ㄍㄨㄟˋ To cut, injure, wound.

　 刽 劊 kùei ㄍㄨㄟˋ To cut, amputate.

7. 剑 劍 chìen ㄐㄧㄢˋ A double-edged sword.

　 剐 剮 kǔa ㄍㄨㄚˇ To hack to pieces (e.g., a criminal).

8. 剧 劇 chǜ ㄐㄩ Severe, intense; very; annoying, troublesome; a play.

力　19

1. 万 萬 wàn ㄨㄢ Ten thousand.

2. 劝 勸 ch'ùan ㄑㄩㄢˋ To urge, persuade.

　 办 辦 pàn ㄅㄢˋ To manage, do, transact.

　 为 爲 wèi ㄨㄟˋ For, because.

　　　　 wéi 　 Is, as.

　 扬 揚 yáng ㄧㄤˊ To expand; bright, glorious.

3. 务 務 wù ㄨ Matter, affair; necessary.

4. 动 動 tùng ㄉㄨㄥˋ To move.

5. 劲 勁 chìng ㄐㄧㄥˋ Strong, muscular.

13

		chìn	ㄐㄣ	(alternate).
劳	勞	lǎo	ㄌㄠ	To toil, suffer, weary; to labor.
		lào		To reward, compensate.
励	勵	lì	ㄌㄧ	To encourage, urge.
6. 执	勢	shìh	ㄕ	Power, influence, strength; aspect, conditions.
7. 勋	勛	hsūn	ㄒㄩㄣ	Merit.
9. 勚	勩	ì	-	Toil, affliction.

ㄅ　20

1. 饣	食	shíh	ㄕ	To eat.　(This is radical 184.)

匚　22

6. 匦	匭	kuěi	ㄍㄨㄟ	A casket, small box.
9. 匮	匱	kuèi	ㄍㄨㄟ	A cupboard, wardrobe; shop-counter.

匚　23

2. 区	區	ch'ǖ	ㄑㄩ	District, region.
		oū	ㄡ	A surname.
5. 医	醫	ī	-	Medicine.

4. 协 協　hsíeh ㄒㄧㄝ　Mutual; cooperate; to aid, help; to harmonize。

　　华 華　húa ㄏㄨㄚ　Flowery, elegant; glory, splendor.

5. 毕 畢　pì ㄅㄧ　To finish, end.

　　卜 蔔　pei ㄅㄛ　Carrot, turnip, or radish.

1. 卫 衛　wei ㄨㄟ　To protect; to escort.

6. 卷 捲　chǔan ㄐㄩㄢ　To gather, grasp; to roll up, curly.

　　厂 廠　ch'ǎng ㄔㄤ　A mill, factory.

2. 历 歷　lì ㄌㄧ　To pass through, successive。

　　历 曆　lì ㄌㄧ　Calendar。

　　厅 廳　t'īng ㄊㄧㄥ　Parlor, court.

3. 厉 厲　lì ㄌㄧ　Severe.

4. 压 壓　yā ㄧㄚ　To press down.

　　厌 厭　yèn ㄧㄢ　To be disgusted; to dislike.

5. 严 嚴　yén ㄧㄢ　Stern, severe; tight.

6. 厕 廁　ts'è ㄘㄜ　The side, prejudiced。

4. 厍 厙　shè ㄕㄜ　A surname.

9. 厌 厭 yěn 一ㄢ Nightmare.

12. 愿 願 yüan ㄩㄢ Willing; to wish.

厶 28

1. 么 麼 ma ㄇㄜ Interrogatory suffix.

2. 云 雲 yún ㄩㄣ Cloud.

5. 县 縣 hsièn ㄒㄧㄢ District, hsien, prefecture.

6. 参 參 ts'ān ㄘㄢ To participate in; to attend.

7. 尝 嘗 ch'áng ㄔㄤ To taste, experience; formerly.

10. 叆 靉 ai ㄞ Cloudy, obscure, nebulous.

12. 叇 靆 tai ㄉㄞ Cloudy sky.

又 29

2. 双 雙 shūang ㄕㄨㄤ A pair (of), a couple.

3. 发 發 fā ㄈㄚ To manifest; send out; to develop (an ailment).

发 髮 fǎ ㄈㄚ Hair on human head.

圣 睪 ì 一 To spy.

6. 变 變 pièn ㄅㄧㄢ To change, alter; rebellion.

口 30

2. 叽 嘰 chī ㄐ A kind of cloth; (used in transliterating).

只 戠 chīh ㄓ A sword; to gather.

只 祇 chīh ㄓ To respect.

16

只 隻 chīh ㄓ A classifier for objects of a pair (e.g. arms, legs).

号 號 hào ㄏㄠ A mark, sign; (ordinal suffix).

台 颱 t'āi ㄊㄞ Strong wind.

台 臺 t'ái ㄊㄞ Terrace, stage, platform.

台 檯 t'ái ㄊㄞ Desk, table.

叹 嘆 t'àn ㄊㄢ To sigh.

叶 葉 yèh ㄧㄝ Leaf.

3. 合 閤 hó ㄏㄜ A small side door.

后 後 hoù ㄏㄡ After, behind; the back; to come after.

吓 嚇 hsìa ㄒㄧㄚ To frighten.

向 嚮 hsiang ㄒㄧㄤ Opposite, to lean towards; to guide; to show one's mind; to encourage.

吗 嗎 ma ㄇㄚ An interrogative suffix.

问 問 wèn ㄨㄣ To ask, inquire; to hold responsible; to sentence (legally).

吁 籲 yǜ ㄩ To beseach, implore.

4. 启 啓 ch'ǐ ㄑㄧ To begin, explain; to open (after addressee's name on envelope).

呛 嗆 ch'īang ㄑㄧㄤ To cough.

呖 嚦 lì ㄌㄧ An exclamation to indicate a clear sound.

呕 嘔 oǔ ㄡ To vomit, barf, puke.

呗 唄 pài ㄅㄞ To recite.

听 聽 t'īng ㄊㄧㄥ To hear, listen; to understand.

吨 噸 tùn ㄊㄨㄣ Ton.

呜 嗚 wū ㄨ Exclamation of regret.

17

4. 员 員 yüan ㄩㄢ An official, a member.

5. 呓 囈 ì – To talk in one's sleep.

   哢 嚨 lúng ㄌㄨㄥ The throat.

   黾 黽 mǐn ㄇㄧㄣ A toad, tree-frog; to put forth effort. Radical 205.

   鸣 鳴 míng ㄇㄧㄥ To make a sound; the sound or cry of an animal.

   咛 嚀 níng ㄋㄧㄥ To enjoin, charge with; to order.

6. 响 響 hsǐang ㄒㄧㄤ Loud; to make a sound.

   哓 嘵 hsīao ㄒㄧㄠ Querulous.

   咸 鹹 hsíen ㄒㄧㄢ Salty.

   哗 嘩 hūa ㄏㄨㄚ Clamour, noise.

   哙 噲 kùai ㄎㄨㄞ A man's name.

           k'ùai ㄎㄨㄞ To swallow; greedy, pleasant, bright.

   骂 罵 mà ㄇㄚ To scold, abuse.

   哑 啞 yǎ ㄚ Mute, dumb; confused.

   哟 喲 yō ㄧㄛ An exclamation.

   哕 噦 yüeh ㄩㄝ To belch, burp; to vomit.

7. 呙 喎 k'ūai ㄎㄨㄞ A wry mouth.

   唠 嘮 láo ㄌㄠ To chatter constantly; gabby; to blabber.

   唡 啢 lǐang ㄌㄧㄤ An ounce.

   唛 嘜 mà ㄇㄚ A brand name or trade mark.

   哝 噥 nūng ㄋㄨㄥ Loquacious.

   哔 嗶 pì ㄅㄧ Crackling of fire.

   唢 嗩 sǔo ㄙㄨㄛ Garrulous.

18

嘶	噝	szū	ㄙ	To hiss, call to come.
哒	噠	tá	ㄊㄚˊ	Name for country.
党	黨	tǎng	ㄉㄤˇ	Party; group.
8. 啭	囀	chǔan	ㄔㄨㄢˇ	To warble like a bird.
啸	嘯	hsiao	ㄒㄧㄠˋ	A hissing sound; to scream, whistle
		sù	ㄙㄨˋ	A moan.
啮	齧	nìeh	ㄋㄧㄝˋ	To gnaw, bite.
啬	嗇	sè	ㄙㄜˋ	Sting.
兽	獸	shòu	ㄕㄡˋ	Animal, beast.
啧	嘖	tsé	ㄗㄜˊ	To call out; to make an uproar.
9. 嚳	嚳	k'ù	ㄎㄨˋ	To inform promptly.
喽	嘍	lóu	ㄌㄡˊ	To chatter, mutter; see 娄.
喷	噴	p'ēn	ㄆㄣ	To blow out, pull out; to spurt out.
10. 嗳	嗳	ai	ㄞˋ	Oh dear. (the exclamation).
嗫	囁	nìeh	ㄋㄧㄝˋ	To move the mouth as in speaking; to chatter.
辔	轡	p'èi	ㄆㄟˋ	Reins, a bridle. Also written 缂.
11. 嘱	囑	chǔ	ㄓㄨˇ	To order, direct; to admonish; to instruct.
嘤	嚶	yīng	ㄧㄥ	Melody of birds; bird songs.
12. 噜	嚕	lǔ	ㄌㄨˇ	Speech; to flatter; to pout.
15. 嚣	囂	hsīao	ㄒㄧㄠ	Din, clamor.

口　31

3. 回	迴	húi	ㄏㄨㄟˊ	To revolve, circle, return.

团	糰	t'úan	ㄊㄨㄢ	Dumplings.
团	團	t'úan		Round.
		t'úan		To crumple.

4.
困	捆	k'ǔn	ㄎㄨㄣ	To tie together, bind: to plait.
困	睏	k'ùn	ㄎㄨㄣ	To sleep, nap, to nod。
卤	鹵	lǔ	ㄌㄨ	Salt, alkaline soil; this is radical 197.
仑	侖	lún	ㄌㄨㄣ	Complete, whole.
围	圍	wéi	ㄨㄟ	To surround; circumference; a span.
园	園	yǔan	ㄩㄢ	Garden, park.

5.
国	國	kúo	ㄍㄨㄛ	A country, state.
图	圖	t'ú	ㄊㄨ	To plan; drawing, plan, figure, illustration, map.

7.
圆	圓	yǔan	ㄩㄢ	Round; a dollar, to explain, tell.

土 32

2.
圣	聖	shèng	ㄕㄥ	Holy, sacred; wise.

3.
尘	塵	ch'én	ㄔㄣ	Dust, dirt.
圹	壙	k'ūang	ㄎㄨㄤ	A vault or tomb; brick grave.

4.
坚	堅	chīen	ㄐㄧㄢ	Hard, firm, durable。
场	場	ch'ǎng	ㄔㄤ	An open space, field.
坟	墳	fén	ㄈㄣ	A grave, mound.
坏	壞	hùai	ㄏㄨㄞ	Bad, spoiled; to ruin, spoil.
块	塊	k'ùai	ㄎㄨㄞ	Lump, piece.
坜	壢	lì	ㄌㄧ	A place name.
坝	壩	pà	ㄅㄚ	An embankment.

20

坛 鐔 t'án ㄊㄢ Earthenware jar.

坛 壇 t'án ㄊㄢ An alter (of earth).

坞 塢 wù ㄨ A low wall, embankment.

5. 坠 隆 chùi ㄔㄨㄟ To fall down, sink.

垆 壚 lú ㄌㄨ Dark clods of earth; a shop or hut; a stove.

垄 壟 lǔng ㄌㄨㄥ A mound of earth.

丧 喪 sāng ㄙㄤ Mourning; to mourn.

　　　　 sàng To lose, ruin.

6. 垲 塏 k'ǎi ㄎㄞ A kind of soil, kaolin, or a paste from that soil, used in making porcelain.

垦 墾 k'ěn ㄎㄣ To open up, reclaim.

垒 壘 lěi ㄌㄟ A wall or rampart.

垫 墊 tien ㄉㄧㄢ To put under as a prop; a cushion.

垩 堊 yà ㄧㄚ White clay, used in making procelain.

茔 塋 ying ㄧㄥ A grave, tomb.

7. 埙 塤 hsün ㄒㄩㄣ An ancient terra-cotta musical instrument, like an ocarina or sweet potato.

埚 堝 kūo ㄍㄨㄛ A crucible.

坝 壩 pà ㄅㄚ A dyke, dam, breakwater.

埘 塒 shih ㄕ Chicken coop.

8. 堑 塹 ch'ien ㄑㄧㄢ Moat, channel.

堕 墮 tò ㄉㄨㄛ To fall, drop.

9. 隳 隳 tò ㄉㄨㄛ To fall, sink; to set.

11. 墙 墻 ch'iang ㄑㄧㄤ A wall.

21

3. 壮 壯 chùang ㄓㄨㄤ Strong, robust.

4. 壳 殼 k'ō ㄎ A skin or husk; egg shell; shed
ㄛ skin of reptiles or arthropods;
shell of a mollusc.

声 聲 shēng ㄕㄥ Voice, noise.

7. 壶 壺 hú ㄏㄨ A kettle, jug; a vase.

8. 壶 壼 k'ǔn ㄎㄨㄣ Apartments; a corridor in a palace;
cf. 壺 .

2. 冬 鼕 t'ūng ㄉㄨㄥ Noise of drums.

2. 处 處 ch'ù ㄔㄨ Place.

6. 复 覆 fú ㄈㄨ To reply, answer; to repeat.

复 複 fù ㄈㄨ Complex, double; double garment.

复 復 fù ㄈㄨ To return to or recover; again.

7. 爱 愛 ai ㄞ To love (to ....).

8. 麸 麩 fū ㄈㄨ Bran.

梦 夢 mèng ㄇㄥ To dream, a dream.

2. 头　頭　t'óu ㄊㄡ　Head.

3. 夹　夾　chia ㄐㄚ　To pinch, squeeze.

   夸　誇　k'ūa ㄎㄨㄚ　To boast.

   关　關　kūan ㄍㄨㄢ　A mountain pass, entry; custom-house.

   买　買　mǎi ㄇㄞ　To buy.

   夺　奪　tó ㄉㄨㄛ　To rob, take by force.

4. 奁　奩　lien ㄌㄧㄢ　A lady's dresser; a bridal trousseau.

5. 奋　奮　fèn ㄈㄣ　To exert oneself.

   卖　賣　mai ㄇㄞ　To sell.

6. 奖　獎　chiǎng ㄐㄧㄤ　A prize, reward; to encourage.

   类　類　lèi ㄌㄟ　Class, species, genus.

3. 妆　妝　chūang ㄓㄨㄤ　Adornment.

   妇　婦　fù ㄈㄨ　Woman, women (generically), wife.

   妈　媽　mā ㄇㄚ　Mother, an old woman.

4. 妫　媯　kūi ㄍㄨㄟ　A river in Shansi; crafty.

   妩　嫵　wǔ ㄨ　To please; to fawn, flatter.

   妪　嫗　yǔ ㄩ　An old woman.

      yǔ　To brood over; to protect.

一

6. 姜 薑 chīang ㄐㄧㄤ Ginger。

娇 嬌 chīao ㄐㄧㄠ Beautiful, graceful.

娆 嬈 jáo ㄖㄠ Graceful, fascinating.

yǎo ㄧㄠ Tender and weak.

娄 嘍 lóu ㄌㄡ To chatter, mutter; see 口娄 .

娄 婁 lǒu ㄌㄡ To follow; to trail behind; to wear。

娈 孌 lǔan ㄌㄩㄢ Beautiful, handsome; admirable。

lǐen ㄌㄧㄢ (Variant)。

娅 婭 yà ㄧㄚ Term of address used between sons-in-law。

7. 娴 嫻 hsíen ㄒㄧㄢ Elegant, refined; accomplished.

娉 嬪 pīn ㄅㄧㄣ A concubine; to become a wife.

pín ㄆㄧㄣ (Variant).

娲 媧 wā ㄨㄚ Sister of Fu Hsi.

8. 婳 嫿 hùa ㄏㄨㄚ Feminine, coy.

婵 嬋 shán ㄕㄢ Beautiful, graceful.

婶 嬸 shěn ㄕㄣ Wife of father's younger brother.

婴 嬰 yīng ㄧㄥ An infant, esp. a girl.

10. 嫒 嬡 ai ㄞ Formal word for daughter.

11. 嫱 嬙 ch'íang ㄑㄧㄤ Women court officials (archaic).

子 39

3. 孙 孫 sūn ㄙㄨㄣ Grandson.

5. 学 學 hsǘeh ㄒㄩㄝ To learn, study, practice; a branch of learning.

6. 孪 孿 lúan ㄌㄨㄢ To bear twins.

亦 孿 shùan ㄕㄨㄢ (Variant).

宀 40

2. 宁 寧 níng ㄋㄧㄥ Peaceful; rather; it is better, would that.

4. 农 農 néng ㄋㄨㄥ To cultivate; agriculture.

5. 宠 寵 ch'ǔng ㄔㄨㄥ To favor; kindness.

宝 寶 păo ㄅㄠ Precious, valuable.

审 審 shěn ㄕㄣ To contest (legally); investigate, examine.

实 實 shíh ㄕ Solid (not hollow).

寫 寫 tìao ㄉㄧㄠ Deep, profound.

6. 宪 憲 hsìen ㄒㄧㄢ A constitution; governmental official.

宾 賓 pīn ㄅㄧㄣ A guest; to submit, entertain.

7. 家 傢 chīa ㄐㄧㄚ Tools, utensils; furniture.

宽 寬 k'ūan ㄎㄨㄢ Broad, ample, spacious; liberal, forgiving.

10. 寝 寢 ch'ǐn ㄑㄧㄣ To sleep, rest; an apartment, bed-chamber.

寸 41

2. 导 導 tăo ㄉㄠ To guide, teach.

对 對 tùi ㄉㄨㄟ Opposite, matching; a pair.

3. 将 將 chīang ㄐㄧㄤ To take; (pretransitive, as 把.

chìang A general.

寻 尋 hsún ㄒㄩㄣ To seek; usual.

4. 寿 壽 shòu ㄕㄡ Span of life-age; a surname.

小　42

2. 尔 爾 ěrh ㄦ You, your.

尢　43

9. 尲 尷 kān ㄍㄢ Embarrassing circumstance.

尸　44

2. 卢 盧 lú ㄌㄨ Rice vessel.
3. 尽 儘 chǐn ㄐㄧㄣ As far as possible; to finish, complete.
　 尽 盡 chìn ㄐㄧㄣ Exhaustive (ly); all, entirely.
4. 层 層 ts'éng ㄘㄥ A story, floor; degree.
8. 属 屬 shǔ ㄕㄨ Belonging to; to be related; sort.
9. 屡 屢 lǚ ㄌㄩ Repeatedly, often, constantly.
12. 屦 屨 chù ㄐㄩ Sandles, straw shoes.
15. 羼 羼 ch'ān ㄔㄢ To laugh out.

山　46

2. 击 擊 chī ㄐㄧ To hit, strike.
3. 岂 豈 ch'ǐ ㄑㄧ How (can it be)? (interrogative particle).
　 　 k'ǎi ㄎㄞ Delighted.

屿	嶼	hsü or yü	亼	A small island.
岁	歲	sui	亼	Year, age, harvest.
4. 岖	嶇	ch'ü	厶	A steep slope.
岘	峴	hsien	丅弓	A steep hill.
岗	岡	kāng	《左	Ridge of a hill.
岚	嵐	lán	为弓	Vapor, mist.
岛	島	tǎo	云	An island.
峄	嶧	i	–	Name of hills in Shantung and Kiangsu.
5. 岿	巋	k'ūei	丂	A range of hills; grand.
		kùei		(Variant).
岭	嶺	líng	为云	A mountain range, mountain pass.
6. 峤	嶠	ch'iao	丂	A mountain ridge or peak.
峡	峽	hsia	丅丫	Hills on each side of a gorge; a gorge, ravine.
峦	巒	lúan	为乂弓	Mountain peaks.
7. 崃	崍	lái	为弓	A place name in Shantung.
崂	嶗	láo	为幺	Mountains in Shantung.
崭	嶄	ch'án	彳弓	A cliff.
9. 嵝	嶁	lǒu	为乂	A mountain in Hunan.
10. 嵘	嶸	yǔng	凵乚	Lofty, prominent, majestic.
		júng	凵乚	(Alternate).
15. 巅	巔	tíen	勿弓	Mountain peak.

2. 坙 巠 chīng ㄑㄥˇ Underground streams.
3. 巩 鞏 kǔng ㄍㄨㄥˇ Secure, solid.

巾　50

1. 巿 幣 pì ㄆㄧˋ Coin, wealth; present.
2. 帅 帥 shùai ㄕㄨㄞˋ To lead, guide, command; leader, commander.
3. 师 師 shīh ㄕ Teacher; military division.
4. 帐 帳 chàng ㄓㄤˋ A tent; a curtain; scrolls; to spread out; accounts.
　　幃 幃 wéi ㄨㄟˊ A curtain; women's apartment.
5. 帜 幟 chìh ㄓˋ A flag; to fasten.
　　帘 簾 lién ㄌㄧㄢˊ A loose-hanging screen, curtain.
6. 帧 幀 chēn ㄓㄣ A picture; one of a pair (as scrolls).
　　带 帶 tài ㄉㄞˋ A belt, zone, ribbon.
7. 帮 幫 pāng ㄅㄤ To help.
8. 帼 幗 kūo ㄍㄨㄛ A cap worn by women.
　　帻 幘 tsé ㄗㄜˊ A conical cap, a turban.

十　51

千 鞦 ch'īen ㄑㄧㄢ A swing.
干 乾 kān ㄍㄢ Dry, clean.
干 幹 kàn ㄍㄢˋ To do, manage.
于 於 yǘ ㄩ With, at, in; concerning, referring to.

28

	广	廣	kǔang ㄍㄨㄤ	Broad, extensive.
2.	庆	慶	ch'ing ㄑㄧㄥ	To congratulate.
3.	庄	莊	chūang ㄓㄨㄤ	Dignified; a farm, village, shop.
4.	库	庫	k'ù ㄎㄨ	A treasury or storehouse, a granary.
	庐	廬	lú ㄌㄨ	Hut.
	庑	廡	wǔ ㄨ	A covered path or walk; a porch.
	应	應	yīng ㄧㄥ	Ought, must.
5.	废	廢	fèi ㄈㄟ	To abolish.
	庙	廟	miào ㄇㄧㄠ	A temple, a monastery.
	庞	龐	p'áng ㄆㄤ	A high house; confused.
9.	赓	賡	kēng	To continue.

5.	张	張	chāng ㄓㄤ	To draw a bow.
	弥	彌	mí ㄇ	To fill; full; long distant; used in transliterating.
	弥	瀰	mí ㄇ	A watery expanse.
			mǐ	Overflowing.
6.	弯	彎	wān ㄨㄢ	To bend; curved.
8.	弹	彈	t'án ㄊㄢ	To strum (an instrument); to snap the finger; to rebound; to press down.

8. 弹 彈 tàn ㄉㄢ A bullet, pellet, shot; a crossbow.

ㄓ 58

1. 丑 醜 ch'ǒu ㄔㄡ Physically or morally unattractive; ugly, deformed.

2. 刍 芻 ch'ú ㄔㄨ To cut grass; hay, straw.

   归 歸 kūei ㄍㄨㄟ Marriage of a woman; return; to restore; to send back.

3. 当 當 tāng ㄉㄤ Just at; ought, suitable.

   当 噹 tàng ㄉㄤ To consider as.

   tāng Dong (sound of bell).

4. 灵 靈 líng ㄌㄧㄥ Spirit; spiritual, devine; super-natural; intelligent, ingenious; a coffin with a corpse.

   录 錄 lù ㄌㄨ To record.

彳 60

4. 彻 徹 ch'è ㄔㄜ To penetrate; discerning; pure.

5. 征 徵 chēng ㄓㄥ To draft (military service); to collect duty.

   径 徑 chìng ㄐㄧㄥ A short cut; diameter; direct, straight.

7. 徕 徠 lài ㄌㄞ To urge, encourage; to induce to come.

9. 御 禦 yǔ ㄩ To withstand, resist, hinder; an opponent.

1. 忆 憶 ì　-　To remember, bring to mind.

3. 忏 懺 ch'àn ㄔㄢ To regret, repent; Buddhist and Taoist ritual.

闷 悶 mén ㄇㄣ Mournful, melancholy; depressed; to cover.

4. 怆 愴 ch'ùang ㄔㄨㄤ Sad.

忾 愾 hsì ㄒㄧ To sigh, groan.

怀 懷 húai ㄏㄨㄞ The bosom; to carry; to be pregnant, to cherish.

怄 慪 òu ㄡ To excite, irritate.

　　 kōu ㄎㄡ Stingy, petty.

怂 慫 sŭng ㄙㄨㄥ To alarm, alert.

　　 tsŭng ㄗㄨㄥ (Variant).

态 態 t'ài ㄊㄞ Attitude.

怃 憮 wŭ ㄨ Disappointed, disraught; to cherish.

　.hsŭ ㄒㄩ Arrogant; to fawn upon.

　　 hū ㄏㄨ Great; arrogant.

忧 憂 yū ㄧㄡ To be worried, anxious; sad.

5. 怅 悵 ch'àng ㄔㄤ Disappointed, dissatisfied.
怿 懌 ì　-　To rejoice, pleased.
怜 憐 lien ㄌㄧㄢ Pity; to pity, sympathize.
总 總 tsŭng ㄗㄨㄥ General, always, ever.
怼 懟 tùi ㄉㄨㄟ To dislike.

6. 恺 愷 k'ăi ㄎㄞ Joyful, good, kind.
恳 懇 k'ĕn ㄎㄣ To request, beg; earnestly; honest.

31

慮	慮	lü	ㄌㄩ	To plan, care for; anxious.
恋	戀	lüan	ㄌㄩㄢ	To hanker after; to dote on, be fond of.
		lìen	ㄌㄧㄢ	(Variant).
恼	惱	nǎo	ㄋㄠ	To get angry; resentful.
恶	惡	ò	ㄜ	Evil, bad; to hate.
恻	惻	ts'è	ㄘㄜ	To pity, sympathize with.
恸	慟	t'ùng	ㄊㄨㄥ	Grief, sadness.
恶	噁	wǔ	ㄨ	Rage.
恹	懨	yèn	ㄧㄢ	Sickly.
恽	惲	yǔn	ㄩㄣ	To deliberate, consult.
7. 悭	慳	ch'īen	ㄑㄧㄢ	Penurious, stingy.
悫	慤	ch'ǜeh	ㄑㄩㄝ	Guileless, upright; ingenuous.
惧	懼	chǜ	ㄐㄩ	To fear.
悬	懸	hsǘan	ㄒㄩㄢ	To suspend; anxious; distant from; separated.
悯	憫	mǐn	ㄇㄧㄣ	To sympathize with; to pity.
8. 惩	懲	ch'éng	ㄔㄥ	To correct, punish; to warn.
惬	愜	ch'ièh	ㄑㄧㄝ	Satisfied, contented; cheerful.
惊	驚	chīng	ㄐㄧㄥ	Alarm.
惯	慣	kùan	ㄍㄨㄢ	Accustomed; experienced.
惫	憊	pèi	ㄅㄟ	Exhausted, worn out, fatigued.
惮	憚	tàn	ㄉㄢ	To shrink from; to dread.
惭	慚	ts'án	ㄘㄢ	Ashamed.
惨	慘	ts'ǎn	ㄘㄢ	Grieved; sad; cruel.

9. 愦 憒 kùei ㄎㄨㄟ Troubled, anxious, concerned; dazed, confused.

k'ùei ㄎㄨㄟ (Variant).

10. 慑 懾 ché ㄓㄜ Afraid, faint hearted.

shè ㄕㄜ To coerce.

愤 憤 fèn ㄈㄣ Zeal, ardor.

13. 懒 懶 lǎn ㄌㄢ Lazy, indolent; reluctant.

lài ㄌㄞ Evil.

14. 蕑 懣 mǐn ㄇㄣ Mournful, melancholy; to stupify; to cover.

21. 戆 戇 chùang ㄔㄨㄤ Stupid, dull, moranic.

戈 62

1. 戋 戔 chiēn ㄐㄧㄢ Small, narrow; prejudiced.
2. 戏 戲 hsì ㄒㄧ A play, drama; to play, jest.
4. 创 創 ch'ùang ㄔㄨㄤ To create, make, invent; to begin.
5. 战 戰 chàn ㄓㄢ War; to fight, contest; to tremble.

手 扌 64

2. 才 纔 ts'ái ㄘㄞ Then, just.

扑 撲 p'ū ㄆㄨ To beat, strike, pound; to rush on; used in rendering sound.

3. 执 執 chíh ㄓ To hold, grip.

扩 擴 k'ùo ㄎㄨㄛ To extend, enlarge, stretch; to escalate.

扪 捫 mén ㄇㄣ To feel, lay hands on; to hold; cover.

扫 掃 sǎo ㄠˇ To sweep.

　　　 sào　　 A broom.

4. 折 摺 ché ㄜˊ To fold.

　　　 chě　　 Pleats

抢 搶 ch'iang ㄑㄧㄤˇ To take by force; to wrestle for; to rob, ravish.

　　　 ch'iang Adverse.

　　　 ch'ūang ㄑㄨㄤ To oppose, rush against.

抚 撫 fǔ ㄈㄨˇ To cherish; to rub.

护 護 hù ㄏㄨˋ To guard, protect; to escort, shelter.

扰 擾 jǎo ㄐㄧㄠˇ To disturb, annoy; to give trouble; to bug.

抠 摳 k'ōu ㄎㄡ To raise; to feel for; to scrape.

抡 掄 lún ㄌㄨㄣˊ To choose, select; in turn; to wave, brandish, to swing.

　　　 lūn ㄌㄨㄣ (Variant).

拟 擬 nǐ ㄋㄧˇ To determine, intend; to compare; to resemble; to estimate, guess.

　　　 ǐ ㄧ (Variant).

报 報 pào ㄅㄠˋ (To) report.

㧐 攫 sǔng ㄙㄨㄥˇ Frightened, terrified.

抟 摶 t'úan ㄊㄨㄢˊ To roll in the hand; to model.

　　　 chùan ㄔㄨㄢˋ To lead.

扬 揚 yáng ㄧㄤˊ To scatter, spread; to publish abroad; to praise; to display.

择 擇 ché ㄓㄜˊ To select, choose.

　　　 tsé ㄗㄜˊ (Variant).

5. 拣 揀 chǐen ㄐㄧㄢˇ   Select; to pick up.

   抔 攦 k'ǔai ㄎㄨㄞˇ   To rub, scratch; to bear an ax on the arm.

   拦 攔 lán ㄌㄢˊ   To obstruct, impede.

   拢 攏 lǔng ㄌㄨㄥˇ   To collect; to grasp; to take action.

   拟 擬 nǐ ㄋㄧˇ   To resemble; decide.

   拧 擰 níng ㄋㄧㄥˊ   To pull about; to create confusion; to twist.

   拨 撥 pō ㄅㄛ   To distribute, disperse, allot; to transfer; to stir up, prod; to pluck (strings).

   担 擔 tān ㄉㄢ   To carry.

   拥 擁 yūng ㄩㄥ   To push; to give (moral) support.

6. 挤 擠 chǐ ㄐㄧˇ   To crawl, push; to squeeze.

   挢 撟 chǐao ㄐㄧㄠˇ   To bend, twist.

   挚 摯 chìh ㄓˋ   To grasp, grab; in advance; to break down.

   拙 擉 ch'ō ㄔㄛ   To pierce, penetrate.

   挟 挾 hsíeh ㄒㄧㄝˊ   To hold under the arm; to put in the bosom.

   挦 撏 hsǐen ㄒㄧㄢˇ   To take, select; to pull out hair.

              hsìen   Appearance of water.

   挥 揮 hūi ㄏㄨㄟ   To move, shake; direct.

   挛 攣 lǘan ㄌㄩㄢˊ   To bend, warp; crooked, winding.

              lǘan   To bind, tie; to take hold of; to drag along.

   挠 撓 náo ㄋㄠˊ   To scratch, vex; to disturb.

   挡 擋 tǎng ㄉㄤˇ   To resist, ward off, oppose, pervert; to stop.

掗	掗	yǎ	ㄚˇ	Snapping of twigs.
7. 捡	撿	chǐen	ㄐㄧㄢˇ	To restrict, bind.
挝	檛	chūa	ㄔㄨㄚ	To beat or strike.
捞	撈	lāo	ㄌㄠ	To drag for, especially in the water; to fish for.
损	損	sǔn	ㄙㄨㄣˇ	To injure, spoil; to destroy; disadvantage.
捣	搗	tǎo	ㄉㄠˇ	To beat, pound; to attack.
8. 据	據	chǜ	ㄐㄩˋ	To hold as base; to base; basis according to; to receive (a communication).
掼	摜	kùan	ㄍㄨㄢˋ	To be familiar with; to take.
㧖	摑	kūo	ㄍㄨㄛ	To slap.
捋	擺	lǒ	ㄌㄨㄛˇ	To split; to choose; to rap, wipe.
掳	擄	lǔ	ㄌㄨˇ	To take captive, to seize; a prisoner, slave.
掺	摻	shān	ㄕㄢ	A delicate hand; tapering, beautiful.
撢	撢	tǎn	ㄉㄢˇ	To grasp; to hit against.
9. 搅	攪	chǐao	ㄐㄠˇ	To agitate or disturb; to cause trouble.
掷	擲	chīh	ㄓ	To throw, fling away.
撳	撳	chìn	ㄑㄧㄣˋ	To press down with the hand; to lean on.
搁	擱	kō	ㄍㄛ	To place, put; to put down.
揽	攬	lǎn	ㄌㄢˇ	To seize, grasp; to monopolize.
搂	摟	lǒu	ㄌㄡˇ	To drag, pull; to hug, embrace.
10. 搀	攙	ch'ān	ㄔㄢ	To sustain, support; assist; to mix.
摆	擺	pǎi	ㄅㄞˇ	To arrange, displace; move back and forth, pendulum.

擯 擯	pìn	ㄅㄧㄣ	To expel, reject; to set in order.
攝 攝	shè	ㄕㄜ	To gather; to control, act for.
攄 攄	shū	ㄕㄨ	To spread, unroll.
攤 攤	t'ān	ㄊㄢ	To spread, apportion.
11. 攖 攖	yǐng	ㄧㄥ	To oppose; to attack.
12. 擷 擷	hsíeh	ㄒㄧㄝ	To collect, take up; a lapful.
攟 攟	měn	ㄇㄣ	To expel, drive out.
攛 攛	ts'ūan	ㄘㄨㄢ	To stir up evil.
13. 擻 擻	shǔ	ㄙㄡ	To shake.
16. 攢 攢	tsūan	ㄗㄨㄢ	To gather together, collect; to hold in the hand.
	ts'úan	ㄘㄨㄢ	(Variant).

攴 攵 66

6. 敵 敵	tí	ㄉㄧ	Opponent, enemy.
7. 斂 斂	lǐen	ㄌㄧㄢ	To gather, accumulate; to arrange, compose; to control oneself.
9. 数 數	shǔ	ㄕㄨ	To count, calculate, estimate.
12. 斓 斕	lán	ㄌㄢ	Variegated, colored.

斗 68

斗 鬥	tòu	ㄉㄡ	To fight, wrangle.

斤 69

8. 断 斷	tùan	ㄉㄨㄢ	To break, cut off.

7.旋 鏇　hsüan ㄒㄩㄢˋ　A pewter flask for keeping spirits warm; a lathe.

无 無　wǔ　ㄨˊ　Not; lacking, without, non-, un-; negative.

1.旧 舊　chìu ㄐㄧㄡˋ　Old.

电 電　tien ㄉㄧㄢˋ　Electricity; electric.

3.旷 曠　k'ùang ㄎㄨㄤˋ　Wild; wasteland, desert, wilderness.

时 時　shíh ㄕ́　Time; period, season.

4.昙 曇　t'án ㄊㄢˊ　Dark clouds.

昜 暘　yáng ㄧㄤˊ　The rising sun.

5.昼 晝　chòu ㄓㄡˋ　Daytime.

显 顯　hsǐen ㄒㄧㄢˇ　Conspicuous; make plain.

昽 曨　lúng ㄌㄨㄥˊ　The rising sun obscured.

6.晓 曉　hsǐao ㄒㄧㄠˇ　Dawn, light; to know, understand; apparent.

晒 曬　shài ㄕㄞˋ　To dry or air in the sun; to be affected by the sun, sunstroke.

晔 曄　yèh ㄧㄝˋ　Sparkling, said of a fire.

晕 暈　yǔn ㄩㄣˇ　A mist, vapors; a halo; to be dizzy.

8.暂 暫　tsàn ㄗㄢˋ　For a time, shortly, suddenly.

　　chàn ㄓㄢˋ　(Variant).

10. 曖 曖 ài ㄞ Obscure, vague.

日 73

2. 曲 麴 ch'ǘ ㄑㄩ Yeast.

月 74

5. 朧 朧 lúng ㄌㄨㄥ The rising moon.

木 75

1. 术 術 shù ㄕㄨ A trick; skill.
2. 朴 樸 p'ǒ ㄆㄛ Sincere, simple; the substance of things.

   p'ǔ ㄆㄨ (Variant).

   朱 硃 chū ㄓㄨ Vermillion; imperial.

   权 權 ch'üan ㄑㄩㄢ Power, authority.

   乐 樂 lè ㄌㄜ Happy.

   yüeh ㄩㄝ Music.

   朴 樸 p'ú ㄆㄨ Simple, plain.

   杀 殺 shā ㄕㄚ To kill.

   杂 雜 tsá ㄗㄚ Mixed; confused.

   东 東 tūng ㄉㄨㄥ East.

3. 来 來 lái ㄌㄞ To come, coming; used in transliteration.

   条 條 t'iao ㄊㄧㄠ (classifier for long slender objects; roads, bridges, river, ribbons.)

束	棗	tsǎo ㄗㄠ	Jujube, "dates".
4. 极	極	chí ㄐㄧ	(Intensifying suffix); very.
枪	槍	ch'īang ㄑㄧㄤ	A lance or spear.
		ch'éng ㄔㄥ	A comet.
枧	梘	chǐen ㄐㄧㄢ	A bamboo tube for carrying water.
枫	楓	fēng ㄈㄥ	Maple.
构	構	kòu ㄍㄡ	To construct; finish; to join to-gether; to grasp, hook.
枥	櫪	lí ㄌㄧ	A kind of oak; a stable.
板	闆	pǎn ㄅㄢ	Board; shop-owner.
枢	樞	shū ㄕㄨ	Pivot, axis, central point; indis-pensible, fundamental.
松	鬆	sūng ㄙㄨㄥ	Loose; to loosen.
枞	樅	ts'ǔng ㄘㄨㄥ	A species of oak (Quercus).
杨	楊	yáng ㄧㄤ	Willow, popular, aspen.
5. 栈	棧	chàn ㄔㄢ	A storehouse, shop.
柽	檉	ch'ēng ㄔㄥ	The tamarisk.
柽	橕	ch'éng ㄔㄥ	A prop, post.
亲	親	ch'ìng ㄑㄧㄥ	With, 家 relatives; with 愛的 dear, beloved.
柜	櫃	kùei ㄍㄨㄟ	A chest, cupboard.
栏	欄	lán ㄌㄢ	A railing, rage.
6. 桢	楨	chēn ㄓㄣ	An evergreen shrub.
栉	櫛	chǐeh ㄐㄧㄝ	A comb; to comb.
桡	橈	jáo ㄖㄠ	An oar; to row.
		náo ㄋㄠ	Crooked; bent wood; unjust; weak, soft; to disperse, scatter.

5. 栎 櫟 lì ㄌ丨 The chestnut-leaved oak, <u>Quercus sinensis</u> and Q. <u>serrata</u>.

栊 櫳 lúng ㄌㄨㄥ A cape or pen.

柠 檸 níng ㄋ丨ㄥ A tree with bark of medicinal value; the lemon.

标 標 pīao ㄅ丨ㄠ Sign, signed, publish.

树 樹 shù ㄕㄨ A tree.

栋 棟 tùng ㄉㄨㄥ Ridge-pole; able man.

6. 桨 槳 chǐang ㄐ丨ㄤ An oar.

桥 橋 ch'íao ㄑ丨ㄠ A bridge.

桩 椿 chūang ㄓㄨㄤ A stump, post.

桦 樺 húa ㄏㄨㄚ A birch (<u>Betula</u> sp.) found in Manchuria.

桧 檜 kùei ㄍㄨㄟ The Chinese juniper.

栾 欒 lúan ㄌㄨㄢ A kind of small tree.

档 檔 tàng ㄉㄤ A cross-piece, as in a ladder chain.

样 樣 yàng 丨ㄤ Shape, kind.

荣 榮 yúng ㄩㄥ Glory, honor; florishing, prospering; beautiful; blood.

7. 检 檢 chǐen ㄐ丨ㄢ A label on a book; to arrange, collate.

楞 櫺 líng ㄌ丨ㄥ A sill, lintel; lattice.

8. 椠 槧 ch'ìen ㄑ丨ㄢ Wood blocks for printing; tablets for memorandum.

椤 欏 ló ㄌㄨㄛ The horse-chestnut (<u>Aesculus</u> sp.).

椟 櫝 tú ㄉㄨ A casket; box.

9. 槛 檻 chǐen ㄐ丨ㄢ Lower section of a tripartite door.

榉 櫸 chǔ ㄐㄩ A large tree used in making furniture; a kind of elm.

楼 樓	lóu ㄌㄡ	An upper-story or tower; a two-storied building.
楕 橢	t'ŏ ㄊㄨㄛ	Ellipse.
榇 櫬	ch'ĕn ㄔㄣ	A coffin; a kind of tree.
槠 櫧	chū ㄓㄨ	A species of live (evergreen) oak.
榄 欖	lăn ㄌㄢ	Chinese olive tree.
10. 榄 欖	chĭa ㄐㄧㄚ	A small evergreen shrub the leaves of which are used in a beverage.
槛 檻	hsĭen ㄒㄧㄢ	Bars, a railing; a cage.
榈 櫚	lǘ ㄌㄩ	A palm.
槟 檳	pìng (pin) ㄅㄧㄥ	Areca nut, betel nut.
11. 樱 櫻	yīng ㄥ	The cherry.
12. 橹 櫓	lŭ ㄌㄨ	A turret on a city wall; a scull, sweep of an oar.
13. 橼 櫞	yŭan ㄩㄢ	Name of any of several kinds of trees.

欠 76

2. 欢 歡	hūan ㄏㄨㄢ	Joyous; to be glad.
3. 欤 歟	yǔ ㄩ	A final particle, indicating admiration, doubt, surprise。
4. 欧 歐	ōu ㄡ	To vomit, barf, puke.

止 77

4. 齿 齒	ch ĭh ㄔ	Tooth. This is radical 211.
6. 涩 澀	sè ㄙㄜ	Rough; astringent.

3. 歼　殲　chīen ㄐㄧㄢ　To destroy.
5. 残　殘　ts'ái ㄘㄞ　To injure, appress.
6. 毙　斃　pì ㄅㄧ　To die a violent death; to kill, execute.
7. 殓　殮　lïen ㄌㄧㄢ　To prepare a corpse for burial.
　　殒　殞　yǔn ㄩㄣ　To perish, die.
8. 殚　殫　tān ㄉㄢ　Quite, entirely.
9. 殨　殨　hùi ㄏㄨㄟ　To open (a sore).
10. 殡　殯　pìn ㄅㄧㄣ　To carry to burial.

殳　79

4. 殴　毆　ōu ㄡ　To brawl, beat with sticks or fists.

毛　82

5. 毡　氈　chān ㄓㄢ　Blanket.
8. 毵　毿　sàn ㄙㄢ　Hirsute, coarse hair.

气　84

　　气　氣　ch'i ㄑㄧ　Air.
5. 氢　氫　ch'īng ㄑㄧㄥ　Hydrogen.

2. 汉 漢 hàn ㄏㄢ The dynasty.

汇 滙 hùi ㄏㄨㄟ To send money; bank draft; to converge, converging waters.

汇 彙 hùi ㄏㄨㄟ A class, series; to classify.

4. 沣 灃 fēng ㄈㄥ A stream in Shensi.

沪 滬 hù ㄏㄨ To fish by trapping; or fish in a weir; Shanghai.

沟 溝 kōu ㄍㄡ A ditch, drain; watercourse.

沩 溈 kūei ㄍㄨㄟ Name of a river.

沥 瀝 lì ㄌㄧ A drop, to drip; detail, in detail.

沦 淪 lún ㄌㄨㄣ Ruined, lost; engulfed; eddies.

浔 漚 òu ㄡ To soak, steep.

         ōu   Bubbles on water.

沈 瀋 shěn ㄕㄣ To pour out water; to leak.

汤 湯 t'āng ㄊㄤ Soup, gravy; to heat; hot water.

沧 滄 ts'āng ㄘㄤ Vast, cold.

5. 泾 涇 chīng ㄐㄧㄥ A large river in Kansuh; to flow straight through.

浅 淺 ch'ǐen ㄑㄧㄢ Shallow, superficial, vulgar, easy to grasp.

泻 瀉 hsieh ㄒㄧㄝ To drain off; to leak. Diarrhea.

泸 瀘 lú ㄌㄨ A <u>hsien</u> in Szechwan; river in Kiangsi, also in Szechwan.

洛 濼 lò ㄌㄛ A river in Shantung.

泷 瀧 lúng ㄌㄨㄥ River in Kwangtung.

泞	濘	nìng	ㄋㄧㄥ	Mud.
		nèng	ㄋㄥ	(Variant).
泼	潑	p'ŏ	ㄆㄛ	To sprinkle, scatter; to dissipate, waste.
泽	澤	ché	ㄔㄜ	A marsh, damp; to fertilize, enrich; glossy, smooth; to deprive of; to point out.
		tsé	ㄗㄜ	(Variant).

6.
济	濟	chì	ㄐㄧ	To succor.
浇	澆	chīao	ㄐㄧㄠ	To wash with water; to pour over.
浃	浹	chíeh		Dampness.
浆	漿	chīang	ㄐㄧㄤ	To starch; thick fluid.
洁	潔	chíeh	ㄐㄧㄝ	Clean, clear, pure.
浸	濜	chìn	ㄐㄧㄣ	A rapid river.
浊	濁	chó	ㄓㄨㄛ	Impure.
浏	瀏	líu	ㄌㄧㄡ	Clear deep water.
泻	瀉	hsìeh	ㄒㄧㄝ	To flow, drain; dysentery.
浔	潯	hsìn	ㄒㄧㄣ	Steep side of a gorge; a river near Kiukiang.
		hsǘn	ㄒㄩㄣ	(Variant).
浒	滸	hǔ	ㄏㄨ	A riverbank.
浑	渾	hún	ㄏㄨㄣ	A turbid current; chaotic, confused.
浍	澮	kùai	ㄎㄨㄞ	Water current; a drain.
		kùei	ㄎㄨㄟ	(Alternate).
滦	灤	lúan	ㄌㄨㄢ	To drip.
洒	灑	sǎ	ㄙㄚ	To sprinkle, spill, scatter.
溮	瀰	shè	ㄕㄜ	Name of a river.

泖	獅	shìh	ㄕ	Name of a river.
洼	窪	wā	ㄨㄚ	Hollow, concavity.
洒	灑	sǎ	ㄙㄚ	To scatter, sprinkle; free.
		hsìn	ㄒㄧㄣ	To shiver; alarmed.
		hsiěn	ㄒㄧㄢ	Solemn, distinguished.
		ts'ǔi	ㄘㄨㄟ	Lofty.
测	測	t'sè	ㄘㄜ	To fathom, measure.
7. 涨	漲	chàng	ㄓㄤ	To rise (water), inundate.
涧	澗	chìen	ㄐㄧㄢ	A swift mountain stream.
润	潤	jùn	ㄖㄨㄣ	To moisten, enrich, fatten; shining, sleep.
涡	渦	kūo	ㄍㄨㄛ	A river in Anwei.
		wō	ㄨㄛ	A whirlpool.
涞	淶	lái	ㄌㄞ	A brook, ripples.
涝	澇	lào	ㄌㄠ	A torrent; great waves; to overflow, flood.
浓	濃	núng	ㄋㄨㄥ	Thick (liquid); dark hue; dense.
涩	澀	sè	ㄙㄜ	Rough, harsh; uneven.
达	達	t'à	ㄊㄚ	Slippery.
涛	濤	t'áo	ㄊㄠ	Billows, large waves.
涂	塗	tú	ㄊㄨ	To smear, dab.
涡	渦	wō	ㄨㄛ	A whirlpool.
8. 渐	漸	chièn	ㄐㄧㄢ	Gradually.
鸿	鴻	húng	ㄏㄨㄥ	Vast, profound.
涟	漣	lién	ㄌㄧㄢ	Flowing water; River in Hunan.
渑	澠	miěn	ㄇㄧㄢ	River in Honan.

澠 澠	shéng	ㄕㄥ	River in Shantung.
滲 滲	shèn	ㄕㄣ	To leak, soak through;
	shēn		Downy growing plumage.
淀 澱	tien	ㄉㄧㄢ	Sediment, dregs. Note: This is not 淀 (tien) - Shallow water; a lake in Hopei.
凟 瀆	tú	ㄉㄨ	A ditch, drain.
渔 漁	yǘ	ㄩ	To fish, seize.
漬 漬	tzù	ㄗ	To soak, steep, soggy.
潁 潁	yíng	ㄥ	River in Shantung.
渊 淵	yūan	ㄩㄢ	Abyss, deep gulf.
9.濺 濺	chīen	ㄐㄧㄢ	Rushing water.
	chìen		To splash.
滯 滯	chìh	ㄓ	To impede; sluggish.
潰 潰	hùi	ㄏㄨㄟ	A stream overflowing; dispersed, scattered.
	k'ùei	ㄎㄨㄟ	(Variant).
溇 漊	lóu	ㄌㄡ	Name of a river.
湿 濕	shīh	ㄕ	Wet.
湾 灣	wān	ㄨㄢ	A bay, cove, bend of a river.
澦 澦	yǜ	ㄩ	Tributary, in Yangtze River.
10.滥 濫	làn	ㄌㄢ	To overflow.
漓 灘	lí	ㄌㄧ	Name of a river.
滤 濾	lǜ	ㄌㄩ	To filter, strain.
滗 潷	pì	ㄅㄧ	To decant.
滨 濱	pīn	ㄅㄧㄣ	A bank, shore
	p'ín	ㄆㄧㄣ	(Variant).

滩 灘	t'ān ㄊㄢ	Rapids, breakers.
滟 灧	yèn ㄧㄢ	Elegant and beautiful, said of a woman.
11. 潋 瀲	lǐen ㄌㄧㄢ	Crystal clear.
潍 濰	wéi ㄨㄟ	A river in Shantung.
12. 潇 瀟	hsīao ㄒㄧㄠ	Sound of beating rain and wind.
澜 瀾	lán ㄌㄢ	Billows, waves.
13. 濑 瀨	lài ㄌㄞ	Water flowing over shallows, ripples; name of a river in Kwangsi.
濒 瀕	pīn ㄆㄧㄣ	A bank, shore, beach.
18. 灏 灝	hào ㄏㄠ	Vast, boundless.

火 灬 86

1. 灭 滅	mìeh ㄇㄧㄝ	To destroy, extinguish.
2. 灯 燈	tēng ㄉㄥ	A lamp.
3. 灵 靈	líng ㄌㄧㄥ	Efficacious; alert, sensitive.
灿 燦	t'sàn ㄘㄢ	Brilliant.
灶 竈	tsào ㄗㄠ	Kitchen; furnace, stove.
4. 炝 熗	ch'iang ㄑㄧㄤ	A species of cookery, using vinegar and vegetables.
炉 爐	lú ㄌㄨ	Stove; to bake.
炜 煒	wěi ㄨㄟ	A raging, glowing.
炀 煬	yáng ㄧㄤ	To roast, sear; to fuse, smelt.
5. 炽 熾	chìh ㄓ	Blaze; splendid, illustrious; to burn.
烂 爛	làn ㄌㄢ	Rotten, over ripe; ragged, broken; bright, glistening.

炼	煉	lìen	ㄌㄧㄢˋ	To smelt, refine, purify.
烁	爍	shùo	ㄕㄨㄛˋ	Bright, splendid.
点	點	tǐen	ㄉㄧㄢˇ	A spot; to spot or dot.
6.烬	燼	chìn	ㄐㄧㄣˋ	Ashes, embers; remains, remnants.
烛	燭	chú	ㄓㄨˊ	Candle, torch; to light.
烦	煩	fán	ㄈㄢˊ	To trouble; to feel vexed.
烩	燴	hùi	ㄏㄨㄟˋ	To cook in a sauce of sesame oil and starch.
热	熱	jè	ㄖㄜˋ	Warm; hot; to heat.
炼	煉	lìen	ㄌㄧㄢˋ	To refine, purify
烧	燒	shāo	ㄕㄠ	To burn, heat; to roast or bake; fever.
烨	燁	yèh	ㄧㄝˋ	A blaze of fire; splendid, glorious.
荧	熒	yíng	ㄧㄥˊ	Shining, sprinkling, sparkling.
7.焖	燜	mēn	ㄇㄣ	To steam food.
烫	燙	t'àng	ㄊㄤˋ	To scald.

父 88

2.爷	爺	yéh	ㄧㄝˊ	Old man.

片 91

8.牍	牘	tú	ㄉㄨˊ	Writing tablets; registers.

牛 牜 93

5.牵	牽	ch'īen	ㄑㄧㄢ	To lead along, pull; to drag.

6. 牺 犧 hsī ㄒ Sacrificial victims; animals of uniform color.

牢 犖 lò ㄌㄛ A brindled ox; open, manifest.

8. 犊 犢 tú ㄉㄨ A sacrificial calf.

犬 犭 94

3. 状 狀 chuàng ㄔㄨㄤ Condition; appearance.

犷 獷 kǔang ㄍㄨㄤ Fierce, rude.

kùang (Variant).

4. 狈 狽 pèi ㄆㄟ A mythical animal with short fore-legs, reputed to ride on the backs of wolves; jerboa.

犹 猶 yú ㄩ As if; still; like.

5. 狞 獰 níng ㄋㄧㄥ Fierce aspect; fur of dogs.

6. 狭 狹 hsía ㄒㄧㄚ Narrow; narrow-minded.

狯 獪 kùai ㄍㄨㄞ Sly, crafty; mischievous.

kùei ㄍㄨㄟ (Alternate).

狲 猻 sūn ㄙㄨㄣ A kind of monkey.

狮 獅 szū ㄙ A lion.

shīh ㄕ (Variant).

独 獨 tú ㄉㄨ Alone, single.

狱 獄 yù ㄩ A prison; a court trial.

7. 猃 獫 hsíen ㄒㄧㄢ Shoddy, sly, and crafty.

8. 猎 獵 lìeh ㄌㄧㄝ To hunt; hunting, field-sports.

猕 獼 mí ㄇㄧ A female monkey.

9.獻 獻 hsìen ㄒㄧㄢˋ To offer, present, report; to show.

13.獺 獺 t'à ㄊㄚˋ The otter.

玉 王 96

2.玑 璣 chī ㄐㄧ An asymmetrical pearl (or woman).

3.玛 瑪 mǎ ㄇㄚˇ Agate; cornelian. Used in transliterating.

玲 瑲 ch'īang ㄑㄧㄤ Tinkling of gems.

现 現 hsìen ㄒㄧㄢˋ Glitter of gems; to see, appear.

环 環 húan ㄏㄨㄢˊ A ring, to encircle.

玮 瑋 wěi ㄨㄟˇ A reddish jade; rare, precious.

5.玺 璽 hsǐ ㄒㄧ The great seal, imperial signet.

珑 瓏 lúng ㄌㄨㄥˊ A gem cut in the form of a dragon.

珲 琿 hún ㄏㄨㄣˊ Fine jade; a precious gem.

莹 瑩 yíng ㄧㄥˊ The sparkle of gems.

7.琐 瑣 sǔo ㄙㄨㄛˇ Fragments; petty, troublesome, annoying.

8.琎 璡 chìn ㄐㄧㄣˋ A decorative article made of jade.

琼 瓊 ch'íong ㄑㄩㄥˊ A red stone; excellent, beautiful.

琼 瓊 chǐang A _hsien_ on Hainan.

琏 璉 lǐan ㄌㄧㄢˇ Royal ceremonial vessel to hold grain.

10.瑷 璦 ài ㄞˋ Beautiful jade.

11.璎 瓔 yīng ㄧㄥ A jewel, gem.

16.瓒 瓚 tsàn ㄗㄢˋ Beautiful jade.

2. 亩 畝　mǔ 　ㄇㄨ　A <u>mou</u>, a Chinese acre.
3. 画 畫　hùa 　ㄏㄨㄚ　Picture, drawing; a mark, line.
　 备 備　pèi 　ㄅㄟ　To prepare.
4. 畅 暢　ch'àng ㄔㄤ　Joyful, pleasant.
　 单 單　tān 　ㄉㄢ　Single, odd, alone.
7. 畴 疇　ch'óu ㄔㄡ　Arable land.

2. 疖 癤　chīeh ㄐㄝ　A small sore, pimple.
　 疗 療　líao 　ㄌㄠ　To cure, heal.
3. 疠 癘　lì 　ㄌ　A sore, ulcer, esp. caused by "varnish poisoning".
　 疟 瘧　yào 　ㄠ　Malaria.
　 　 　nüeh 　ㄋㄝ　(Variant).
4. 疮 瘡　ch'ūang ㄔㄨㄤ　A sore abscess.
　 疯 瘋　fēng 　ㄈㄥ　Insane, insanity; leprosy.
　 疬 癧　lì 　ㄌ　Lump or swellings.
　 疡 瘍　yáng 　ㄤ　Ulcers, sores.
5. 症 癥　chēng 　ㄓㄥ　Obstructions of the bowels.
　 痉 痙　chìng 　ㄐㄥ　Convulsions, fits.
　 痈 癰　yūng 　ㄩㄥ　A boil, abscess.
6. 痒 癢　yǎng 　ㄤ　To itch.
7. 痫 癇　hsién 　ㄒㄢ　Fits, convulsions.

癆 癆 láo ㄌㄠˊ Wasting away; consumption; injurious.

8. 癉 癉 tàn ㄉㄢˋ Weared, fatigued; distressed from overwork.

9. 瘞 瘞 ì ㄧˋ A secluded spot; to bury.

瘻 瘻 lú ㄌㄩˊ A running sore, an ulcer.

10. 瘪 瘪 pǐeh ㄅㄧㄝˇ Shrivelled, empty, flaccid, limp.

癱 癱 t'ān ㄊㄢ To be paralized.

11. 癭 癭 yǐng ㄧㄥˇ A goiter; a knob or a tree.

12. 癮 癮 yǐn ㄧㄣˇ A rash; a yearning for drink or a drag.

13. 癩 癩 lài ㄌㄞˋ Skin blemishes; mange; leprosy.

14. 癬 癬 hsüan ㄒㄩㄢˇ Ringworm, dermatitis.

16. 癲 癲 tien ㄉㄧㄢ Insane, mad; convulsions.

白 106

6. 皚 皚 ái ㄞˊ Whiteness.

皮 107

5. 皺 皺 chòu ㄓㄡˋ Facial wrinkles, or creases in clothes.

6. 皸 皸 chūn ㄐㄩㄣ Chapped skin.

皿 108

5. 盞 盞 chǎn ㄓㄢˇ A shallow cup for oil; a wine cup. Classifier for oil-burning lamps.

監 監 chǐen ㄐㄧㄢ To supervise.

　　　 chìen ㄐㄧㄢ Supervisor; eunuch; to examine.

塩 鹽 yén ㄧㄢ Saline, salty.

6. 盖 蓋 kài ㄍㄞ To cover, lid.

盘 盤 pán ㄆㄢ A plate, dish, bathtub.

目 四 109

4. 眍 瞘 k'ōu ㄎㄡ Deeply-sunk eyes.

7. 睑 瞼 chǐen ㄐㄧㄢ Eye (archaic).

睐 睞 lài ㄌㄞ To squint at.

9. 䁩 瞜 lóu ㄌㄡ Eye (archaic).

11. 瞩 矚 chǔ ㄓㄨ To gaze.

瞒 瞞 mán ㄇㄢ To deceive; to blind; eyes half-closed.

矢 111

6 矫 矯 chǐao ㄐㄧㄠ To dissemble.

石 112

2. 矶 磯 chī ㄐㄧ An obstruction in the water; a jetty.

3. 矾 礬 fán ㄈㄢ Alum; sulphate

矿 礦 k'ùang ㄎㄨㄤ A mine, ore

码 碼 mǎ ㄇㄚ Weights for money; one yard (measure).

4. 砖 磚 chūan ㄓㄨㄢ A brick or slab; square tile; brick tea.

砀 碭	tàng	ㄊㄤ	A colored veined stone; to overflow, exceed.	
砚 硯	yèn	ㄧㄢ	Stone on which ink is rubbed.	
5. 础 礎	ch'ǔ	ㄔㄨ	Clear; painful.	
砺 礪	lì	ㄌㄧ	Sandstone, a coarse whetstone; to grind.	
砻 礱	lúng	ㄌㄨㄥ	To grind, sharpen; a mill.	
6. 硗 磽	ch'iao	ㄑㄧㄠ	Stony soil.	
硖 硤	hsia	ㄒㄧㄚ	Ancient town near Ichang (Hupeh).	
砾 礫	lì	ㄌㄧ	Small stones, rubble; broken pottery.	
硕 碩	shùo	ㄕㄨㄛ	Great, large, full, ripe.	
	shíh	ㄕ	(Variant).	
硙 磑	wèi	ㄨㄟ	A mill; to grind or pulverize.	
7. 硷 鹼	chien	ㄐㄧㄢ	Soda, alkali.	
确 確	ch'üeh	ㄑㄩㄝ	Solid, as a rock; really, actually.	
8. 碍 礙	ai	ㄞ	To impede.	
碜 磣	ch'en	ㄔㄣ	Sand, grit.	
碛 磧	ch'i	ㄑㄧ	Exposed rock on ocean shore.	

示 礻 113

1. 礼 禮	lǐ	ㄌㄧ	Propriety; rite.	
4. 袄 襖	ǎo	ㄠ	A short jacket.	
祎 禕	i	—	Rare, excellent, precious.	
5. 祢 禰	ni	ㄋㄧ	A deceased father after his tablet has been placed in the ancestral temple.	

6. 祯 禎　chēn ㄓㄣ　Lucky, auspicious.

7. 祸 禍　hùo ㄏㄨㄛ　Calamity, misfortune; tough luck.

　　祷 禱　tǎo ㄊㄠ　To pray.

8. 禅 禪　ch'án ㄔㄢ　Zen Buddhism.

　　　　　shán ㄕㄢ　To meditate.

　　　　　shàn　To clear and level land for an alter; to abdicate.

禾　115

4. 秋 鞦　ch'iu ㄑㄧㄡ　A swing; a crupper.

　　种 種　chǔng ㄓㄨㄥ　A seed; kind, species

　　　　　chùng　To plant.

5. 称 稱　ch'ēng ㄔㄥ　To address; call; a name, title; to praise.

　　积 積　chī ㄐㄧ　To accumulate; to store(a supply or cache).

6. 秽 穢　hùi ㄏㄨㄟ　Dirt, dirty, foul; a growth of weeds。

　　　　　wèi ㄨㄟ　(Variant).

8. 稣 穌　sū ㄙㄨ　To revive, rise again.

　　颖 穎　yǐng ㄧㄥ　A full, heavy head of grain; a writing brush.

9. 稳 穩　wěn ㄨㄣ　Firm, stable, secure.

11. 穑 穡　sè ㄙㄜ　To harvest; husbandry.

穴　116

2. 穷 窮　ch'iung ㄑㄩㄥ　Poor; thoroughly, the end.

4.	窃	竊	ch'ìeh	ㄑㄧㄝ	To steal; surreptitiously, furtively.
5.	窍	竅	ch'ìao	ㄑㄧㄠ	A hole, cavity; the mind, intelligence.
7.	窜	竄	ts'úan	ㄘㄨㄢ	To sneak away, escape.
	窝	窩	wō	ㄨㄛ	A nest, hole, den; a depression.
8.	窥	窺	k'ūei	ㄎㄨㄟ	To pry into, to spy.
	窦	竇	tòu	ㄉㄡ	A hole; a drain.
9.	窭	窶	chǜ	ㄐㄩ	Rustic, unceremonious.

立 117

4.	竖	豎	shù	ㄕㄨ	To establish; upright, vertical, perpendicular; a perpendicular stroke.
5.	竞	競	chìng	ㄐㄧㄥ	To compete; emulate; to quarrel.

竹 ⺮ 118

3.	笔	筆	pǐ	ㄅㄧ	A writing instrument.
	笃	篤	tǔ	ㄉㄨ	True, genuine; stable.
5.	笺	箋	chīen	ㄐㄧㄢ	A tablet or pad of paper; a document, note.
	笼	籠	lúng	ㄌㄨㄥ	A cage or basket, or similar ventilated container.
6.	筑	築	chú	ㄓㄨ	To beat down, tamp or ram earth; to build.
	筚	篳	pì	ㄅㄧ	A wooden comb.
	笾	籩	pīen	ㄅㄧㄢ	A woven basket, used for giving fruits in offering.
	筛	篩	shāi	ㄕㄞ	A sieve; to strain or sift.

7. 简	簡	chiĕn ㄐㄧㄢ		A slip of bamboo for notes; documents.
簽	籤	ch'īen ㄑㄧㄢ		A tally stick, bamboo slip.
签	簽	ch'īen ㄑㄧㄢ		To sign; slips, lots.
筹	籌	ch'óu ㄔㄡ		To calculate, devise.
8. 箧	篋	ch'ieh ㄑㄧㄝ		A trunk; a portfolio.
箫	簫	hsīao ㄒㄧㄠ		A panpipe; a flute of bamboo.
8. 箩	籮	ló ㄌㄨㄛ		Deep open baskets; sieve; crate.
箪	簞	tān ㄉㄢ		A small basket for cooked rice.
箨	籜	t'ò ㄊㄨㄛ		First leaves of bamboo shoots; the sheath enveloping emerging leaves.
箦	簀	tsé ㄗㄜ		A mat, bed-mat.
9. 篑	簣	k'ùei ㄎㄨㄟ		A basket for carrying earth.
篓	簍	lŏu ㄌㄡ		A hamper, basket.
10. 篮	籃	lán ㄌㄢ		A basket.
篱	籬	lí ㄌㄧ		A bamboo fence.
11. 断	籲	tùan ㄉㄨㄢ		To stop; interrupt.
13. 籁	籟	lài ㄌㄞ		A three-reed musical pipe.

米 119

2. 籴	糴	tí ㄉㄧ		To buy up grain.
5. 粝	糲	lì ㄌㄧ		Coarse (applied to grain).
粜	糶	t'iao ㄊㄧㄠ		To sell grain.
6. 粪	糞	fèn ㄈㄣ		Manure, night-soil; worthless.

58

7. 粮 糧 liàng Provisions.

絲 糸 120

1. 系 繫 chì ㄐㄧ To tie.
   系 係 hsì ㄒㄧ Related to; connected with.

2. 纠 纖 chì ㄐㄧ Used for transliteration.
   纠 糾 chiu ㄐㄧㄡ A confederacy; to collect.

3. 纪 紀 chì ㄐㄧ Records, chronicles.
   纤 縴 ch'ien ㄑㄧㄢ A tow-rope; to pull, lead; to bring together.
   纣 紂 chòu ㄓㄡ A crupper: traces.
   纥 紇 hó ㄏㄜ Tassels, end of a fringe.
   纤 纖 hsien ㄒㄧㄢ Small, fine, delicate.
   红 紅 húng ㄏㄨㄥ Red; symbol of good luck.
   纫 紉 jén ㄖㄣ To thread (as a needle), to string, to join together to sew, stitch.
   纩 纊 k'uang ㄎㄨㄤ Fine floss silk.
   丝 絲 szū ㄙ Silk, wire, fiber; strings of musical instruments.
   纨 紈 wán ㄨㄢ White silk, white.
   纡 紆 yū ㄩ To twist, distort.
   约 約 yüeh ㄩㄝ A covenant, agreement; to bind, restrain.

4. 纼 紖 ch'ěn ㄔㄣ A lead for cattle, rope.
   纸 紙 chǐh ㄓ Paper, stationery.
   紧 緊 chin ㄐㄧㄣ Urgent, important.
   纯 純 ch'ún ㄔㄨㄣ Purely.

4. 纺 紡 făng ㄈㄤ To spin, twist.

紛 紛 fēn ㄈㄣ Confused, mixed.

纲 綱 kāng ㄍㄤ Large rope of a net; lanes, principles.

绘 綸 kūan ㄍㄨㄢ A silk hankerchief.

lún ㄌㄨㄣ Silken threads, to twist silk.

纳 納 nà ㄋㄚ To give or receive; to enter, be appointed; to insert.

纽 紐 nĭn ㄋㄧㄡ A knot; to tie.

紕 紕 p'ī ㄆㄧ Spoiled silk.

p'í Tassel, silk fringe.

纱 紗 shā ㄕㄚ Gauze, thin silk; yarn; muslin.

纾 紓 shū ㄕㄨ Slow, remiss; little by little.

纵 縱 tsùng ㄗㄨㄥ To permit, relax, loosen; to let go, be indulgent.

tsūng Perpendicular, vertical.

纬 緯 wĕi ㄨㄟ The wool of a web; parallels of latitude; tassels.

纹 紋 wén ㄨㄣ Stripes, line, figures; a crack.

纭 紜 yŭn ㄩㄣ Tangled, confused; numerous.

5. 织 織 chīh ㄓ To weave.

经 經 chīng ㄐㄧㄥ Classic books; to plan, manage; constant, recurring; (indicator for past tense).

绋 紼 fú ㄈㄨ Rope for pulling a bier.

绉 縐 chòu ㄓㄡ Wrinkled, shrunk; crepe.

绌 紬 ch'óu ㄔㄡ A thread, clue; to investigate.

绌 絀 ch'ú ㄔㄨ Crimson silk; deficiency, impediment.

cho ㄓㄨㄛ (Variant).

终 終 chūng The end; the whole of; after all.

绂 紱 fú A sash.

细 細 hsǐ Fine, minute, delicate; carefully.

绁 紲 hsïeh To tie with cords; a bridle.

线 綫 hsïen Thread, wire; a line, clue, fuse.

绎 繹 i To unravel silk, to get the clue; to explain; continuous.

累 纍 léi To join, bind; to cling to; to creep.

练 練 lìen To practice, drill; to select, train.

绊 絆 pàn Obstacle; to trip.

绍 紹 shào To connect, join; to hand down, continue.

绅 紳 shēn A girdle, to bind; the gentry.

绐 紿 tài To fool, cheat; pretend.

组 組 tsǔ A silk band, girdle, fringe; group, section.

6. 给 給 chǐ To give to, grant; to issue.

　　　　 kěi (more common pronunciation)

绛 絳 chìang Deep red.

绞 絞 chǐao To bind, twist; to wrap.

结 結 chíeh To incur an obligation; to contract; cohesion; to flourish, bear fruit.

絷 縶 chíh To tie up, connect, fetter.

绝 絕 chǘeh To interrupt, break off; extinct.

缬 纈 háng Printed fabric.

绚 絢 hsǔan Silken pouch hung from the girdle; stylish; ornamental.

绘 繪 huì To draw, sketch; to paint.

绕	繞	jǎo	ㄐㄠ	To surround, to coil; to wind round; to make a detour.
绒	絨	júng	ㄖㄨㄥ	Sponge, velvet, wool; nap, down.
绀	紺	kàn	ㄍㄢ	Violet or purple.
绔	絝	k'ù	ㄎㄨ	Trousers, pants, slacks.
络	絡	lò	ㄌㄨㄛ	Unreeled silk, hemp, cotton; to spin silk; continuous, to connect; blood vessels; a halter.
绖	絰	tieh	ㄉㄧㄝ	A white hemp cloth worn by mourners.
统	統	t'ǔng	ㄊㄨㄥ	To govern, rule, control.
縈	縈	yúng	ㄩㄥ	To wind about, reel, coil.
7. 继	繼	chì	ㄐㄧ	To follow, continue; to adapt; to inherit.
绢	絹	chüan	ㄐㄩㄢ	Cheap silk; pongee.
绡	綃	hsiao	ㄒㄧㄠ	Raw silk.
绣	繡	hsiu	ㄒㄧㄡ	To embroider, embellish; variegated, illustrated.
綆	綆	kěng	ㄍㄥ	A well-rope.
綏	綏	siu	ㄙㄨㄟ	To comfort; to retreat.
绦	縧	t'āo	ㄊㄠ	A sash cord
绨	綈	t'í	ㄊㄧ	Coarse dark pongee.
8. 绽	綻	chàn	ㄓㄢ	A ripped seam; to split, rent.
绮	綺	chǐ	ㄑㄧ	Open work silk fabric; beautiful, pretty.
绯	緋	fēi	ㄈㄟ	Dark red.
绩	績	chī	ㄐㄧ	To spin or join threads.
绰	綽	ch'ò	ㄔㄨㄛ	Spacious, ample; kind generous.
绸	綢	ch'óu	ㄔㄡ	Thin silk; silk good.

缀 綴	chùi ㄔㄨㄟ	To baste; to connect, continue; to mix, variegated.
	chò ㄔㄛ	To stop, cease.
续 續	hsù ㄒㄩ	To connect, join, add; continuous.
绪 緒	hsù ㄒㄩ	The end of a ball of thread; a clue; to connect.
绲 緄	kǔn ㄎㄨㄣ	An embroidered sash; a cord; to sew.
绫 綾	líng ㄌㄧㄥ	Damask, thin silk.
绺 綹	liǔ ㄌㄧㄡ	A skein of silk; a pocket.
绿 綠	lù ㄌㄩ	Green; chlorine.
	lù ㄌㄨ	(Variant).
绵 綿	mién ㄇㄧㄢ	Soft, downy; prolonged, drawn out, continuous.
绷 綳	pèng ㄅㄥ	To bind, tape, or bandage.
绳 繩	shéng ㄕㄥ	Rope, cord, a marking line; to measure; to restrain.
绶 綬	shòu ㄕㄡ	To give to, confer; to transmit.
缁 緇	tzū ㄗ	Blade silk; a dark color.
综 綜	tsùng ㄗㄨㄥ	Arranging threads for weaving; to sum up, inquire into.
绾 綰	wǎn ㄨㄢ	To string together; to bind up, to put up (hair).
维 維	wéi ㄨㄟ	To tie, hold together; to hold fast.
9. 缜 縝	chěn ㄔㄣ	Close-woven; to tie.
缉 緝	ch'i ㄑㄧ	To twist; to join, continue, to follow up; to arrest, catch.
缄 緘	chīen ㄐㄧㄢ	To bind. seal.
缣 縑	chīen ㄐㄧㄢ	A kind of waterproof silk fabric.
·缍 綣	ch'üan ㄑㄩㄢ	Bound in a league; a parasite.

緗 緗	hsīang	ㄒㄧㄤ	Light-yellow.
緩 緩	hŭan	ㄏㄨㄢ	Slow, leasurely; gradually; to delay, retard.
緱 緱	kòu	ㄎㄡ	Cord binding on the hilt of a sword.
纜 纜	làn	ㄌㄢ	A hawser, cable, rope, line.
縷 縷	lŭ	ㄌㄩ	Hempen or silkey threads; to state in detail.
緲 緲	mĭao	ㄇㄧㄠ	Minute, infinitesimal; indistinct.
緬 緬	mĭen	ㄇㄧㄢ	To think of, to recall.
緡 緡	mín	ㄇㄧㄣ	A fishing line; a cord.
綁 綁	păng	ㄅㄤ	To tie, bind.
編 編	pīen	ㄅㄧㄢ	To compile, add; to weave manually.
緦 緦	szū	ㄙ	Coarse cotton cloth, used for mourning.
緞 緞	tùan	ㄉㄨㄢ	Satin.
緹 緹	t'í	ㄊㄧ	A light red silk.
締 締	t'í	ㄊㄧ	A knot, connection.
10.纏 纏	ch'án	ㄔㄢ	To bind up, wrap; to involve.
縉 縉	chìn	ㄐㄧㄣ	Red silk.
縋 縋	chùi	ㄓㄨㄟ	A cord; to let down, lower; to suspend.
縛 縛	fú	ㄈㄨ	To tie.
縊 縊	ì	—	To strangle oneself.
縟 縟	jù	ㄐㄩ	Adorned, beautiful; gay, elegant.
縞 縞	kăo	ㄍㄠ	Plain white silk.
縭 縭	lí	ㄌㄧ	A bridal ornament.
繽 繽	pīn	ㄅㄧㄣ	A colorful (object).

縗 縗 ts'ui ㄘㄨㄟ A part of a mourning garment.

緣 緣 yüan ㄩㄢ Destiny; connection, cause, reason; to follow, climb; the hem of a garment.

緼 縕 yün ㄩㄣ Ravelled silk.

yün ㄩㄣ Vague, confused.

wěn ㄨㄣ Orange color.

11. 縫 縫 féng ㄈㄥ To sew, stitch.

縲 縲 léi ㄌㄟ To bind with ropes; a bond.

縵 縵 mán ㄇㄢ Silk thread; thin silk, unpatterned.

繆 繆 miu ㄇㄧㄡ Error; in error; to mislead.

繆 繆 móu ㄇㄡ To wind around.

chīu ㄐㄧㄡ To tie, bind.

縹 縹 p'iǎo ㄆㄧㄠ Clear, bright, misty, indistinct.

繰 繰 sāo ㄙㄠ To reel silk from cocoons.

tsǎo ㄗㄠ Elegant, of paintings.

縮 縮 shū ㄕㄨ To draw in, shrink; to bind fast; straight, upright.

sō ㄙㄨ (Variant).

纓 纓 yīng ㄧㄥ A neck or chin band on a hat; a tassel or fringe.

12. 纈 纈 hsieh ㄒㄧㄝ To tie silk into skeins; a knot.

繚 繚 liáo ㄌㄧㄠ To bind, wrap; fetters; lines for a sail.

繕 繕 shàn ㄕㄢ To write out, copy.

繒 繒 tseng ㄗㄥ Silken fabrics.

13. 繮 繮 chīang ㄐㄧㄤ A bridle, reins.

繳 繳 chiǎo ㄐㄧㄠ To bind, wind about; to involve.

65

繯繯 húan ㄏㄨㄢ Fine silk; to bind, tie.

繰繰 sāo ㄙㄠ To reel silk from cocoons.

tsǎo ㄘㄠ Crimson silk.

14. 繾繾 ch'ien ㄑㄧㄢ Involved with, loving.

辮辮 pien ㄅㄧㄢ Pigtail.

16. 纘纘 tsǔan ㄗㄨㄢ To carry on, continue; to imitate.

缶 121

8. 罌罌 yīng ㄧㄥ An earthenware jar with a small mouth and two or four ears; a pitcher.

网 罒 122

3. 罗 羅 ló ㄌㄨㄛ Gauze, netting; a surname. A net for birds; to arrange; for trans- literating.

罗 囉 ló ㄌㄨㄛ To chatter, prattle.

4. 罚 罰 fá ㄈㄚ To punish.

5. 罢 罷 pà ㄅㄚ To desist, quit; indicating sugges- tion (at the end of a clause).

9. 罴 羆 p'í ㄆㄧ A kind of bear.

12. 羁 羈 chī ㄐㄧ A halter; to restrain; to block.

羊 123

5. 羟 羥 ch'īang ㄑㄧㄤ A wild goat.

羽 124

6. 翘 翹 ch'íao ㄑㄧㄠ Long curved tail feathers; to ele- vate, raise the head; warped; women's head ornaments.

翚 翬 hūi ㄏㄨㄟ Variegated. A kind of pheasant.

66

4. 斋 齋　chāi ㄔㄞ　A fast; to abstain; a studio, shop; pure, refined; a study, library.

耒　127

7. 耢 耮　lăo ㄌㄠ　A wooden seive.

9. 耧 耬　lóu ㄌㄡ　A drill for sowing seed.

10. 耙 耰　pá ㄅㄚ　A rake; to rake.

耳　128

3. 闻 聞　wén ㄨㄣ　To hear; smell; perceive.

4. 聂 聶　nieh ㄋㄝ　To whisper; to pick up one's skirts.

　　　　 chè ㄔㄜ　To slice meat into their stripes; to close up.

　 筲 簹　sŭng ㄙㄥ　To excite, provoke; to agitate, stir up.

5. 职 職　chíh ㄓ　To govern, supervise, direct; only particularly; numerous.

　 尤 龍　lúng ㄌㄥ　A deaf person.
　 聍 聹　níng ㄋㄧㄥ　(An intensifying auxiliary verb, used with advice).

6. 联 聯　lien ㄌㄢ　To unite; joined, associated, united.

9. 聩 聵　k'ūei ㄎㄟ　Deaf; born deaf.

　　　　 hùi ㄏㄨㄟ　(Variant).

　 聪 聰　t'sūng ㄘㄥ　Astute; acute (hearing); clever.

肉 月　130

67　4. 肮 骯　āng ㄊ　Dirty, soiled.

胀	脹	chàng ㄔㄤ	Swollen abdomen; inflated, bloated.	
肠	腸	ch'áng ㄔㄤ	The bowels; feelings, affections.	
肕	膞	chúan ㄔㄨㄢ	A part of a muscle.	
肿	腫	chǔng ㄔㄨㄥ	Swollen, bloated; to swell.	
肤	膚	fū ㄈㄨ	The skin, flesh; superficial.	
胁	脅	hsieh ㄒㄧㄝ	The ribs, flank; to coerce; to be forced.	
肾	腎	shèn ㄕㄣ	Kidneys, testes; gizzard.	
5. 胫	脛	chìng ㄐㄧㄥ	The shinbone.	
		hsing ㄒㄧㄥ	(Alternate).	
胡	鬍	hú ㄏㄨ	Beard, mustache.	
胪	臚	lú ㄌㄨ	The skin; abdomen.	
胜	勝	shēng ㄕㄥ	To endure, be able to endure; deserving.	
		shèng	To win.	
胆	膽	tǎn ㄉㄢ	The gall bladder; bravery, courage.	
6. 胶	膠	chīao ㄐㄧㄠ	Glue; sticky.	
脍	膾	kùai ㄎㄨㄞ	Minced meat or fish.	
脔	臠	lǚan ㄌㄩㄢ	Sliced meat.	
脑	腦	nǎo ㄋㄠ	Brain.	
脏	臟	tsāng ㄗㄤ	Dirty; fat, obese.	
		tsàng	The viscera, entrails.	
7. 脸	臉	lǐen ㄌㄧㄢ	The face.	
脓	膿	núng ㄋㄨㄥ	Pus.	
8. 腊	臘	là ㄌㄚ	To sacrifice, a year; the twelfth lunar month; dried meat.	
9. 腻	膩	nì ㄋㄧ	Grease, fat; oily; glossy.	

9. 騰 騰 t'éng ㄊㄥˊ To mount, ascend; to move, to turn
out.

10. 膑 臏 pìn ㄅㄧㄣˋ To expell, reject.

14. 螣 螣 t'éng ㄊㄥˊ A kind of fish.

16. 臜 臢 tsān ㄗㄢ A hair-lip; dirty.

tsāng ㄗㄤ (Variant).

至 133

4. 致 緻 chìh ㄓˋ To mend, patch; soft, delicate;
secret.

舟 137

4. 舰 艦 chìen ㄐㄧㄢˋ A warship.
舱 艙 ts'āng ㄘㄤ The hold of a ship.

5. 舻 艫 lú ㄌㄨˊ The stem or prow of a ship.

艮 138

2. 艰 艱 chīen ㄐㄧㄢ Hardship; difficult.

色 139

4. 艳 艷 yèn ㄧㄢˋ Beautiful, glamorous; wanton.

艹 ++ 140

1. 艺 藝 ì - Skill, art.

2. 节 節 chiéh㄄ Verse; festival, a fair.

　　　 chǐeh Knot (in wood).

3. 芗 薌 hsīangㄒ An aromatic plant.

4. 苋 莧 hsìenㄒ Edible forbs.

　 苈 藶 lǐ ㄌ A plant with hooks on the seed.

　 芦 蘆 lǘ ㄌ Reed, rushes.

　 苏 蘇 sū ㄙ To relieve; surname; thyme.

　 苏 囌 sū ㄙ Garrulous; loquacious.

　 苍 蒼 ts'āngㄘ Green; old.

　 苁 蓯 ts'úngㄘ A small edible plant, like water cress.

　 苇 葦 wěi ㄨ A reed.

　 芜 蕪 wú ㄨ A dense stand of weeds; neglected, waste lands.

　 芸 蕓 yǔn ㄩ Rue; used for girls name.

5. 茕 煢 ch'íungㄑ Alone, desolate.

　 范 範 fàn ㄈ Normal; mean; a law, a surname.

　 茎 莖 hsíng ㄒ A stem or stalk; the hilt of a sword.

　　　 chīngㄐ (Alternate).

　 茏 蘢 lúng ㄌ A kind of waterweed, or duckweed, <u>Polygonum</u>.

　 茑 蔦 niǎo ㄋ A morning glory; a parasitic plant such as mistletoe.

　 苹 蘋 p'íngㄆ Apple; duckweed.

6. 荠 薺 chì ㄗ The shepherd's purse (<u>Capsella</u> sp.).

　 荞 蕎 ch'íaoㄑ Buckwheat.

　 荚 莢 chīehㄐ Seeds of legumes.

茧	繭	chǐen ㄐㄧㄢ	Cocoon.
荐	薦	chìen	To recommend (a person).
荃	藎	chìn ㄐㄧㄣ	A plant whose root produce a yellow dye; loyal.
荟	薈	huì ㄏㄨㄟ	To flourish, as in plants.
荤	葷	hūn ㄏㄨㄣ	A meat (non-vegetarian) diet.
荛	蕘	jáo ㄖㄠ	Grass, rushes, stubble, fuel.
荭	葒	k'úng ㄎㄨㄥ	A red-leaved vegetable.
苹	蓽	pì ㄅㄧ	Plant in hemp family.
荪	蓀	sūn ㄙㄨㄣ	The iris (flower).
荨	蕁	t'án ㄊㄢ	Nettle.
药	藥	yào ㄧㄠ	Drug, medicine; to prescribe medicine.
荥	滎	yúng ㄩㄥ	Dashing of waves; streams of water; brooks.

7.	劳	藭	ch'iung ㄑㄩㄥ	Poor, impoverished; exhausted; to investigate thoroughly, sift out.
	莼	蓴	ch'ún ㄔㄨㄣ	A water plant (Brasenia purpurea).
	莸	獲	hùo ㄏㄨㄛ	To take in hunting; to bag (game); to obtain.
		穫		To harvest a crop.
	莱	萊	lái ㄌㄞ	Goosefoot (Chenopodium sp.); wild herbs; fallow fields.
	裣	襝	líen ㄌㄧㄢ	Front part of an old-fashioned jacket.
	莳	蒔	shíh ㄕ	To plant, erect.
	荡	蕩	tàng ㄊㄤ	Large, vast, magnificent.
	莴	萵	wō ㄨㄛ	Plants similar to lettuce.
	荫	蔭	yìn ㄧㄣ	Shade, shady; to shelter, protect.

71

菸	蕕	yú	ㄩˊ	A foul-smelling aquatic plant.
8. 萧	蕭	hsīao	ㄒㄧㄠ	A kind of <u>Artemesia</u>; sighing of wind, mournful; annoying, troublesome; reverent.
莲	蓮	lien	ㄌㄧㄢˊ	Water lily.
萝	蘿	ló	ㄌㄨㄛˊ	Creeping plants.
萚	蘀	t'ò	ㄊㄨㄛˋ	Fallen leaves and bark.
9. 藹	藹	ai	ㄞˇ	Kind, gentle, friendly.
蔵	蔵	ch'ăn	ㄔㄢˇ	To prepare; complete; command.
蒋	蔣	chīang	ㄐㄧㄤ	An edible aquatic grass.
蒉	蕢	k'ùei	ㄎㄨㄟˋ	A straw basket.
萎	蔞	lóu	ㄌㄡˊ	A species of <u>Artemisia</u>.
萨	薩	sā	ㄙㄚ	Pusa, (used in transliterating.)
营	營	yíng	ㄧㄥˊ	A camp, barracks; a scheme or plan.
10. 蓟	薊	chì	ㄐㄧˋ	A thistle.
蓝	藍	lán	ㄌㄢˊ	Blue, indigo.
11. 蔷	薔	ch'íang	ㄑㄧㄤˊ	A red rose.
薮	薮	lien	ㄌㄧㄢˊ	A wild grape (<u>Vitis pentaphylla</u>).
蔺	藺	lìn	ㄌㄧㄣˋ	Kind of rush used for mats.
蔑	衊	mìeh	ㄇㄧㄝˋ	Defiled with blood; to calumniate.
12. 靳	靳	ch'í	ㄑㄧˊ	To beg, beseech.
13 薮	藪	sǒu	ㄙㄡˇ	A marshy wildlife preserve.
		shǔ	ㄕㄨˇ	A pad for the head.
蕴	蘊	yùn	ㄩㄣˋ	To collect, bring together.
		wèn	ㄨㄣˋ	(Variant).

14. 蘚 蘚 hsǐen ㄒㄧㄢˇ Moss on damp walls.

虍 141

2. 房 盧 lú ㄌㄨˊ Rice vessel, surname.

虫 142

虫 蟲 ch'úng ㄔㄨㄥˊ Insect, reptile, small crawling animal, worm.

2. 虮 蟣 chī ㄐㄧ A louse (<u>Anoplura</u>).

3. 蛮 蠆 ch'ài ㄔㄞˋ Scorpion-like insect. Dragon.

虾 蝦 hsia ㄒㄧㄚ A shrimp, prawn.

蚁 蟻 ǐ ㄧˇ An ant; used for the first person in petitions.

吗 螞 mǎ ㄇㄚˇ A leech; locust; ant.

虽 雖 súi ㄙㄨㄟˊ Although, even if.

4. 蚬 蜆 hsǐen ㄒㄧㄢˇ Small smooth clams.

蚕 蠶 ts'án ㄘㄢˊ Silkworm.

5. 蛏 蟶 ch'ēng ㄔㄥ Mussels, bivalve.

蛊 蠱 kǔ ㄍㄨˇ Internal worms; insanity; poison.

蛎 蠣 lì ㄌㄧˋ Rock-oysters.

6. 蛴 蠐 ch'í ㄑㄧˊ A large maggot.

蛱 蛺 chíeh ㄐㄧㄝˊ A butterfly.

蛰 蟄 chíh ㄓ To hibernate, become torpid.

蛲 蟯 jáo ㄖㄠˊ Intestinal worms.

蠻 蠻 mán ㄇㄢˊ Aboriginal tribes south of China; fierce, uncivilized.

蝍 螄 szū ㄙ A spiral shell.

shih ㄕ˗ (Variant).

螢 螢 yíng ㄧㄥˊ A glow-worm, firefly.

7. 蝸 蝸 wō ㄨㄛˉ A snail.

kūa ㄍㄨㄚ (Variant).

8. 蟬 蟬 ch'án ㄔㄢˊ Cicada.

蟈 蟈 kūo ㄍㄨㄛ A small green frog; a cicada.

蠟 蠟 là ㄌㄚˋ A candle; wax., waxy, glazed.

蠅 蠅 yíng ㄧㄥˊ Flies.

9. 螻 螻 lóu ㄌㄡˊ The mole-cricket.

10. 蠑 蠑 yúng ㄩㄥˊ A kind of lizard.

12. 蟏 蟏 hsīao ㄒㄧㄠ A small, long-legged spider.

血 143

5. 衅 釁 hsìn ㄒㄧㄣ˗ To offer a blood sacrifice; to annoint before worship; to embalm; a quarrel, a wrong.

衣 衤 145

2. 补 補 pǔ ㄅㄨˇ To mend, patch, repair; billion.

3. 衬 襯 ch'èn ㄔㄣˋ To be lined with; underclothing; to assist.

表 錶 piǎo ㄅㄧㄠˇ A watch, clock; to manifest.

4. 祆 襖 ǎo ㄠˇ Heavy padded coat; overcoat.

丧 喪 sàng ㄙㄤˋ To lose, die; to destroy.

              sāng To mourn for parents.

5. 袭 襲 hsí ㄒㄧˊ Garment lining; (classifier for clothing); to wear; to inherit; to invade.

       袅 裊 niǎo ㄋㄧㄠˇ To curl, as smoke.

       袜 襪 wà ㄨㄚˋ Stockings, socks, hose.

6. 装 裝 chuāng ㄓㄨㄤ Attire, dress; to fill up, pack.

       亵 褻 hsieh ㄒㄧㄝˋ Vile, irreverant; to revile.

       裆 襠 tāng ㄉㄤ Breeches, trousers.

7. 裥 襇 chien ㄐㄧㄢ Part of garment.

       裤 褲 k'ù ㄎㄨˋ Trousers, pants, slacks. See 绔

8. 裢 褳 lien ㄌㄧㄢˊ A pouch, pocket.

9. 褛 褸 lǚ ㄌㄩˇ Lapel of a coat; soiled, ragged.

10. 褴 襤 lán ㄌㄢˊ Ragged clothes.

見 见 147

2. 观 觀 kūan ㄍㄨㄢ Behold; observe.

4. 规 規 kūei ㄍㄨㄟ Compasses; circle; a rule, regulation.

       觅 覓 mì ㄇㄧˋ To search for; to look after.

       视 視 shìh ㄕˋ To look at, inspect; to regard.

5. 觇 覘 chān ㄔㄢ To spy, keep under close observation.

       觉 覺 chüeh ㄐㄩㄝˊ To feel.

              chiao ㄐㄧㄠˋ To wake up; to sleep.

       览 覽 lǎn ㄌㄢˇ To look at; inspect.

6. 覬 覬 chì ㄐㄧˋ To covet, desire.

7. 覡 覡 hsì ㄒㄧ A wizard.

8. 靚 靚 chìng ㄓㄥˋ To decorate; to paint the face.

   覿 覿 tí ㄊㄧˊ Face to face; to be granted an audience.

9. 覦 覦 yú ㄩˊ To long for, covet; to spy upon.

10. 覯 覯 kòu ㄍㄡˋ To meet suddenly; unforeseen.

11. 覲 覲 chìn ㄐㄧㄣˋ To be granted an appointment or audience.

    覷 覷 ch'ü ㄑㄩˋ To spy, watch for.

角　148

6. 觴 觴 shāng ㄕㄤ A goblet, feast.

   ch'áng ㄔㄤˊ (Variant).

   觸 觸 ch'ù ㄔㄨˋ To butt, gore, knock against.

言 訁 149

2. 訊 譏 chī ㄐㄧ To ridicule; to inspect.

   計 計 chì ㄐㄧˋ A plan, sheme, device; to calculate.

   訃 訃 fù ㄈㄨˋ Parent's obituary.

   认 認 jèn ㄖㄣˋ To recognize, know; to confess, acknowledge.

   订 訂 tìng ㄉㄧㄥˋ To arrange, settle; to edit.

3. 记 記 chì ㄐㄧˋ To remember; to record.

   讫 訖 ch'ē ㄑㄧˋ To stop, finish; to settle, complete; until.

3. 许 許 chǐeh ㄐㄧㄝ To accuse, charge.

 訓 訓 hsùn ㄒㄩㄣ To advise, counsel, instruct.

 讧 訌 húng ㄏㄨㄥ To slander; discord, revolution.

 议 議 i ㄧ To discuss, talk over, consult; to criticize; an agreement.

 让 讓 jàng ㄖㄤ To let, allow, permit; polite, yielding.

 讯 訊 jèn ㄐㄩㄣ Slow or cautious in speech.

 讪 訕 shān ㄕㄢ To abuse, revile.

 讨 討 t'ǎo ㄊㄠ To beg, demand; to punish, put to death.

4. 讲 講 chǐang ㄐㄧㄤ To speak; to argue, discuss.

 诀 訣 chǔeh ㄐㄩㄝ Mystery, secret; esoteric.

 访 訪 fǎng ㄈㄤ To inquire about.

 讽 諷 fěng ㄈㄥ To chant, recite; to ridicule.

 䜣 訢 hsīn ㄒㄧㄣ Joy and pleasure.

   hsī ㄒㄧ Vapor-rising from the ground.

   yǐn ㄧㄣ Respectful.

 讻 訩 hsiung ㄒㄩㄥ To brawl, sold.

 许 許 hsǔ ㄒㄩ To promise, allow; perhaps; excess, very; final particle.

 讳 諱 hùi ㄏㄨㄟ To conceal; to shun, avoid the use of.

 论 論 lùn ㄌㄨㄣ To discuss, speak; to argue. An essay, thesis.

 讷 訥 nà ㄋㄚ To raise the voice.

   nò ㄋㄛ To speak cautiously.

 讹 訛 ó ㄜ To cheat, deceive; false.

讴	謳	ōu	ㄡ	To sing ballads; songs, ballads.
设	設	shè	ㄕㄜ	To establish, found; to arrange devise; supposing (interrogative).
讼	訟	sùng	ㄙㄨㄥ	Litigation, dispute.
讶	訝	yà	ㄧㄚ	Exclamation of surprise.
5. 诈	詐	chà	ㄔㄚ	To deceive; bogus.
诏	詔	chào	ㄔㄠ	To proclaim, as a king, to appeal to.
诊	診	chěn	ㄔㄣ	To examine (medically), to give treatment (medically).
证	證	chèng	ㄔㄥ	Proof, evidence, to give evidence.
讵	詎	chǜ	ㄐㄩ	How? (to indicate surprise).
诎	詘	ch'ǖ	ㄑㄩ	To squat, bend down; to stammer.
诃	訶	hó	ㄏㄜ	To blame.
诇	詗	hsiung	ㄒㄩㄥ	To dispense information; to gossip to spy; clever, shrewd.
诒	詒	i	ㄧ	To bequeath, send.
		t'ài	ㄊㄞ	To deceive; to ridicule.
译	譯	i	ㄧ	To explain, interpret; to translate.
诂	詁	kǔ	ㄍㄨ	To comment, explain.
评	評	p'íng	ㄆㄧㄥ	To arrange, criticize; to comment on, a commentary.
识	識	shìh	ㄕ	To know, be acquainted with; to recognize, distinguish.
		chìh	ㄓ	To remember, record.
诉	訴	sù	ㄙㄨ	To tell, inform, to slander, complain.
诋	詆	tǐ	ㄉㄧ	To slander, defame.
诌	謅	tsōu	ㄗㄡ	To jest; to bawl.

诅 詛	tsŭ	ㄗ	To curse.
词 詞	tz'ú	ㄘ	Phrase(s), word; stories.
6. 诧 詫	ch'à	ㄔ	To wonder at.
诤 諍	chēng	ㄓㄥ	To remonstrate (with), to caution.
诚 誠	ch'éng	ㄔㄥ	Sincere, honest; certainly.
诘 詰	chieh	ㄐㄧㄝ	To investigate; to preserve order; to punish.
诛 誅	chū	ㄓㄨ	To punish, execute; to extirpate.
诠 詮	ch'üan	ㄑㄩㄢ	To explain, comment, illustrate; to enforce.
话 話	hùa	ㄏㄨㄚ	Words, speech.
诙 詼	hūi	ㄏㄨㄟ	To ridicule; to banter.
诨 諢	hùn	ㄏㄨㄣ	Obscene jibes; off-color banter; a unisexual joke, usually concerning illicit sexual relations, or excretion.
诣 詣	ì	-	To arrive, attain.
诟 詬	kòu	ㄍㄡ	Shame; to abuse.
该 該	kāi	ㄍㄞ	Ought, should; obligation.
详 詳	hsiang	ㄒㄧㄤ	In detail; to examine with care, to judge; carefully; to report to a superior; to roam.
诩 詡	hsŭ	ㄒㄩ	To boast; to make known; harmony; bold, vigorous; to flatter。
诖 詿	kùa	ㄍㄨㄚ	To impose upon; to disturb.
诓 誆	k'ūang	ㄎㄨㄤ	To swindle; deceive.
诡 詭	kŭei	ㄍㄨㄟ	To feign, cheat.
诔 誄	lĕi	ㄌㄟ	To praise the dead; a eulogy.
诗 詩	shīh	ㄕ	Poetry, a poem, ode.
试 試	shìh	ㄕ	To test, try; to examine; trained, disciplined.

79

眷 謄	t'éng ㄊㄥ	To copy, transcribe.
誉 譽	yǔ ㄩ	To flatter, praise.
语 語	yǔ ㄩ	To speak; words, language, conversation; soft speech.
	yù ㄩ	To tell to.

7. 谄 諂 ch'ǎn — To flatter, distinguish.

诫 誡 chiai ㄐㄞ — A warning, admonishment; command; to distinguish.

诮 誚 ch'iao ㄑㄠ — To blame, scold; to ridicule.

诶 誒 è ㄜ — (An interjection).

诰 誥 kào ㄍㄠ — A title (of nobility); a patent.

诳 誑 k'úang ㄎㄨㄤ — Lies; to deceive.

说 説 shúo ㄕㄨㄛ — To say, speak, talk.

诵 誦 sùng ㄙㄨㄥ — To hum, recite, chant; a song.

诬 誣 wú ㄨ — To malign falsely; false.

误 誤 wù ㄨ — To obstruct, impede; to be mistaken.

诱 誘 yǔ ㄧㄡ — To induce, entice; to lead on.

8. 请 請 ch'ǐng ㄑㄧㄥ — To invite, request; please.

谆 諄 chūn ㄓㄨㄣ — To reiterate, repeatedly; to impress upon.

诽 誹 fěi ㄈㄟ — To slander.

谊 誼 ì — — Suitable, proper; related, connected, friendships.

课 課 k'ò ㄎㄛ — A lessen, assignment.

谅 諒 liang ㄌㄧㄤ — To excuse; to consider.

谂 諗 shěn ㄕㄣ — To consult, to seek counsel; to announce.

谂	讅	shěn ㄕㄣ	To cross examine, interrogate.
谁	誰	shúi ㄕㄨㄟ	Who, which?
		shéi	(Alternate).
许	誶	sui ㄙㄨㄟ	To vilify; to scold, abuse, acuse; to question.
诞	誕	tàn ㄊㄢ	A birthday; to have children.
谈	談	t'án ㄊㄢ	To chat.
调	調	t'íao ㄊㄧㄠ	To stir up, mix, blend, harmonize; to train.
诹	諏	tsōu ㄗㄡ	To plan, consult, deliberate.
诿	諉	wěi ㄨㄟ	To excuse oneself; to decline; to lay blame on others.
谀	諛	yú ㄩ	To flatter.
9. 谙	諳	ān ㄢ	To have knowledge of.
谌	諶	ch'én ㄔㄣ	Sincere, faithful.
谏	諫	chièn ㄐㄧㄢ	To admonish, to plead with.
诸	諸	chū ㄓㄨ	All, every.
谐	諧	hsieh ㄒㄧㄝ	To harmonize, accord with; to agree.
谞	諝	hsŭ ㄙㄩ	Knowledge, discrimination; prudence.
谖	諼	hsüan ㄒㄩㄢ	False, deceptive; to forget.
诺	諾	nò ㄋㄛ	To respond, answer; to promise; used in transliterating.
谑	謔	nüeh ㄋㄩㄝ	To jest, mock.
		hsüeh ㄒㄩㄝ	(Variant).
谝	諞	p'ien ㄆㄧㄢ	To boast.
谛	諦	ti ㄉㄧ	To judge, examine; to discriminate.
谍	諜	tíeh ㄉㄧㄝ	To spy.

諮	諮	tzŭ	ㄗ	To consult, plan; a dispatch.
谓	謂	wèi	ㄨㄟ	To speak about; to be called.
谒	謁	yèh	ㄜ	A visit.
谚	諺	yèn	ㄢ	A proverb.
谕	諭	yŭ	ㄩ	To proclaim; an official order.

10. 谗 讒 ch'án ㄢ To slander.

谦 謙 ch'īen ㄐㄢ Retiring, modest, self-effacing; humility.

谢 謝 hsieh ㄒㄝ To thank; be grateful; to decline; to confess; to hand over.

谎 謊 hŭang ㄏㄨㄤ To misstate, lie; falsehood.

谜 謎 mú ㄇ A riddle, puzzle.

谧 謐 mì ㄇ To whisper; quiet; inattentive.

谤 謗 pàng ㄅㄤ To slander.

谥 謚 shìh ㄕ A posthumous title for royalty.

谡 謖 shù ㄙㄨ To raise; to rise.

　 　 sù ㄙㄨ (Variant).

谣 謠 yáo ㄠ To sing; rumor.

11. 谪 謫 ché ㄓㄝ To blame, to find fault, to disgrace an official.

谫 譾 chĭen ㄐㄢ Stupid, shallow.

谨 謹 chĭn ㄐㄣ Attentive; carefully, judiciously.

谩 謾 mán ㄇㄢ To deceive, insult.

谬 謬 miu ㄇㄡ Falsehood, error, exaggeration.

谟 謨 mò ㄇㄛ A plan, course of action; to imitate; false.

　 　 mù ㄇㄨ (Variant).

12. 谯 譙 ch'iao ㄑㄠ To blame, ridicule.

譙 譙 ch'iao ㄑㄠˊ A lookout, tower.

譎 譎 chúeh ㄐㄩㄝˊ To pretend, deceive.

讕 讕 lán ㄌㄢˊ To make a false charge.

譜 譜 p'ǔ ㄆㄨˇ A register, family register; a treatise.

譚 譚 t'án ㄊㄢˊ To boast.

13. 讇 讇 chān ㄓㄢ Loquacious.

讞 讞 yèn ㄧㄢˋ To decide judicially, negotiate.

14. 譴 譴 ch'ien ㄑㄧㄢˋ To reprimand, scold.

辯 辯 pien ㄅㄧㄢˋ To argue, debate; to discuss.

16. 讎 讎 ch'óu ㄔㄡˊ An enemy, rival; to hate; to compare; a mate or class.

17. 讖 讖 ch'èn ㄔㄣˋ To verify; an omen.

20. 讌 讌 yèn ㄧㄢˋ A feast; to entertain; to rest, quiet.

谷　150

谷 穀 kǔ ㄍㄨˇ Grain, corn.

豕　152

5. 象 像 hsiàng ㄒㄧㄤˋ Appearance, resemblance; like, similar; image.

7. 蒙 濛 méng ㄇㄥˊ Mist, drizzle.

蒙 曚 méng ㄇㄥˊ Sun below horizon, down.

蒙 懞 měng ㄇㄥˇ Stupid, dull.

10. 豶 豶 fén ㄈㄣˊ To geld a pig.

2. 貞 貞 chēn ㄔㄣ Chaste.

貟 負 fù ㄈㄨ To bear, to support on the shoulders.

3. 貢 貢 kùng ㄍㄨㄥ Tribute.

財 財 ts'ái ㄘㄞ Wealth; bribe.

賬 賬 chàng ㄓㄤ An account, bill, check.

4. 質 質 chíh ㄓ Disposition; matter, substance, elements; to confront, call as a witness.

　　 chìh A pledge, pawn.

貯 貯 chǔ ㄓㄨ To hoard, store.

販 販 fàn ㄈㄢ To traffic in; to deal in.

賢 賢 hsíen ㄒㄧㄢ Virtuous, good, worthy; used in transliterating

貨 貨 hùo ㄏㄨㄛ Goods, commodities, produce.

購 購 kòu ㄍㄡ To buy, hire.

貫 貫 kùan ㄍㄨㄢ To pierce, to string on a thread.

敗 敗 pài ㄅㄞ To defeat.

貧 貧 p'ín ㄆㄧㄣ Poor, impoverished.

貪 貪 t'ān ㄊㄢ To covet, want; avaricious.

責 責 tsé ㄗㄜ To upbraid; to ask of; to punish.

　　 chái ㄔㄞ (Variant).

5. 賤 賤 chìen ㄐㄧㄢ Mean, worthless; to hold lightly.

6. 貳 貳 èrh ㄦ Double; changeable.

費 費 fèi ㄈㄟ To waste, spend; expenditure, expensis.

賀 賀 hò ㄏㄜ To congratulate; to send a gift of congratulations.

贻	貽	í	-	To give to, hand down; to leave to.
贶	貺	k'ùang	ㄎㄨㄤ	To give, grant; to confer.
		hùang	ㄏㄨㄤ	(Variant).
贵	貴	kùei	ㄍㄨㄟ	Honorable; expensive, valuable.
贸	貿	mào	ㄇㄠ	To barter, trade.
贲	賁	pì	ㄆㄧ	A military emblem, or symbol, or banner.
贬	貶	pìen	ㄅㄧㄢ	To exile.
赊	賒	shih	ㄕ	To buy on credit; to borrow; to let on hire.
贷	貸	tài	ㄊㄞ	To loan for interest; to borrow.
贴	貼	t'īeh	ㄊㄧㄝ	To paste, attach.

6.
贾	賈	chǐa	ㄐㄧㄚ	Price.
		kǔ	ㄍㄨ	To trade; a merchant.
贽	贄	chìh	ㄓ	A gift (to a superior) or offering.
赆	贐	chìn	ㄐㄧㄣ	Farewell or parting gifts.
贿	賄	hùi	ㄏㄨㄟ	Riches, wealth.
赅	賅	kāi	ㄍㄞ	To give.
赁	賃	lín	ㄌㄧㄣ	To rent, lease.
		jēn	ㄖㄣ	(Variant).
赃	贓	tsāng	ㄗㄤ	Plunder, stolen goods; bribes, corruption.
贼	賊	tséi	ㄗㄟ	A thief, rebel; to hurt, plunder; a term of abuse.
		tse	ㄗㄜ	(Variant).
资	資	tzū	ㄗ	Wealth, property; to aid; to rely upon; disposition.

7.
赈	賑	chèn	ㄔㄣ	Liberal; to aid the needy or distressed.

来	來	lài ㄌㄞ	To confer; to reward, bestow (on an inferior).
赊	賒	shē ㄕㄜ	To buy or sell on credit; distant; to shirk, put off.
8. 賫	賷	chī ㄐㄧ	To grasp and offer, subserviently.
賧	賤	ch'ien ㄐㄧㄢ	Mean, cheap, worthless.
賙	賙	chōu ㄓㄡ	To give alms.
賠	賠	p'éi ㄆㄟ	To restore, indemnify; to apologize.
賞	賞	shǎng ㄕㄤ	To reward, grant; an award, praise; to enjoy, appreciate.
賻	贖	shú ㄕㄨ	To redeem, ransom; to atone for.
賭	賭	tǔ ㄉㄨ	To gamble, risk.
賜	賜	tz'ù ㄘ	To give.
9. 賦	賦	fù ㄈㄨ	To spread, diffuse.
賴	賴	lài ㄌㄞ	To rely upon, to trust.
10. 賺	賺	chùan ㄔㄨㄢ	To earn, profit; to cheat.
賻	賻	fù ㄈㄨ	Funeral gifts.
賽	賽	sài ㄙㄞ	To compete; to contend, rival; to emulate.
11. 贅	贅	chùi ㄓㄨㄟ	To repeat; tautology; irrelevants useless, parasitic
12. 贊	贊	tsàn ㄗㄢ	To assist; to second; to praise, admire; to inform; to bring to light.
贈	贈	tsèng ㄗㄥ	To bestow, confer, give (a gift).
贋	贋	yèn ㄧㄢ	False, counterfeit; spurious; fake.
13. 贍	贍	shàn ㄕㄢ	To give, aid, supply; to be sufficient for.
贏	贏	yíng ㄧㄥ	Full, replete; to produce; profit, gain.

17. 贛 贛 kàn ㄎㄢ Region south of Po-yang Lake, Kiangsi Province.

赤　155

6. 赬 赬 ch'ēng ㄔㄥ Deep red; to blush.

走　156

2. 趙 趙 chào ㄓㄠ To hasten to; to visit; surname.
3. 趕 趕 kǎn ㄍㄢ To hurry.
5. 趨 趨 ch'ú ㄔㄨ Yeast; mother of vinegar.
16. 趲 趲 tsǎn ㄗㄢ To hasten, hurry.

足 足　157

3. 尳 尳 tǔn ㄉㄨㄣ To store.
4. 跄 蹌 ch'iang ㄑㄧㄤ To walk rapidly.
   跃 躍 yùeh ㄩㄝ To jump.
5. 踐 踐 chièn ㄐㄧㄢ To trample upon.
6. 跻 躋 chī ㄐㄧ To increase, augment.
   跷 蹺 ch'iao ㄑㄧㄠ To raise or cross the legs when
   sitting.

   蹕 蹕 pì ㄅㄧ To clear the way for the emperor;
   imperial stopping place.

7. 躊 躊 ch'óu ㄔㄡ Embarrassed.
   躚 躚 hsiēn ㄒㄧㄢ To walk aimlessly, meander.
   踊 踊 yǔng ㄩㄥ To leap, jump; exult, enthusiastic;
   to have one's toes cut off as punishment.

8. 跛 蹟　chíh 业　To walk with a limp.

9. 躑 躑　chíh 业　Embarrassed; bewildered.

10. 蹣 蹣　mán ㄇㄢ　To jump over.

蹑 躡　nieh ㄋㄧㄝ　To tread, step; to ascend.

12. 躥 躥　ts'uan ㄘㄨㄢ　To leap; spurt out, eject.

15. 躝 躝　lin ㄌㄧㄣ　A cart-rut; to run over, trample.

16. 躜 躜　tsúan ㄗㄨㄢ　To jump.

ts'úan ㄘㄨㄢ　(Variant).

身　158

4. 躯 軀　ch'ǖ ㄑㄩ　The human body; oneself.

車车　159

1. 轧 軋　yà ㄚ　To crush.

chà ㄔㄚ　To crowd about; a creaking sound.

2. 轨 軌　kǔei ㄍㄨㄟ　A rut or track; axel of a wheel; a law.

军 軍　chūn ㄐㄩㄣ　Military.

3. 轩 軒　hsǖan ㄒㄩㄢ　A porch, balcony, side room; merry, jovial; a surname.

轫 軔　jèn ㄖㄣ　To skid, to stop; a catch, an impediment; hard, firm, tough.

4. 斩 斬　chǎn ㄓㄢ　To behead, bisect.

6. 缲 繰　p'èi ㄆㄟ　Reins, a bridle. Also written 辔 .

9. 毂 轂　kǔ ㄍㄨ　Hub of a wheel.

11. 转 轉　chǔan ㄓㄨㄢ　To change direction, alter course, a revolution, to turn around, revolve; to cause to turn; to transfer, transmit.

88

轟	轟	hūng	ㄏㄨㄥ	To rumble, roar; to blow up, explode.
软	軟	juǎn	ㄖㄨㄢˇ	Soft, yielding; weak.
轮	輪	lún	ㄌㄨㄣˊ	To turn; a turn, revolution.
轭	軛	ò	ㄜˋ	A yoke, collar; to restrain.
载	載	tsài	ㄗㄞˋ	To load, contain; to carry in a vehicle; to enter in a register; to go to work.

5. 轸 軫 chěn ㄔㄣˇ Distressed, distraught, upset, saddened.

轻 輕 ch'īng ㄑㄧㄥ Light (eight)

轴 軸 chú ㄓㄨˊ An axel; a dowel on which maps or scrolls are rolled.

轶 軼 ì ㄧˋ To overtake (in a vehicle); to rush out; to surpass; exceeding.

轲 軻 k'ō ㄎㄜ A pair of wheels.

轱 軲 kū ㄍㄨ A wheel; to revolve.

6. 较 較 chiǎo ㄐㄧㄠˇ To test; than; relatively.

chiǎo ㄐㄧㄠˇ To compare.

轿 轎 chiǎo ㄐㄧㄠˋ A sedan-chair, palanquin.

轾 輊 chìh ㄓˋ A kind of chariot.

辂 輅 lù ㄌㄨˋ A carriage, chariot.

轼 軾 shìh ㄕˋ A stretcher in a palanquin.

7. 辅 輔 fǔ ㄈㄨˇ Auxiliary; props.

辄 輒 ch'è ㄓㄜˊ Sides of a chariot; at once, abruptly.

辆 輛 liàng ㄌㄧㄤˋ A pair of wheels; classifier for vehicles.

8. 辍 輟 ch'ò ㄔㄛˋ To mend.

辉 輝 hūi ㄏㄨㄟ Brightness, shining; glory.

89

辊 輥	kǔn	ㄍㄨㄣˇ	To revolve; a stone roller.
辇 輦	niǎn	ㄋㄧㄢˇ	A chair used as a hand carriage; the emperor's carriage; the royal court.
辈 輩	pèi	ㄅㄟˋ	Generation.
辎 輜	tzū	ㄗ	A baggage wagon; baggage.
辋 輞	wǎng	ㄨㄤˇ	Rim or tire of a wheel; felloe, felly.

9. 辑 輯 chì ㄐㄧ To collate, edit.

辐 輻 fú ㄈㄨˊ Spokes or blades in a wheel.

输 輸 shū ㄕㄨ To pay (as tribute); an offering; to transport, introduce; to loses to submit; to report to a superior; to overturn.

辏 輳 ts'òu ㄊㄡˋ The hub of a wheel.

10. 辗 輾 chǎn ㄓㄢˇ To turn half over; to roll over.

辖 轄 hsía ㄒㄧㄚˊ Linch - pin of a wheel; to govern or control.

舆 輿 yú ㄩ The bottom of a carriage; to contain, hold; earth, people, public.

辕 轅 yǔan ㄩㄢˇ The shafts of a horsedrawn vehicle.

11. 车鹿 轆 lù ㄌㄨˋ A pulley, windless, block.

12. 车散 轍 ch'è ㄔㄜˋ The track of a wheel; a precedent.

辚 轔 lín ㄌㄧㄣˊ Rumbling of vehicles; a threshold.

15. 车樂 轢 lì ㄌㄧˋ A wheel-rut.

辛 160

6. 辟 闢 p'ì ㄆㄧˋ To cleave, split open; to develop.

辞 辭 tz'ú ㄘ Words, speech; instructions; to

shirk, make excuses; to resign.

辵辶 162

2. 辽 遼 liao ㄌㄧㄠˊ Liao Dynasty.

　 边 邊 pien ㄅㄧㄢ Side.

3. 迁 遷 ch'ien ㄑㄧㄢ To move, remove.

　 过 過 kùo ㄍㄨㄛˋ To pass through; to experience.

　 迈 邁 mài ㄇㄞˋ To take a trip; to surpass.

　 达 達 tá ㄉㄚˊ To open; inform; to reach; attain.

4. 这 這 chè ㄓㄜˋ This (thing), this, these.

　 迟 遲 ch'íh ㄔˊ Slow, late.

　 进 進 chìn ㄐㄧㄣˋ To enter, advance.

　 还 還 húan ㄏㄨㄢˊ Yet, still.

　 　 　 hái ㄏㄞˊ Yet, still.

　 连 連 lian ㄌㄧㄢˊ To connect, join; including, together with; even; a company of soldiers.

　 违 違 wéi ㄨㄟˊ To object, oppose, disobey; to avoid.

　 远 遠 yǔan ㄩㄢˇ Far (away).

　 运 運 yùn ㄩㄣˋ To move about, transport.

5. 迩 邇 ěrh ㄦˇ Near, close.

　 迭 疊 tíeh ㄉㄧㄝˊ To fold; layer.

6. 选 選 hsǔan ㄒㄩㄢˇ To select.

　 逊 遜 hsǔn ㄒㄩㄣˋ To yield; humble, modest.

　 适 適 shih ㄕ To go to; to reach; a bride's moving to husband's house; to marry (of women); to suit, succeed; pleasure; amusements suddenly, just now.

7. 遜 邐 lǐ ㄌㄧˇ To walk in crowds.

   遞 遞 tì ㄊㄧˋ To hand over; transmit.

8. 逻 邏 ló ㄌㄛˊ To patrol, make a circuit; to watch.

9. 遗 遺 í ㄧˊ To hand down, bequeath; to lose, neglect, abandon; to forget.

邑 阝 163

2. 邓 鄧 tèng ㄊㄥˋ District in Honan; surname.

3. 邝 鄺 kǔang ㄎㄨㄤˇ A surname.

4. 邬 鄔 wū ㄨ A place name.

5. 邻 鄰 lín ㄌㄧㄣˊ A neighbor.

   邹 鄒 tsōu ㄗㄡ Ancient state, in present Shantung (where Mencius was born).

   邺 鄴 yèh ㄧㄝˋ Place name, north of Honan.

   邮 郵 yú ㄧㄡˊ Mail, post.

6. 郑 鄭 chèng ㄔㄥˋ Surname.

   郏 郟 chīa ㄐㄧㄚ A district in Honan.

   郁 鬱 yǜ ㄩˋ Anxious, sullen; surname.

   郐 鄶 kùai ㄎㄨㄞˋ A small feudal state in area of present day Honan.

   郓 鄆 yǔn ㄩㄣˇ An ancient city in Lu.

7. 郦 酈 lì ㄌㄧˋ Place-name in State of Lu.

8. 郸 鄲 tān ㄊㄢ A place name.

酉 164

4. 酝 醞 yǜn ㄩㄣˋ To brew, ferment.

92

6. 将 將 chiang4 ㄐㄧㄤ Jam, soy-sauce.
7. 酿 釀 niang4 ㄋㄧㄤ To brew (by fermentation).
   酽 釅 yèn ㄧㄢ Strong, rich (as applied to fluids).

米   165

5. 释 釋 shih4 ㄕ To release, open out; to explain;
   used in transliterating.

里   166

    里 裏 li3 ㄌㄧ Inside, interior.

金 釒 167

1. 钇 釔 i3 - The element yttrium (Y).
   钆 釓 ká ㄍㄚ The element gadolinium (Gd).
2. 钊 釗 cháo ㄔㄠ An ancient weapon.
   针 針 chēn ㄓㄣ A needle, pin, probe; a sting, a
   stitch.
   钌 釕 líao ㄌㄧㄠ The element ruthenium (Ru).
   钋 釙 p'ò ㄆㄛ The element polonium (Po).
   钉 釘 tīng ㄉㄧㄥ A nail, spike.
3. 钗 釵 ch'āi ㄔㄞ A hairpin; womankind.
   钏 釧 ch'ùan ㄔㄨㄢ A bracelet.
   钒 釩 fán ㄈㄢ The element vanadium (V).
   钎 釬 hàn ㄏㄢ To solder.
   钔 鍆 mén ㄇㄣ The element mendelevium (Md).

钕	釹	nǚ	ㄋㄩˊ	The element neodymium (Nd).
钚	鈈	pu	ㄅㄨ	The element plutonium (Pu).
钐	釤	sān	ㄕㄢ	The element samarium (Sm).
钓	釣	tiao	ㄉㄧㄠˋ	To fish with a hook and line.
钍	釷	t'ù	ㄊㄨˇ	The element thorium (Th).

4.

钞	鈔	ch'ào	ㄔㄠˋ	A money order; paper money; taxes.
钤	鈐	ch'íen	ㄑㄧㄢˊ	A stamp, seal.
钦	欽	ch'īn	ㄑㄧㄣ	Respectful; to command respect; to hope for.
钟	鐘	chūng	ㄓㄨㄥ	Gong; clock.
钟	鍾	chūng	ㄓㄨㄥ	An ancient measure, equalling four <u>tou</u> ㄉㄡ or about a peck; a cup or goblet; to bring together.
钧	鈞	chǔn	ㄐㄩㄣ	A unit of weight (30 catties).
钫	鈁	fáng	ㄈㄤˊ	The element francium (Fr).
钖	錫	hsī	ㄒㄧ	The element tin (Sn). See 锡.
铏	鉶	hsíng	ㄒㄧㄥˊ	A sacrificial caldron.
钬	鈥	hǔo	ㄏㄨㄛˇ	The element holmium (Ho).
钢	鋼	kāng	ㄍㄤ	Hard, strong; steel.
钪	鈧	k'àng	ㄎㄤˋ	The element scandium (Sc).
钩	鉤	kōu	ㄍㄡ	A hook, barb; to connect.
钙	鈣	kài	ㄍㄞˋ	The element calcium (Ca).
铆	鉚	mǎo	ㄇㄠˇ	A spike, large nail.
钠	鈉	nà	ㄋㄚˋ	To sharpen wood; to hammer metal to a point; the element sodium (Na).
钮	鈕	niu	ㄋㄧㄡˇ	A knob, button.
钯	鈀	pà	ㄅㄚˋ	The element palladium (Pd).

钡 鋇 pèi ㄅㄟ The element barium (Ba).

钛 鈦 t'ài ㄊㄞ The element titanium (Ti).

钭 鈄 tǒu ㄊㄡ Wine flask.

钝 鈍 tùn ㄊㄨㄣ Blunt, obtuse; dull-witted.

钨 鎢 wū ㄨ The element tungsten (W).

钥 鑰 yò ㄧㄛ A key; lock.

                  yào ㄧㄠ (Variant).

5. 钲 鉦 chēng ㄔㄥ A gong.

钾 鉀 chǐa ㄐㄧㄚ The element potassium (K).

鉴 鑒 chìen ㄐㄧㄢ A metal mirror; to view.

铅 鉛 ch'īen ㄑㄧㄢ The element lead (Pb).

钱 錢 ch'íen ㄑㄧㄢ Money, wealth.

钳 鉗 ch'íen ㄑㄧㄢ Forceps, pincers, pliers; manacles.

铉 鉉 hsǔan ㄒㄩㄢ Rings on a tripod; a decorated pole for carrying a tripod.

钶 鈳 k'ō ㄎㄛ The element columbium (Cb); also written 铌.

钴 鈷 kǔ ㄍㄨ A flat-iron; the element cobalt (Co).

铃 鈴 líng ㄌㄧㄥ Small bells.

钼 鉬 mù ㄇㄨ The element molybdenum (Mo).

铌 鈮 ní ㄋㄧ The element niobium (Nb), now columbium.

铋 鉍 pì ㄅㄧ The element bismuth (Bi).

铍 鈹 p'í ㄆㄧ The element beryllium (Be).

铂 鉑 pó ㄅㄛ The element platinum (Pt).

钷 鉕 p'á ㄆㄚ The element promethium (Pm). See 钷.

铈 鈰 shih ㄕ The element cerium (Ce).

铄	鑠	shùo ㄕㄨㄛ	To melt, to polish; shinning.
钽	鉭	t'ǎn ㄊㄢ	The element tantalium (Ta).
铁	鐵	t'ǐeh ㄊㄧㄝ	Firmness; firm, decided; the element iron (Fe).
钿	鈿	t'íen ㄊㄧㄢ	Silver or gold filagree hairpin.
		tìen ㄊㄧㄢ	(Variant).
铊	鉈	t'ó ㄊㄛ	A stone roller, a weight.
铎	鐸	tó ㄊㄛ	A bell with a clapper.
钻	鑽	tsūan ㄗㄨㄢ	To drill into, bore, pierce; to enter deeply, penetrate.
		tsān ㄗㄢ	(Variant).
铀	鈾	yú ㄧㄡ	The element uranium (U).
钰	鈺	yǜ ㄩ	(A given name.)
钺	鉞	yǜeh ㄩㄝ	A battle-axe.

6.
铡	鍘	chā ㄓㄚ	A knife for cutting chaff.
铲	鏟	ch'ǎn ㄔㄢ	A shovel, spade; to cut, pare.
铮	錚	chēng ㄓㄥ	A small gong; clang of metals.
铛	鐺	ch'ēng ㄔㄥ	A griddle.
铪	鉿	chīa ㄐㄧㄚ	A sound of creaking.
铰	鉸	chǐao ㄐㄧㄠ	A hinge.
铗	鋏	chīeh ㄐㄧㄝ	Tongs; a sword.
铢	銖	chū ㄓㄨ	Ancient silver coin.
		shú ㄕㄨ	(Variant).
铳	銃	ch'ùng ㄔㄨㄥ	A kind of firearm.
铨	銓	ch'ūan ㄔㄨㄢ	To estimate quality or quantity; to select.
铒	鉺	ér ㄦ	The element erbium (Er).

衒	銜	hsien I ㄢ		A bit; to hold in the mouth; to gag, control.
铣	銑	hsien ㄒㄧㄢˇ		A small chisel; burnished, bright.
鉶	鉶	hsíng ㄒㄧㄥ		A sacrificial cauldron; also written 鈃.
铧	鏵	húa ㄏㄨㄚˊ		A spade or shovel.
铟	銦	ī	-	The element indium (In).
铱	銥	ī	-	The element iridium (Ir).
铷	銣	jú ㄖㄨˊ		The element rubidium (Rb).
铠	鎧	k'ǎi ㄎㄞˇ		Armor (on a person).
铐	銬	k'ào ㄎㄠˋ		Handcuffs; manacles.
铬	鉻	kò ㄍㄜˋ		The element chromium (Cr).
铑	銠	láo ㄌㄠˊ		The element rhenium (Rh).
鑾	鑾	lúan ㄌㄨㄢˊ		Bells on a royal chariot; imperial, a term of respect.
铭	銘	míng ㄇㄧㄥˊ		To engrave, carve.
铙	鐃	náo ㄋㄠˊ		Bells, cymbals.
钷	鉕	p'ō ㄆㄛ		The element promethium (Pm). Sometimes written 钷.
铯	銫	sè ㄙㄜˋ		The element cesium (Cs).
铛	鐺	tāng ㄊㄤ		A small gong used by peddlers.
铫	銚	t'íao ㄊㄧㄠˊ		A spear.
		tiao ㄊㄧㄠˋ		A pan with a long handle.
		yáo ㄧㄠˊ		A weeding implement ; a surname.
铥	銩	tīu ㄉㄧㄡ		The element thulium (Tm).
铜	銅	t'úng ㄊㄨㄥˊ		Brass, bronze; the element copper (Cu).
铕	銪	yǔ ㄧㄡˇ		The element europium (Eu).

7. 锏 鐗 chīen ㄐㄧㄢ A knife used in execution.

锓 鍥 ch'īen ㄑㄧㄢ To engrave.

锔 鋦 chǖ ㄐㄩ The element curium (Cm).

铸 鑄 chù ㄓㄨ To cast metals; to coin.

锄 鋤 ch'ú ㄔㄨ A hoe.

锋 鋒 fēng ㄈㄥ A sharp tip of spear or lance.

锈 鏽 hsiu ㄒㄧㄡ Rust; to corrode.

销 銷 hsīao ㄒㄧㄠ To melt, fuse.

锌 鋅 hsīn ㄒㄧㄣ The element zinc (Zn).

tzǔ ㄗ Hard.

锐 銳 jùi ㄖㄨㄟ A sharp-pointed weapon; acute, zealous, valiant.

锎 鐦 k'āi ㄎㄞ The element californium (Cf).

锆 鋯 kào ㄍㄠ The element zirconium (Zr).

铿 鏗 k'ēng ㄎㄥ Tinkling or jingling of metals.

锅 鍋 kūo ㄍㄨㄛ A cooking pot, saucepan.

铼 錸 lái ㄌㄞ The element rhenium (Rh)。

锒 鋃 láng ㄌㄤ An ornament.

铹 鐒 láo ㄌㄠ The element lawrencium (Lw).

锂 鋰 lí ㄌㄧ The element lithium (Li).

铝 鋁 lǚ ㄌㄩ The element aluminum (Al).

铓 鋩 máng ㄇㄤ A sharp point.

锇 鋨 óu ㄡ The element osmium (Os).

铺 鋪 p'ū ㄆㄨ To spread out, arrange.

锁 鎖 shǔ ㄕㄨ A lock, chains; to lock。

铽	鋱	t'è	ㄊㄜ	The element terbium (Tb).
锑	銻	t'ī	ㄊㄧ	The element antimony (Sb).
铤	鋌	t'ǐng	ㄊㄧㄥ	Iron or copper ore; ingots or bars.
锉	銼	ts'ò	ㄘㄨㄛ	A file; iron pan.
银	銀	yín	ㄧㄣ	Riches, wealth, treasure; the element silver (Ag).

8.
锕	錒	ā	ㄚ	The element actinium (Ac).
锸	鍤	ch'á	ㄔㄚ	A spade.
锗	鍺	ché	ㄓㄜ	The element germanium (Ge).
锧	鑕	chǐh	ㄓ	A metallic substance.
锦	錦	chǐn	ㄐㄧㄣ	Delicate brocade; elegant.
锥	錐	chūi	ㄓㄨㄟ	An awl; to bore, pierce; a trifle.
锤	錘	ch'úi	ㄔㄨㄟ	Ancient Chinese weight, 12 ounces.
锯	鋸	chǜ	ㄐㄩ	A saw; to saw; serrate.
锡	錫	hsī	ㄙ	Tin, pewter; the element tin (Sn). See 钖.
锞	錁	k'ǒ	ㄎㄜ	A grease-pot; small ingots.
锢	錮	kù	ㄍㄨ	To pour molten metal into cracks; to close, stop.
链	鏈	lìen	ㄌㄧㄢ	A chain or cable.
锣	鑼	ló	ㄌㄨㄛ	A gong.
锰	錳	měng	ㄇㄥ	The element manganese (Mn).
锫	錇	p'éi	ㄆㄟ	The element berkelium (Bk).
锝	鍀	té	ㄉㄜ	The element technetium (Tc).
锭	錠	tìng	ㄉㄧㄥ	An ingot.
錾	鏨	tsàn	ㄗㄢ	A cold chisel; to engrave, cut out.

99

锘 錯	ts'ò	ㄘㄛ	Fault; error; to be confused; alternately.
锱 錙	tzū	ㄗ	An ancient measure of weight, equal to one <u>chu</u> 銖.

9. 鑀 鎄 āi ㄞ The element einsteinium (Es).

鎮 鎮 chèn ㄔㄣ To repress, hold down; to guard; to keep off evil; a market; a regiment.

锵 鏘 ch'īang ㄑㄧㄤ Tinkling of small bells.

锹 鍬 ch'īao ㄑㄧㄠ A hoe.

鍥 鍥 ch'ieh ㄑㄧㄝ A sickle; to cut, oppress.

键 鍵 chìen ㄐㄧㄢ A door bolt; piano key.

镄 鐨 fèi ㄈㄟ The element fermium (Fm).

鍰 鍰 húan ㄏㄨㄢ A metal ring; a weight of more than six taels (archaic).

镏 鎦 líu ㄌㄧㄡ The element lutetium (Lu).

镂 鏤 lòu ㄌㄡ To engrave, carve.

锚 錨 máo ㄇㄠ An anchor.

镅 鎇 méi ㄇㄟ The element americium (Am).

镁 鎂 měi ㄇㄟ The element magnesium (Mg).

锘 鍩 nù ㄋㄨ The element nobelium (No).

镀 鍍 tù ㄉㄨ To plate, gild.

锻 鍛 tùan ㄉㄨㄢ To forage metal.

镃 鎡 tzū ㄗ A hoe or mattock.

10. 镓 鎵 chīa ㄐㄧㄚ The element gallium (Ga).

镒 鎰 î - A piece of gold weighing 20 taels; wealth.

回 鎬 kǎo ㄎㄠ A tool.

鎘 鎘	kè	ㄎㄜ	The element cadmium (Cd).
錼 錼	nà	ㄋㄚ	The element neptunium (Np).
鑷 鑷	nieh	ㄋㄧㄝ	Tweezers, forceps; to pull out.
鎳 鎳	nieh	ㄋㄧㄝ	The element nickel (Ni).
鎊 鎊	pàng	ㄆㄤ	A pound (measure).
鎸 鎸	shàn	ㄕㄢ	A metal fan.
钂 钂	t'ăng	ㄊㄤ	An ancient weapon.

11. 鏡 鏡 chìng ㄐㄧㄥ A mirror, speculum.

鐫 鐫	chūan	ㄐㄩㄢ	To engrave.
鏝 鏝	mán	ㄇㄢ	A trowel.
鏢 鏢	piao	ㄅㄧㄠ	A metal dart.
鎪 鎪	sōu	ㄙㄡ	To engrave on metal or wood.
鏜 鏜	t'āng	ㄊㄤ	Roll or boom of drums.
鏑 鏑	tí	ㄉㄧ	The point of an arrow or spear.
鏃 鏃	tsù	ㄗㄨ	Head of an arrow or spear.
	ts'ù	ㄘㄨ	(Variant).
鏞 鏞	yūng	ㄩㄥ	A large bell.

12. 錂 錂 chĭang ㄐㄧㄤ Money, coins.

	ch'ĭang	ㄑㄧㄤ	(Variant).
鐝 鐝	chūeh	ㄐㄩㄝ	A pick, hoe.
鑭 鑭	lán	ㄌㄢ	The element lanthanum (la).
鐐 鐐	liao	ㄌㄧㄠ	Manacles, fetters; furnace.
鏷 鏷	p'ŭ	ㄆㄨ	The element protactinium (Pa).
鐠 鐠	p'ŭ	ㄆㄨ	The element praseodymium (Pr).
饊 饊	săn	ㄙㄢ	Fried round cakes of wheat flour.

鐙	鐙	tèng ㄉㄥ	·A stirrup.	
鑹	鑹	ts'ùan ㄘㄨㄢ	A temper (a metal).	
鐓	鐓	tūn ㄉㄨㄣ	Anvil.	
13.鐲	鐲	chó ㄓㄨㄛ	A small bell; bracelets, bangles.	
鐶	鐶	húan ㄏㄨㄢ	A metal ring; a weight of more than six taels (archaic).	
鐿	鐿	i ─	The element ytterbium (Yb).	
鐳	鐳	lèi ㄌㄟ	A pot; small copper coin; element radium (Ra).	
鐮	鐮	lían ㄌㄧㄢ	A sickle, sythe.	
14.鑊	鑊	hùo ㄏㄨㄛ	A boiler, cauldron; a skillet.	
15.鑞	鑞	là ㄌㄚ	Tin, copper, pewter. See 锡 and 锡.	
鏢	鏢	pīao ㄆㄧㄠ	A metal dart.	
17.鑲	鑲	hsīang ㄒㄧㄤ	To inlay, esp. with jewels.	
20.钁	钁	kùo ㄍㄨㄛ	A mattock.	

長 長 长 168

长	長	ch'áng ㄔㄤ	Long.

門 门 169

门	門	mén ㄇㄣ	Entrance. (This is radical 169).
1. 闩	閂	shūan ㄕㄨㄢ	A bolt used to bar a door.
2. 闪	閃	shǎn ㄕㄢ	To flash, as lightning.
3. 闯	闖	ch'ǔang ㄔㄨㄤ	To rush in; suddenly.
闭	閉	pì ㄅ	To close.

4. 间 閒 chīen ㄐㄧㄢ In, among, on.

    chìen To divide, separate.

  闲 閑 hsíen ㄒㄧㄢ A bar, fence, corral; to defend; trained.

  闰 閏 jùn ㄖㄨㄣ Extra; inserted between others, intercalate.

  闵 閔 mǐn ㄇㄧㄣ To mourn, weep; to encourage.

  闱 闈 wéi ㄨㄟ Doors leading to women's quarters.

5. 闸 閘 chá ㄓㄚ A flood-gate, a lock (in a canal), a barrier.

  闹 鬧 nào ㄋㄠ A disturbance; to make a disturbance; noise, bustle.

6. 阂 閡 ài ㄞ To shut others out; obstructed.

    hè ㄏㄜ (Variant).

  阀 閥 fá ㄈㄚ Ranking, classification.

  闿 閫 k'ǎi ㄎㄞ To loosen or open.

  阁 閣 kó ㄍㄜ A pavilion; vestibule; bookcase.

  闺 閨 kūei ㄍㄨㄟ Women's apartment; lady-like, feminine.

  闽 閩 mǐn ㄇㄧㄣ A kind of snake; Fukien Province.

7. 阄 鬮 chīu ㄐㄧㄡ A ticker or lot (of chance); to draw lots.

  阃 閫 k'ǔn ㄎㄨㄣ A threshold; entrance to women's apartments.

  阆 閬 lǎng ㄌㄤ A high door.

  闾 閭 lǘ ㄌㄩ Gate of a village.

  闼 闥 t'à ㄊㄚ The door of an inner room.

  阅 閱 yüeh ㄩㄝ To examine, inspect, review; to pass through.

8. 阐 闡 ch'ǎn ㄔㄢ To open; explain.

103 阊 閶 ch'āng ㄔㄤ The gates of heaven; west wing.

闃	闃	ch'ǖ ㄑㄩ	To live alone; still, quiet.	
鬩	鬩	hsì ㄒㄧ	To quarrel; animosity, resentment.	
閽	閽	hūn ㄏㄨㄣ	A door-keeper, an entrance.	
閼	閼	ò ㄜ	To close, obstruct; to conceal.	
閿	閿	wén ㄨㄣ	To look at closely.	
閹	閹	yēn ㄧㄢ	To castrate, emasculate.	
閭	閭	yén ㄧㄢ	Gate to a village; a hamlet.	
		nién ㄋㄧㄢ	(Variant).	
閾	閾	yǜ ㄩ	A door-sill, threshold.	

9. 闋 闋 ch'üeh ㄑㄩㄝ To close a door; to close, rest.

闊 闊 k'ùo ㄎㄨㄛ Broad, ample; affluent.

闌 闌 lán ㄌㄢ A door screen; to cut off.

10. 闕 闕 ch'üeh ㄑㄩㄝ A look-out tower at a city gate. An imperial city.

闔 闔 hó ㄏㄜ Leaf of a door.

闐 闐 t'íen ㄊㄧㄢ To fill up; rumbling sounds.

　　　 tìen ㄉㄧㄢ A place name.

11. 闞 闞 k'àn ㄎㄢ To peep; a pavilion.

阜阝 170

2. 队 隊 tùi ㄉㄨㄟ A regiment or group of men, air-planes, warships.

4. 阵 陣 chèn ㄓㄣ A group of soldiers; a battle; a time, occasion.

阶 階 chīeh ㄐㄧㄝ Steps, degrees.

阳 陽 yáng ㄧㄤ Male principle; sun.

阴 陰	yīn	ㄣ	Female principle; cloudy, shady, dark.
5. 陈 陳	ch'én	ㄣ	Stale; to arrange, spread out.
际 際	chì	ㄐ	Interval; limit; border.
陉 陘	hsing	ㄒㄥ	A gorge, pass; niche near a stove.
陆 陸	lù	ㄌㄨ	Land; six.
陇 隴	lúng	ㄌㄨㄥ	A dike or bank.
6. 陕 陝	shǎn	ㄕㄢ	Mountain passes; the Province of Shensi.
7. 险 險	hsiěn	ㄒㄧㄢ	A narrow pass; danger, dangerous, risk.
陨 隕	yǔn	ㄩㄣ	To fall.
9. 隐 隱	yǐn	ㄣ	To avoid, conceal; retired, hidden; small, minute; painful, sore; grieved.
	yèn	ㄣ	To lean on.
10. 随 隨	súi	ㄙㄨㄟ	To follow.

隶　171

隶 隸	lì	ㄌㄧ	Attached to, belonging to; to control, to rule. (This is not radical 171).

隹　172

2. 难 難	nán	ㄋㄢ	Difficult, hard。
5. 雏 雛	ch'ú	ㄔㄨ	A chick, fledgling; to brood.

雨　173

4. 雳 靂	lì	ㄌㄧ	Peal of thunder.

5. 霧 霧 wù ㄨ Fog, mist, vapor.

6. 霽 霽 chǐ ㄗ A clearing sky.

7. 霉 黴 méi ㄇㄟ Moldy and black; bacteria; lichens; to rot. Sometimes written 霉

面 176

面 麵 mien ㄇㄧㄢ Flour. (This is not radical 176.)

6. 靥 靨 yèh ㄧㄝ The jaws, cheeks.

革 177

7. 鞑 韃 tá ㄊㄚ A nomadic tribe, formerly of north-west China.

10. 鞯 韉 chǐen ㄐㄧㄢ A saddle-cloth.

韦 韋 178

3. 韧 韌 jèn ㄐㄣ Pliable but strong, like leather.

5. 韨 韍 fú ㄈㄨ A leather knee-pad; a leather strap for a seal.

8. 韩 韓 hàn ㄏㄢ A fence, a surname; old name for Korea.

9. 韪 韙 wěi ㄨㄟ Right; that which is right, correct, proper.

10. 韬 韜 t'āo ㄊㄠ A bow-case, sheath; just, liberal.

韫 韞 yǔn ㄩㄣ An orange color.

頁 页 181

2. 顷 頃 ch'ǐng An instant, a short time; one hundred <u>mou</u>, 畝 , ca 15 acres.

106

2. 顶 頂 tǐng ㄉㄧㄥˇ The top; extremely, utmost, very.

3. 頇 頇 hān ㄏㄢ A large face.

项 項 hsiang ㄒㄧㄤˋ The nape; an item, kind; a term, as in algebra.

须 鬚 hsū ㄒㄩ Mustache, beard.

须 須 hsū ㄒㄩ Necessary, must; a moment, to wait.

顺 順 shùn ㄕㄨㄣˋ Favorable, prosperous; to obey, agree; in accordance with; to allow, indulge; to persist in.

4. 顼 頊 hsū ㄒㄩ Anxious, worried.

顾 顧 kù ㄍㄨˋ To care for, look after.

颃 頏 háng ㄏㄤˊ To fly down.

颂 頌 sùng ㄙㄨㄥˋ To praise, commend; hymns, odes.

顿 頓 tùn ㄉㄨㄣˋ A time, turn; to injure; suddenly; classifier for times.

顽 頑 wán ㄨㄢˊ Obstinate, wayward; stupid; corrupt; bigoted.

预 預 yù ㄩ To prepare, before hand; to be at ease, pleased, comfortable.

5. 颇 頗 p'ō ㄆㄛ Inclined to one side, leaning; somewhat, rather.

p'ū ㄆㄨ (Variant).

颈 頸 ching ㄐㄧㄥˇ The neck, throat.

顾 顧 kù ㄍㄨˋ To care for.

领 領 lǐng ㄌㄧㄥˇ The throat; collar; to lead, guide or direct; to receive.

颅 顱 lú ㄌㄨˊ The skull, forehead.

6. 颊 頰 chia ㄐㄧㄚˊ The jaw, cheeks.

颏 頦 hái ㄏㄞˊ The chin.

107

頜 頜 hó ㄏㄜˊ The jowls.

　　 kó ㄍㄜˊ (A variant).

頡 頡 hsieh ㄒㄧㄝˊ To soar, ascend in flight.

7. 頷 頷 hàn ㄏㄢˋ The chin, jaws.

頤 頤 i ㄧˊ The chin, jaws; to nurish, to rear.

頻 頻 p'in ㄆㄧㄣˊ Urgent, hurried; imminent; a shore, a band.

頹 頹 t'úi ㄊㄨㄟˊ To fall, descend; ruin.

8. 顆 顆 k'ō ㄎㄜ A kernel; classifier for small objects.

9. 顓 顓 chūan ㄓㄨㄢ Good, sedate, simple.

額 額 ó ㄜˊ Forehead; amount, a fixed number.

題 題 t'í ㄊㄧˊ The forehead; a heading, item, subject.

顏 顏 yén ㄧㄢˊ Color; to dye.

10. 顳 顳 nieh ㄋㄧㄝˋ The temporal bones.

顙 顙 sǎng ㄙㄤˇ The forehead.

顛 顛 tīen ㄉㄧㄢ To jolt.

11. 顢 顢 mān ㄇㄢ A large face; dawdling.

12. 顥 顥 hào ㄏㄠˋ Luminous, bright; hoary, white.

13. 顫 顫 chàn ㄓㄢˋ A cocked head; shaking, unsteady.

　　 ch'àn ㄔㄢˊ (Variant).

14. 顬 顬 jú ㄐㄨˊ The temporal bone.

15. 顰 顰 p'in ㄆㄧㄣˊ To knit the brows; to look disraught.

18. 顴 顴 ch'üan ㄑㄩㄢˊ The cheek-bones.

風 风 182

风 風	fēng	ㄈㄥ	Wind. (This is radical 182).
5. 颯 颯	sà	ㄙㄚ	The sound of wind; a gust suddenly.
8. 颶 颶	chǜ	ㄐㄩ	Hurricane, typhoon.
9. 飀 飅	líu	ㄌㄧㄡ	Sighing of the wind.
11. 飄 飄	p'īao	ㄆㄧㄠ	To whirl (like wind); floating, graceful.
颼 颼	sōu	ㄙㄡ	A chilling wind; a whizzing sound.
12. 飆 飆	pīao	ㄆㄧㄠ	Whirlwind.

飛 飞 183

飞 飛	fēi	ㄈㄟ	To fly. (This is radical 183).

食 食 饣 184

2. 饥 饑	chī	ㄐ	Hunger, famine; scarcity.
3. 饷 饗	hsiǎng	ㄒㄧㄤ	To offer in sacrifice or at a feast.
4. 饬 飭	ch'ìh	ㄔ	To direct; to prepare.
饭 飯	fàn	ㄈㄢ	Cooked rice; food; a meal.
饩 餼	hsì	ㄒㄧ	A sacrificial victim; to give a ration of grain.
饪 飪	jěn	ㄖㄣ	To cook thoroughly.
饮 飲	yǐn	ㄧㄣ	To drink, swallow.
饫 飫	yǜ	ㄩ	To overeat.
5. 饯 餞	chìen	ㄐㄧㄢ	A bye-bye gift or party.
饱 飽	pǎo	ㄅㄠ	Satiated, replete.

饰	飾	shìh	ㄕ	To adorn; to set off; to deceive; ornaments.
饲	飼	szù	ㄙ	To feed, nurish; provision, food.
6. 饺	餃	chǐao	ㄐㄧㄠ	A meat dumpling.
饵	餌	ěrh	ㄦ	Cakes; dumplings.
饷	餉	hsǐang	ㄒㄧㄤ	Rations or pay for troops; revenue; gifts of provisions.
饶	饒	jáo	ㄖㄠ	To forgive, spare, overlook; to be liberal, indulgent.
饼	餅	pǐng	ㄅㄧㄥ	Cake, biscuit.
蚀	蝕	shíh	ㄕ	To eat, consume slowly; an eclipse.
餍	饜	yèn	ㄧㄢ	To eat to repletion; to be replete.
7. 馁	餒	něi	ㄋㄟ	To be hungry, famished; feeble.
饿	餓	ò	ㄜ	Hungry.
8. 馅	餡	hsìen	ㄒㄧㄢ	Fruit, meat, sugar, etc., as stuffing in pastry; a secret.
馄	餛	hún	ㄏㄨㄣ	Dumpling.
馃	餜	kūo	ㄍㄨㄛ	Cakes or biscuits.
馆	館	kǔan	ㄍㄨㄢ	A place to lodge; a tavern; a public office.
9. 馈	饋	k'ùei	ㄎㄨㄟ	Provisions, food; to offer a gift, esp. of food.
馋	饞	ch'án	ㄔㄢ	Gluttonous.
10. 馏	餾	lìu	ㄌㄧㄡ	To steam food.
11. 馑	饉	chìn	ㄐㄧㄣ	A dearth; famine.
馐	饈	hsǐu	ㄒㄧㄡ	Delicacies.
馒	饅	mán	ㄇㄢ	Steamed breed.
馊	餿	sōu	ㄙㄡ	Rancid, sour.

12. 饌饌 chùan ㄔㄨㄢ To give food to; delicacies.

馬马 187

马 馬 mǎ ㄇㄚ A horse; at once; used in transliterating.

2. 冯 馮 féng ㄈㄥ A surname.

  p'íng ㄆㄧㄥ To ford a stream.

  驭 馭 yü ㄩ To drive (a chariot); to manage; to wait on, set before; an attendant; imperial.

  yà ㄧㄚ To invoke; to meet.

3. 驰 馳 ch'íh ㄔ To go quickly.

  驯 馴 hsǜn ㄒㄩㄣ Tame; docile, well-bred。

  驮 馱 t'ó ㄊㄨㄛ To carry on the back; to bear.

4. 驱 驅 ch'ü ㄑㄩ To expel, to drive.

  驴 驢 lü ㄌㄩ An ass, donkey.

  驳 駁 pó ㄅㄛ To refute.

5. 驾 駕 chìa ㄐㄧㄚ To ride; to yoke, control.

  驻 駐 chù ㄓㄨ To halt; to reside temporarily.

  驹 駒 chü ㄐㄩ A colt; strong.

  驸 駙 fù ㄈㄨ An extra harnessed by the side of a team.

  驿 驛 i — A government post.

  驽 駑 nú ㄋㄨ Worn-out old horses; referring to a man in the intellectual menopause.

  驶 駛 shǐh ㄕ To ride in; to be driven; to proceed to.

  驷 駟 szù ㄙ A team of four horses.

马台	駘	t'ái ㄊㄞˊ		A worn-out horse, a nag.
驼	駝	t'ó ㄊㄛˊ		The camel.
马且	駔	tsăng ㄗㄤˇ		A powerful horse; broken, inferior, coarse.
		tsŭ ㄗㄨˇ		A cord attached to a badge.

6.
骄	驕	chīao ㄐㄧㄠ	A high spirited horse; proud, haughty.
骇	駭	hài ㄏㄞˋ	To terrify; startled.
马匆	騶	tsōu ㄗㄡ	To go; a mythical animal.
骁	驍	hsīao ㄒㄧㄠ	A good horse; brave, strong skillful.
骅	驊	hūa ㄏㄨㄚ	A chestnut horse.
骆	駱	lò ㄌㄛˋ	Camel.
骈	駢	p'íen ㄆㄧㄢˊ	A pair of horses; to associate, join together
		p'ín ㄆㄧㄣˊ	(Variant).

7.
骋	騁	ch'ěng ㄔㄥˇ	To gallop, hasten.
骎	駸	ch'īn ㄑㄧㄣ	A fleet horse.
骏	駿	chŭn ㄐㄩㄣˋ	A spirited, vigorous horse; swift; lofty.
骊	驪	lí ㄌㄧˊ	A fine horse, black horse.
验	驗	yèn ㄧㄢˋ	To verify, fulfill; to examine.

8.
骐	騏	ch'í ㄑㄧˊ	A piebald horse; spotted.
骑	騎	ch'í ㄑㄧˊ	To mount, ride.
骓	騅	chūi ㄓㄨㄟ	A piebald horse.
骒	騍	k'ò ㄎㄜˋ	A mare.
骖	驂	ts'ān ㄘㄢ	The two outside horses of a team of four abreast.

9.
鹙	鶖	ch'īu ㄑㄧㄡ	A long-legged wading bird.
骝	騮	líu ㄌㄧㄡˊ	A bay horse with a black mane.

马扁 騙 p'ien ㄆㄧㄢˋ To cheat, swindle.

马蚤 騷 sāo ㄙㄠ To annoy: sad, grieved; moved; lascivious; poetic.

10. 寋 騫 ch'ien ㄑㄧㄢ Defective, jailing; to raise the head.

陟 騭 chìh ㄓˋ A stallion; to promote; to determine.

骟 騸 shàn ㄕㄢˋ To geld a horse or ass.

11. 马累 騾 ló ㄌㄨㄛˊ A mule.

马票 驃 p'iao ㄆㄧㄠˋ A charger; fleet, rapid.

piao (Variant).

11. 马悤 驄 ts'ūng ㄘㄨㄥ A piebald horse

14. 马聚 驟 tsòu ㄗㄡˋ A fast horse; sudden and violent; long continued.

16. 马冀 驥 chì ㄐㄧˋ A thoroughbred.

17. 马襄 驤 hsiang ㄒㄧㄤ To prance, like a spirited horse.

骨 188

9. 骨娄 髏 lóu ㄌㄡˊ Skull.

髟 190

10. 髟宾 鬢 pìn ㄅㄧㄣˋ Hair on the temples.

鬼 194

6. 厭 魘 yěn ㄧㄢˇ Nightmare.

7. 鬼两 魎 hǎng ㄌㄧㄤˇ A fairy, sprite.

2. 魛 鮂刀 tāo ㄊㄠ The mullet (Family Mugilidae).

4. 魴 鲂 fáng ㄈㄤ A kind of bream.

鮜 鮢 hù ㄏㄨ The shad (Family Clupeidae).

魯 鲁 lǔ ㄌㄨ Stupid; common, vulgar; Shantung.

鲅 鲅 pān ㄆㄢ A flounder or sole (Heterosomata).

魨 魨 t'ún ㄊㄨㄣ A fresh water porpoise, the "white-flag" dolphin, Lipotes vexillifer.

鱿 鱿 yú ㄩ A kind of squid.

鼋 鼋 yüan ㄩㄢ A sea turtle.

5. 鲊 鲊 chǎ ㄓㄚ Sweets made from fish concentrate; preserved fish.

鮒 鮒 fù ㄈㄨ A perch-like fish.

鱟 鱟 hoù ㄏㄡ The king crab.

鲈 鱸 lú ㄌㄨ A sea-perch, or seabass (Serranidae); a generic term for bass-like fish.

鮎 鮎 nien ㄋㄧㄢ The sheat-fish.

鲅 鲅 pá ㄆㄚ A species of threadfin, (Family Polynemidae): 马鲅

鮑 鲍 pào ㄆㄠ Salted, pickled or dried fish; abalone.

鮃 鮃 p'ing ㄆㄧㄥ A flatfish or sole (Family Soleidae or Cynoglossidae).

鲐 鲐 t'ái ㄊㄞ A puffer (Tetraodontidae).

鮀 鮀 t'ó ㄊㄛ A snakefish (Family Ophichthyidae).

鲫 鲫 yin ㄧㄣ The shark-sucker (Family Echeneidae).

鲉 鲉 yīu Rockfish or scorpionfish (Family Scorpaenidae).

6. 鲛 鲛 chīao ㄐㄧㄠ A shark, or other elasmobranch.

鮰 鮰 húi ㄏㄨㄟˊ A kind of catfish (Family Amblycepidae); sometimes a sturgeon (Family Acipenseridae).

鯗 鯗 hsiǎng ㄒㄧㄤˇ Dried, salted fish.

鮮 鮮 hsiēn ㄒㄧㄢ Fresh (pert. to fruit, flowers, meat, fish); delicious.

鱏 鱏 hsín ㄒㄧㄣˊ A sturgeon (Family Acipenseridae).

hsǖn ㄒㄩㄣ (Variant).

鯶 鯶 hùn ㄏㄨㄣˋ A kind of tench (Family Cyprinidae).

鱠 鱠 kùai Minced meat or fish.

鮭 鮭 kúei ㄍㄨㄟˊ Fresh-water porpoise (<u>Lipotes sinensis</u>); also a species of salmon (Family Salmonidae).

鰂 鰂 tsé ㄗㄜˊ A cuttlefish, squid.

鮦 鮦 t'úng ㄊㄨㄥˊ A snakefish (Family Ophichthyidae).

鮠 鮠 wéi ㄨㄟˊ A kind of shad (Family Clupeidae).

鮪 鮪 wěi ㄨㄟˇ A shovel-nosed sturgeon; a tuna (Family Thunnidae).

7. 鯁 鯁 kěng ㄍㄥˇ Fish bones, things that stick in the throat. Unyielding, blunt of speech.

鯀 鯀 kǔei ㄍㄨㄟˇ A large fish.

鯉 鯉 lǐ ㄌㄧˇ The carp; also a small fish (topminnow) (Cyprinodontidae).

鮰 鱺 lì ㄌㄧˋ An eel, 鰻 鮰 , (Family Anguillidae).

鯆 鯆 p'ù ㄆㄨˋ A ray or skate; an elasmobranch fish.

鰷 鰷 t'iáo ㄊㄧㄠˊ A slender fish.

鰣 鰣 shíh ㄕˊ An anadromous fish, a shad (Family Clupeidae).

8. 鰂 鰂 chì ㄐㄧˋ A large carp-like fish (Family Cyprinidae).

鯕 鯕 ch'í ㄑㄧˊ Dolphin, written 鯕 鰍

鯖 鯖 ch'īng ㄑㄧㄥ Mackerel, mullet.

ching ㄐㄧㄥ To fry.

鯨 鯨 ch'íng ㄑㄧㄥ A whale; gigantic.

chīng ㄐㄧㄥ (Alternate).

鯡 鯡 féi ㄈㄟ A herring (Family Clupeidae).

鯤 鯤 k'ūn ㄎㄨㄣ A sea monster; fry of fish.

鰱 鰱 lien ㄌㄧㄢ A tarpon (Family Elopidae); a species of bream.

鯪 鯪 líng ㄌㄧㄥ A dace, a small cyprinid fish.

鯢 鯢 ní ㄋㄧ The giant salamander, <u>Megalobatrachus davidianus</u>; the young of fish.

鯰 鯰 nien ㄋㄧㄢ A sturgeon (Acipenseridae); or sheath-fish (Siluridae).

鱔 鱔 shàn ㄕㄢ A rice-field eel (Family Symbranch-iidae).

鯛 鯛 tĭao ㄉㄧㄠ Generic word for perch; more speci-fically a fish called the John Dory
t'ĭao ㄊㄧㄠ (Family Zeidae), or the seabreams (Family Sparidae).

鯧 鯧 ts'āng ㄘㄤ The pomfret (Family Stromateidae) or man-of war fish (Family Nomeidae).

ch'āng (Variant).

鯫 鯫 tsōu ㄗㄡ A small fish.

tsòu ㄘㄡ A petty person.

鯔 鯔 tzù ㄗ A mullet (Family Mugilidae).

9. 鱨 鱨 ch'áng ㄔㄤ A kind of flying fish (Family Exocoetidae) yellow in color.

鯽 鯽 chĭ ㄐ The bastard carp.

鰍 鰍 ch'īu ㄑㄧㄡ The loach (Family Cobitidae). See 鯕 .

116

鰍	鰌	ch'íu	ㄑㄧㄡ	The loach (Family Cobitidae).
鰆	鰆	ch'ún	ㄔㄨㄣ	A fish of the family Cybiidae.
鰉	鰉	húang	ㄏㄨㄤ	A sturgeon (Family Acipenseridae).
鰐	鰐	ò	ㄜ	Crocodile.
鯿	鯿	pǐen	ㄅㄧㄢ	A kind of bream.
鰓	鰓	sāi	ㄙㄞ	Gills of a fish.
鰈	鰈	tǐeh	ㄉㄧㄝ	A flatfish, sole (Heterosomata).
鰮	鰮	wèn	ㄨㄣ	A round-herring (Family Dussumieriidae); also a sardine (Clupeidae).

10. 鰭 鰭 ch'í ㄑㄧ Fin (of a fish).

鰥	鰥	kūan	ㄍㄨㄢ	A large fish in the Yellow River; a widower; solitary.
鰨	鰨	t'à	ㄊㄚ	A flat fish (Heterosomata); sole, flounder, etc.
鰩	鰩	yáo	ㄧㄠ	A flying fish (Family Exocoetidae); a skate or ray.
歔	歔	yú	ㄩ	To fish, seize.

11. 鰲 鰲 aó ㄠ A sea monster.

鱈	鱈	hsüeh	ㄒㄩㄝ	The codfish (Family Gadidae).
		hsìeh		(Variant).
鰳	鰳	lè	ㄌㄜ	A kind of shad.
鰻	鰻	mán	ㄇㄢ	An eel; also a kind of catfish (Plotosidae or Ariidae). See 鮰
鰵	鰵	mǐn	ㄇㄧㄣ	A kind of perch or cod.
鰾	鰾	pǐao	ㄆㄧㄠ	The air-bladder or swim-bladder of a fish.
鱅	鱅	yúng	ㄩㄥ	A kind of tench.

12. 鱘 鱘 hsún ㄒㄩㄣ A sturgeon (Family Acipenseridae) or a trout (Family Salmonidae).

117

鱖 鱥 kùei ㄍㄨㄟ A kind of large-mouth striped perch.

鱗 鱗 lín ㄌㄧㄣ Fish scales; scaly, imbricate.

13. 鱣 鱣 chán ㄔㄢ A sturgeon (Family Acipenseridae).

鱧 鱧 lǐ ㄌㄧ The snakefish, snakehead (Family Ophiocephalidae).

鳥 鸟 196

2. 鸡 鷄 chī ㄐ Chickens, fowl; grouse or partridge; a plover.

鳩 鳩 chīu ㄐㄧㄨ A pigeon, dove (<u>Streptopelia</u> sp. or <u>Oenopopelia</u> sp.)

鳬 鳬 fú ㄈㄨ Wild ducks; the shelldrake.

3. 鴞 鴞 hsiao ㄒㄧㄠ An owl, said to eat its mother; an unfilial son; brave and unscrupulous; highest throw in dice.

鳲 鳲 shíh ㄕ A turtle dove (<u>Streptopelia</u>) (Family Columbidae).

鳶 鳶 yūan ㄩㄢ A hawk, kite.

4. 鴆 鴆 chèn ㄓㄣ A predator bird; deadly.

tān ㄊㄢ Addicted to.

鴟 鴟 ch'īh ㄔ An owl.

鴂 鴂 chǘeh ㄐㄩㄝ A cuckoo (Cuculidae).

鷗 鷗 ōu ㄡ Gulls, terns (Family Laridae).

鴇 鴇 pǎo ㄅㄠ A goose-like bird; a bustard; a procuress.

鳾 鳾 shíh ㄕ A nuthatch (<u>Sitta</u>), of the family Sittidae.

鶬 鶬 ts'āng ㄘㄤ A species of crane.

| 鴉 鵶 | yā | ㄚ | A crow, rook, raven (Family Corvidae). |

5. 鸲 鴝 ch'ü ㄑ A species of mynah; a species of ruby-throat (Luscenia, Turdidae).

鴞 鴞 hsīao ㄒㄧㄠ An owl, said to eat its mother, but leaving the head (Family Strigidae).

鷽 鷽 hsíao ㄒㄧㄠ A kind of magpie (Family Corvidae).

鴣 鴣 kū ㄍㄨ A partridge.

鴒 鴒 líng ㄌㄧㄥ A wagtail (Motacilla sp.). See 鹡

鸕 鸕 lú ㄌㄨ A cormorant used for fishing.

鴅 鴅 tān ㄉㄢ A species of nightingale.

鴕 鴕 t'ó ㄊㄜ The ostrich, emu.

鶇 鶇 tùng ㄉㄨㄥ A species of thrush (Turdus or Monti-cola) of the family Turdidae.

鴨 鴨 yā ㄚ A duck.

鴦 鴦 yāng ㄤ Female mandarin duck.

䳬 䳬 yù ㄩ Eagles flying fast; to swoop.

鴛 鴛 yūan ㄩㄢ The drake of the mandarin duck.

6. 鷮 鷮 chíao ㄐㄧㄠ A long-tailed pheasant.

鵁 鵁 chíao ㄐㄧㄠ A species of crane or heron, with a red crest.

鷙 鷙 chìh ㄓ Predatory birds; violent, rapacious.

鴴 鴴 hèng ㄏㄥ A species of pratincole (a wading bird) (Family Glareolidae); or a plover, (Family Charadriidae).

鵂 鵂 hsīu ㄒㄧㄡ An owl, esp. a horned owl; bird of ill omen.

鴿 鴿 kō ㄍㄜ A dove, pigeon. (Columba sp.);鳩鴿.

鴰 鴰 kūa ㄍㄨㄚ A crane-like wader.

鴷	鴷	lìeh ㄌㄝ	A wryneck (<u>Jynx torquilla</u>)or a woodpecker (Family Picidae).
鸞	鸞	lúan ㄌㄨㄢ	A mythical bird; bells whose sound is like the voice of this bird.
鶯	鶯	yīng ㄥ	A species of willow-warbler (<u>Cettia</u>, <u>Phylloscopus</u>, <u>Regulus</u>, etc.), (Family Sylviidae).

7. 鵑 鵑 chūan ㄔㄨㄢ — A cuckoo (Family Cuculidae).

鷳	鷳	hsíen ㄒㄧㄢ	The silver pheasant; once a badge of civil officials 5th grade.
鷴	鷴	ㄒㄧㄢ	
鵠	鵠	kŭ ㄍㄨ	The snow-goose (<u>Chen hyperborea</u>); a swan; hoary, white-haired.
鸝	鸝	lí ㄌㄧ	An oriole (<u>Oriolus</u> sp.), (Family Oriolidae).
鵝	鵝	ó ㄜ	The domestic goose; a swan (<u>Cygnus</u> sp.).
鵓	鵓	pó ㄅㄛ	Wood pigeon.
鷥	鷥	szū ㄙ	An egret.
鵜	鵜	t'é ㄊㄧ	A pelican, 鵜鶘 , (Family Pelicanidae).
鴝	鴝	yǜ ㄩ	The mynah.

8. 鵪 鵪 ān ㄢ — The quail (<u>Coturnix</u> sp.).

鵮	鵮	ch'īen ㄑㄧㄢ	To peck.
鶉	鶉	ch'ún ㄔㄨㄣ	The quail, partridge.
鶵	鶵	chúi	A turtledove.
鵲	鵲	ch'ǜeh ㄑㄩㄝ	The magpie; small corvid birds.
		ch'ìao ㄑㄧㄠ	(Variant).

9. 鶘 鶘 hù ㄏㄨ — Pelican.

鶊	鶊	kēng ㄍㄥ	The oriole.
鵬	鵬	p'éng ㄆㄥ	A large mythical bird, the roc.

鵰鳥 鵰	tiao ㄊㄠ	A large raptorial bird.
鵡鳥 鵡	wǔ ㄨ	A cockatoo (<u>Psittacula</u> sp.) or parrot.
鵩鳥 鵩	fú ㄈㄨ	A small owl.
鶡鳥 鶡	hó ㄏㄛ	A kind of long-tailed pheasant; an emblem of courage; the crossbill (<u>Loxia</u> <u>curvirostra</u>).
鶘鳥 鶘	hú ㄏㄨ	The pelican (Family Pelicanidae).
鶥鳥 鶥	mēi ㄇㄟ	A species of thrush (<u>Moupinia</u>, <u>Babax</u>, or <u>Garrulax</u>) of the family Turdidae.
鶩鳥 鶩	mù ㄇㄨ	Ducks.
	wù ㄨ	(Variant).
鶚鳥 鶚 鶚鳥 鶚	ò ㄜ	Osprey (Family Pandionidae). See 鵙.
鶿鳥 鶿	tz'u ㄘ	A cormorant (Family Phalacrocoracidae), esp. trained for fishing.
10.鶺鳥 鶺	chí ㄐㄧ	A wagtail (<u>Motacilla</u> sp.), 鶺鴒 See 鴒 .
鶼鳥 鶼	chīen ㄐㄧㄢ	A mythical bird with one eye and one wing.
鶻鳥 鶻	kù ㄍㄨ	A falcon.
	hù ㄏㄨ	(Variant).
鷉鳥 鷉	t'í ㄊㄧ	A species of grebe (Family Colymbidae).
鷀鳥 鷀	ts'ú ㄘㄨ	A cormorant (Family Phalacrocoraiidae). See 鶿 .
鷂鳥 鷂	yaò ㄧㄠ	A generic term for diurnal raptors: sparrow-hawk (<u>Accipiter</u> sp.), Kite (<u>Milvus</u> sp.), etc.
11.鷓鳥 鷓	chè ㄓㄜ	A partridge.

鶴 鶴	hó	ㄏㄜ	A crane (Family Gruidae) symbol of longevity.
鷖 鷖	ī	ㄧ	The widgeon; sometimes the phoenix.
鷚 鷚	liao	ㄌㄧㄡ	A species of pipit (Anthidae) or hedge-sparrow (Prunellidae).
鸚 鸚	yīng	ㄧ	A parrot, cockatoo, etc.
12. 鷦 鷦	chāo	ㄓㄠ	A species of wren - warbler (<u>Prinia</u>) (Family Sylviidae); or 鷦 鷯 , a true wren (Family Troglodytidae).
	chīao	ㄐㄧㄠ	(Variant).
鷲 鷲	chìu	ㄐㄧㄡ	A condor, vulture; a buzzard (Family Accipitridae).
	chìu	ㄐㄧㄡ	Rapacious.
鷯 鷯	liao	ㄌㄧㄠ	Small, dull-colored passerine birds: wrens, tits, etc.
鷸 鷸	yǜ	ㄩ	A snipe or sandpiper (Scolopacidae); turquoise kingfisher.
13. 鸇 鸇	chān	ㄓㄢ	A sparrow-hawk (<u>Accipiter</u> sp.); swift in flight.
鷺 鷺	lū	ㄌㄨ	A species of the heron family (Ardeidae).
鷿 鷿	p'ì	ㄆㄧ	A species of grebe (Family Colymbidae).
鷹 鷹	yīng	ㄧ	A hawk, eagle, falcon; a falconer, 鷹 師
18. 鸛 鸛	kùan	ㄍㄨㄢ	A species of the crane family (Gruidae) or stork (Ciconiidae).

鹵 卤 lŭ ㄌㄨ Salt, rock-salt. Radical 197.

鹵 滷 lŭ ㄌㄨ Salt, alkaline soil; bitter.

9. 鹺 鹾 ts'ó ㄘㄜ Brine, salt.

麥 麦 199

麥 麦 maí ㄇㄞ Wheat. Used in transliterating.

4. 麩 麸 fū ㄈㄨ Bran.

黃 201

5. 黌 黉 húng ㄏㄨㄥ A school.

黑 203

6. 黶 黡 yěn ㄧㄢ Black spots on body; moles.

8. 黷 黩 tú ㄊㄨ To blacken, soil; to insult.

黽 黾 205

黽 黾 mǐn ㄇㄧㄣ A toad, frog; to put forth effort.

4. 黿 鼋 yüan ㄩㄢ A marine turtle.

12. 鼉 鼍 t'ó ㄊㄜ An iguana; monitor lizard (Varanus sp.)

齊 文 210

0. 斉 齊 ch'í ㄑㄧˊ Even, equal; to arrange. This is radical 210.

6. 斋 齋 chāi ㄓㄞ A fast; to abstain; a vegetarian meal; a studio.

齒 齒 211

2. 齔 齔 ch'èn ㄔㄣˋ Time of loss of milk teeth; i.e. young.

5. 齡 齡 líng ㄌㄧㄥˊ The front teeth; (human) age.

齠 齠 t'íao ㄊㄧㄠˊ To shed milk teeth, exuviate.

齟 齟 tsǔ ㄗㄨˇ Unevenly fitting teeth; irregular; malocclusion.

6. 齦 齦 k'ěn ㄎㄣˇ To gnaw; to girdle a tree.

yén ㄧㄣˊ The gums.

齜 齜 tzū ㄗ Projecting teeth.

7. 齬 齬 yǔ ㄩˇ Irregular teeth.

齪 齪 ch'ō ㄔㄛ To grate one's teeth.

9. 齲 齲 ch'ǚ ㄑㄩˇ Tooth decay.

齷 齷 wò ㄨㄛˋ Small, petty; dirty.

龍 龙 212

龙 龍 lúng ㄌㄨㄥˊ A dragon; a surname. Radical 212.

6. 龚 龔 kūng ㄍㄨㄥ To give; to present to; decorous.

龜电213

龟 龜 kūei Tortoise.

The Standard Forms and the Simplified Equivalents,

Arranged According to Radicals

乙　5

10. 乾 干 kān ㄍㄢ Dry, clean.

13. 亂 乱 lùan ㄌㄨㄢ Disorderly, reckless, rebellion, anarchy; to confuse.

二　7

6. 亞 亚 yǎ ㄧㄚ Transliteration, for a; 亚洲.

人 亻 9

6. 來 来 lái ㄌㄞ To come.

侖 仑 lún ㄌㄨㄣ To think; to arrange.

7. 係 系 hsì ㄒㄧ Related to; connected with.

俠 侠 hsía ㄒㄧㄚ Generous, heroic, bold; a knight-errant.

8. 倀 伥 ch'āng ㄔㄤ Rash, wildly.

個 个 kò ㄍㄜ (Classifier for persons or things).

倆 俩 lǐa ㄌㄧㄤ Two.

倫 伦 lún ㄌㄨㄣ Constant, ordinary, regular; natural relationships; degrees (in comparison).

們 们 mén ㄇㄣ Plural suffix, applied to pronouns or personal nouns.

倉 仓 ts'āng ㄘㄤ Granary; a surname.

9. 偵 侦 chēn ㄓㄣ A scout, spy.

側	側	ts'è ㄘㄜ	The side; prejudiced; mean, to incline to.
偉	伟	wěi ㄨㄟ	Admirable, powerful; fine looking.
偽	伪	wèi ㄨㄟ	False.
10.傢	家	chīa ㄐㄚ	Tools, utensils; furniture.
僂	偻	lóu ㄌㄡ	Hunchback; bent, deformed.
		lü ㄌㄨ	To bend.
備	备	pèi ㄅㄟ	To prepare.
傘	伞	sǎn ㄙㄢ	Umbrella.
傖	伧	ts'āng ㄘㄤ	Confused, disorderly.
11.債	债	chài ㄔㄞ	To be in debt.
償	偿	cháng ㄔㄤ	To recompense; indemnity.
僉	佥	ch'īen ㄑㄧㄢ	All, unanimous.
僅	仅	chǐn ㄐㄧㄣ	Merely, barely, barely enough.
傾	倾	ch'īng ㄑㄧㄥ	To upset; to be overthrown; to collapse; to fall flat.
傳	传	ch'úan ㄔㄨㄢ	To preach, promulgate, perpetuate; to interpret; to spread, as a rumor or conduct electricity.
傷	伤	shāng ㄕㄤ	To hurt, wound; distressed.
傴	伛	yǔ ㄩ	Hunchbacked.
傭	佣	yūng ㄩㄥ	To employ, hire.
12.僥	侥	chǐao ㄐㄧㄠ	By luck or chance.
僑	侨	ch'íao ㄑㄧㄠ	An inn; to sojourn; tall.
像	象	hsiang ㄒㄧㄤ	Appearance, resemblance; like, similar; image.
僕	仆	p'ú ㄆㄨ	Servant.

13. 儕 侪 ch'ái ㄔㄞˊ A class, company.

價 价 chìa ㄐㄧㄚˋ Value.

僨 偾 fèn ㄈㄣˋ To ruin.

儉 俭 chǐen ㄐㄧㄢˇ Frugal, economical.

億 亿 ì ㄧˋ A hundred thousand.

儀 仪 ì ㄧˋ To discuss, talk over; to consult.

儈 侩 k'ùai ㄎㄨㄞˋ A broken, middleman; to hint.

儂 侬 núng ㄋㄨㄥˊ First personal pronoun (archaic).

14. 儘 尽 chǐn ㄐㄧㄣˇ As far as possible; to finish complete.

儔 俦 ch'óu ㄔㄡˊ A group of four people; friends.

優 优 yū ㄧㄡ Superior.

15. 儲 储 ch'ú ㄔㄨˊ To collect, store; savings.

19. 儷 俪 lì ㄌㄧˋ A pair, couple.

儺 傩 nó ㄋㄨㄛˊ To exorcise the devil.

儻 傥 t'ǎng ㄊㄤˇ If, supposing.

20. 儼 俨 yěn ㄧㄢˇ Majestic, stern; like, as.

儿 10

6. 兒 儿 éhr ㄦˊ Diminutive suffix.

入 11

6. 兩 两 lǐang ㄌㄧㄤˇ Two (used with 個).

128

8. 凍 冻 tùng ㄊㄨㄥˋ To freeze, jell; very cold.

10. 凱 凯 k'ǎi ㄎㄞˇ Victory; victorious return.

6. 劑 剂 chì ㄑㄧˋ To trim; to adjust; to compound medicine.

7. 剄 剄 chǐng ㄐㄧㄥˇ To cut the throat.

剋 克 k'ò ㄎㄜˋ To subdue, control, overcome.

則 则 tsé ㄗㄜˊ A rule, standard, patterns; a particle denoting responses in accordance with.

8. 剗 划 ch'ǎn ㄔㄢˇ To level off, trim.

剛 刚 kāng ㄍㄤ Hard; constant, enduring.

9. 剮 剐 kǔa ㄍㄨㄚˇ To hack to pieces (e.g., a criminal).

10. 創 创 ch'ùang ㄔㄨㄤˋ To create, invent; to begin.

12. 劃 划 hùa ㄏㄨㄚˋ To designate; to mark all.

13. 劍 剑 chìen ㄐㄧㄢˋ A double-edged sword.

劇 剧 chü ㄐㄩˋ Severe, intense; very; annoying, troublesome; a play.

劊 刽 kuei ㄍㄨㄟˋ To cut, amputate.

劉 刘 líu ㄌㄧㄡˊ A surname; to slay, destroy.

14. 劌 刿 kùei ㄍㄨㄟˋ To cut, injure, wound.

7. 勁 劲　chìng ㄐㄧㄥ　Strong, muscular.

　　　　　chìn　　　(Alternate).

9. 動 动　tùng ㄉㄨㄥ　To move.

　務 务　wù ㄨ　Matter, affair; necessary.

10. 勛 勋　hsūn ㄒㄩㄣ　Merit.

　勞 劳　lǎo ㄌㄠ　To toil, suffer; weary; to labor.

　　　　　lào　　　To reward, compensate.

11. 勢 势　shìh ㄕ　Power, influence strength; aspect, conditions.

12. 勩 勩　ì -　Toil, affliction.

13. 勵 励　lì ㄌㄧ　To encourage, urge.

ㄈ　22

9. 匭 匦　kǔei ㄍㄨㄟ　A casket, small box.

12. 匱 匮　kùei ㄍㄨㄟ　A cupboard, wardrobe; shop counter.

匚　23

9. 區 区　ch'ü ㄑㄩ　District, region.

　　　　　oū ㄡ　A surname.

十　24

6. 協 协　hsíeh ㄒㄧㄝ　Mutual; cooperate; to aid, help; to harmonize.

7. 厙 厙 shè ㄕㄜˋ A surname.

9. 厠 厕 ts'è ㄘㄜˋ The side, prejudiced.

12. 厲 厉 lì ㄌㄧˋ Severe.

厭 厌 yèn ㄧㄢˋ To be disgusted; to dislike.

9. 叅 参 ts'ān ㄘㄢ To participate in; to attend.

17. 叢 丛 ts'úng ㄘㄨㄥˊ Thicket, a grove; crowded.

7. 呗 呗 pài ㄆㄞˋ To recite.

員 员 yǔan ㄩㄢ An official, a member.

8. 啓 启 ch'ǐ ㄑㄧˇ To begin, explain; to open (after addressee's name on envelope).

唡 唡 liǎng ㄌㄧㄤˇ An ounce.

問 问 wèn ㄨㄣˋ To ask, inquire, to hold responsible; to sentence (legally).

啞 哑 yǎ ㄧㄚˇ Mute, dumb; confused.

9. 喬 乔 ch'íao ㄑㄧㄠˊ Tall, lofty; a surname.

喎 喎 k'ūai ㄎㄨㄞ A wry mouth.

嘍 喽 lóu ㄌㄡˊ To chatter, mutter.

嗎	吗	ma	ㄇㄚ	An interrogatory suffix.
喪	丧	sāng	ㄙㄤ	Mourning; to mourn.
		sàng		To lose, ruin.
嗇	啬	sè	ㄙㄜ	Sting.
單	单	tān	ㄉㄢ	Single, odd, alone.
嗚	呜	wū	ㄨ	Exclamation of regret.
喲	哟	yō	ㄧㄛ	An exclamation.
嗆	呛	ch'iang	ㄑㄧㄤ	To cough.
鳴	鸣	míng	ㄇㄧㄥ	To make a sound; the sound or cry of an animal.
嗶	哔	pì	ㄅㄧ	Crackling of fire.
嗩	唢	suǒ	ㄙㄨㄛ	Garrulous.
11. 嘗	尝	ch'áng		To taste, experience; formerly.
嘜	唛	mà	ㄇㄚ	A brand name or trademark.
嘔	呕	ǒu	ㄡ	To vomit, barf, puke.
嘆	叹	t'àn	ㄊㄢ	To sigh.
嘖	啧	tsé	ㄗㄜ	To call out; to make an uproar.
12. 嘰	叽	chī	ㄐㄧ	A kind of cloth; (used in transliterating).
嘵	哓	hsiāo	ㄒㄧㄠ	Querulous.
嘩	哗	hūa	ㄏㄨㄚ	Clamor, noise.
嘮	唠	láo	ㄌㄠ	To chatter constantly; gabby; to blabber.
嘶	嘶	szū	ㄙ	To hiss, call to come.
嗒	哒	tá	ㄉㄚ	Name for country.
噁	噁	wǔ	ㄨ	Rage.

13. 嘍嘍 ai ㄞ "Oh dear" (the exclamation).

嘯嘯 hsiao ㄒㄧㄠˋ A hissing sound; to scream, whistle.

   sù A moan.

嘴噲 kuài ㄎㄨㄞˋ To swallow; greedy, pleasant, bright.

罵駡 mà ㄇㄚˋ To scold, abuse.

嚀咛 níng ㄋㄧㄥˊ To enjoin, charge with; to order.

嚨噥 nūng ㄋㄨㄥ Loquacious.

噴噴 p'ēn ㄆㄣ To blow out, pull out; to spurt out.

噹噹 tāng ㄉㄤ "Dong" (sound of a bell).

   tàng To consider as.

14. 嚇吓 hsia ㄒㄧㄚ To brighten.

嚒吨 tùn ㄉㄨㄣˋ A ton.

嚒嗳 yüeh ㄩㄝˊ To belch, burp; to vomit, barf, puke.

15. 嚮向 hsiang ㄒㄧㄤˋ Opposite; to lean towards; to guide; to show one's mind; to encourage.

嚕嚕 lǔ ㄌㄨˇ Speech; to flatter; to pout.

齧啮 nieh ㄋㄧㄝˋ To gnaw or bite.

16. 囑嘱 chǔ ㄓㄨˇ To order, direct; to admonish, to instruct.

嚦呖 li ㄌㄧˋ An exclamation to indicate a clear sound.

嚨咙 lúng ㄌㄨㄥˊ The throat.

17. 嚳喾 k'ù ㄎㄨˋ To inform promptly.

嚴严 yén ㄧㄢˊ Stern, severe; tight.

嚶嘤 yīng ㄧㄥ Melody of birds, bird song.

18.	嚮 响	hsiang ㄒㄧㄤˇ	Loud; to make a sound.
	嚣 嚣	hsiao ㄒㄧㄠˊ	Din, clamor.
	囁 嗫	nieh ㄋㄧㄝˋ	To move the mouth, as in speaking.
19.	囅 辗	ch'ān ㄔㄢˇ	To laugh out.
	囀 啭	chǔan ㄓㄨㄢˋ	To warble like a bird.
	囈 呓	ì -	To talk in one's sleep.
	囉 罗	ló ㄌㄨㄛˊ	To chatter, prattle.
	轡 辔	p'èi ㄆㄟˋ	Reins, a bridle.
21.	囌 苏	sū ㄙㄨ	Garrulous; loquacious.

囗 31

8.	國 国	kúo ㄍㄨㄛˊ	A country, state.
	圇 囵	lún ㄌㄨㄣˊ	Complete, whole.
9.	圍 围	wéi ㄨㄟˊ	To surround; circumference, a span.
10.	圓 圆	yüan ㄩㄢˊ	Round, a dollar; to tell, explain.
	園 园	yüan ㄩㄢˊ	Garden, park.
11.	團 团	t'úan ㄊㄨㄢˊ	Round; to crumple.
12.	圖 图	t'ú ㄊㄨˊ	To plan; illustrate; a drawing, plan, figure, map.

土 扌 32

8.	埡 垭	yà ㄧㄚˋ	White clay used in making porcelain.
9.	場 场	ch'ăng ㄔㄤˇ	An open space, field.
	堅 坚	chīen ㄐㄧㄢ	Hard, firm, durable.

塯	埚	kūo ㄎㄨㄛ		A crucible.
報	报	pào ㄅㄠ		(To) report.
塢	坞	wù ㄨ		A low wall, enbankment.
堯	尧	yáo ㄠ		Lofty; Emperor Yao。
10. 塤	埙	hsūn ㄒㄩㄣ		An ancient terra-cotta musical instrument, like an ocarina or sweet potato.
塏	垲	k'ǎi ㄎㄞ		A kind of soil, kaolin, or a paste from that soil, used in making porcelain.
塊	块	k'ùai ㄎㄨㄞ		Lump, piece.
塒	埘	shíh ㄕ		A chicken coop.
塗	涂	tú ㄊㄨ		To smear, dab.
塋	茔	yíng ㄧㄥ		A grave, tomb.
11. 塵	尘	ch'én ㄔㄣ		Dust, dirt.
塹	堑	ch'íen ㄑㄧㄢ		A moat or channel.
墊	垫	tìen ㄉㄧㄢ		To put under as a prop; a cushion.
墮	堕	tò ㄊㄨㄛ		To fall, drop.
12. 墜	坠	chùi ㄔㄨㄟ		To fall down, sink.
墳	坟	fén ㄈㄣ		A grave mound.
墾	垦	k'ěn ㄎㄣ		To open up, reclaim.
墜	堕	tò ㄊㄨㄛ		To fall, sink; to set
13. 墻	墙	ch'íang ㄑㄧㄤ		A wall.
14. 壙	圹	k'ūang ㄎㄨㄤ		A vault or tomb; brick grave.
壇	坛	t'án ㄊㄢ		An alter (of earth).
壓	压	yā ㄧㄚ		To press down.
15. 壘	垒	lěi ㄌㄟ		A wall or rampart.

16. 壞 坏 hùai ㄏㄨㄞ Bad, spoiled; to ruin, spoil.

　　壢 坜 lì ㄌㄧ A place name.

　　壚 垆 lú ㄌㄨ Dark clods of earth; a shop or hut; a stove.

　　壠 垄 lǔng ㄌㄨㄥ A mound of earth.

21. 壩 坝 pà ㄅㄚ An embankment.

　　壩 埧 pà ㄅㄚ A dyke, dam, breakwater.

士　33

4. 壯 壮 chùang ㄔㄨㄤ Strong, robust.

9. 壺 壶 hú ㄏㄨ A kettle, jug; vase.

10. 壼 壸 k'ǔn ㄎㄨㄣ Apartments; a corridor in a palace.

11. 壽 寿 shòu ㄕㄡ Span of life, age; a surname.

夕　36

11. 夥 伙 hǔo ㄏㄨㄛ A band, group of companions; buddies.

　　夢 梦 mèng ㄇㄥ To dream; a dream.

大　37

4. 夾 夹 chīa ㄐㄚ To pinch, squeeze.

11. 獎 奖 chǐang ㄐㄤ A prize, reward; to encourage.

　　奩 奁 líen ㄌㄧㄢ A lady's dresser; a bridal trousseau.

　　奪 夺 tó ㄊㄨㄛ To rob, take by force.

13. 奮 奋 fèn ㄈㄣ To exert one'self; to spread wings; determined.

4. 妝 妆 chuāng ㄔㄨㄤ Adornment.

8. 嬦 妇 fù ㄈㄨ Woman, women (generically), wife.

婁 娄 lǒu ㄌㄡ To follow; to trail behind; to wear. See 嘍 .

婭 娅 yà ㄧㄚ Term of address used between sons-in-law.

9. 媯 妫 kūi ㄍㄨㄟ A river in Shansi; crafty.

媧 娲 wā ㄨㄚ Sister of Fu Hsi.

10. 媽 妈 mā ㄇㄚ Mother, an old woman.

11. 嫗 妪 yù ㄩ An old woman.

yù To brood over; to protect.

12. 嬌 娇 chiāo ㄐㄧㄠ Beautiful, graceful.

嫻 娴 hsién ㄒㄧㄢ Elegant, refined; accomplished.

嫿 姮 hùa ㄏㄨㄚ Feminine, coy.

嬈 娆 jáo ㄖㄠ Graceful, fascinating.

yǎo ㄧㄠ Tender and weak.

嬋 婵 shán ㄕㄢ Beautiful, graceful.

嫵 妩 wǔ ㄨ To please; to fawn, flatter.

14. 嬡 嫒 ai ㄞ Formal word for daughter.

嬰 婴 yīng ㄧ An infant, especially a girl.

15. 嬪 嫔 pīn ㄆㄧㄣ A concubine; to become a wife.

pín (Variant).

嬸 婶 shěn ㄕㄣ Wife of father's younger brother.

19. 孌 娈 lǔan ㄌㄨㄢ Beautiful, handsome; admirable.

lǐen (Variant).

6. 孫　孙　sūn ㄙㄨㄣ　Grandson.

13. 學　学　hsüeh ㄒㄩㄝ　To learn, study, practice; a branch of learning.

19. 䜌　亦　lúan ㄌㄨㄢ　To bear twins.
　　 孿　孪　shùan ㄕㄨㄢ　(Variant).

10. 寬　宽　k'ūan ㄎㄨㄢ　Broad, ample, spacious; liberal, forgiving.

　　 寫　窵　tìao ㄊㄧㄠ　Deep, profound.

11. 寢　寝　ch'ǐn ㄑㄧㄣ　To sleep, rest; an apartment, bed chamber.

　　 寧　宁　níng ㄋㄧㄥ　Peaceful; rather; it is better, would that.

12. 寫　写　hsǐeh ㄒㄧㄝ　To write.

　　 寶　宝　pǎo ㄅㄠ　Precious, valuable.

　　 賓　宾　pīn ㄅㄧㄣ　A guest; to submit, entertain.

　　 審　审　shěn ㄕㄣ　To contest (legally); to examine, investigate.

　　 實　实　shíh ㄕ　Solid (not hollow).

14. 憲　宪　hsìen ㄒㄧㄢ　A constitution; governmental official.

16. 寵　宠　ch'ǔng ㄔㄨㄥ　To favor; kindness.

8. 將　将　chīang ㄐㄧㄤ　To take; (pretransitive, as 把).

		chiàng	A general.
專	专	chūan ㄔㄨㄢ	Only, specially; alone, unassisted; to assume responsibility.
9. 尋	寻	hsǔn ㄒㄩㄣ	To seek, usual.
11. 對	对	tùi ㄉㄨㄟ	Opposite, matching; a pair.
13. 導	导	tǎo ㄉㄠ	To guide, teach.

尢 43

14. 尷	尴	kān ㄎㄢ	Embarrassing circumstance.
		chīen ㄑㄧㄢ	(Variant).

尸 44

10. 屢	屡	lǚ ㄌㄩ	Repeatedly, often, constantly.
12. 層	层	ts'éng ㄘㄥ	A story, floor; degree.
13. 屨	屦	.chǜ ㄐㄩ	Sandles, straw shoes.
18. 屬	属	shǔ ㄕㄨ	Belonging to, related to; sort.

山 46

5. 岡	冈	kāng ㄍㄤ	Ridge, hill; a mound.
7. 峽	峡	hsía ㄒㄧㄚ	Hills on each side of a gorge; a gorge, ravine.
	峴	岘	hsǐen ㄒㄧㄢ	A steep hill.
8. 崗	岗	kāng ㄍㄤ	Ridge of a hill.
9. 嵐	岚	lán ㄌㄢ	Vapor, mist.

11. 嶃 嶄 ch'án ㄔㄢˊ A cliff.

嶇 岖 ch'ū ㄑㄩ A steep, slope.

嶁 嵝 lǒu ㄌㄡˇ A mountain in Hunan.

12. 嶠 峤 ch'iao A mountain ridge or peak.

嶼 屿 hsǜ ㄒㄩˋ A small island.

yü ㄩ (Variant).

嶗 崂 láo ㄌㄠˊ Mountains in Shantung.

13. 嶧 峄 i ㄧ Name of hills in Shantung and Kiangsu.

14. 嶺 岭 líng ㄌㄧㄥˊ A mountain range, mountain pass.

嶸 嵘 yǔng ㄩㄥˇ Lofty, prominent, majestic.

júng ㄐㄩㄥˊ (Variant).

17. 巋 岿 k'ūei ㄎㄨㄟ A range of hills; grand.

kùei (Variant).

18. 巔 巅 tien ㄉㄧㄢ Mountain peak.

19. 巒 峦 lúan ㄌㄨㄢˊ Mountain peaks.

川 巛 47

4. 巠 圣 chīng ㄐㄧㄥ Underground streams.

干 51

10. 幹 干 kàn ㄍㄢˋ To do, manage.

幺 52

9. 幾 几 chī ㄐㄧ Very nearly.

chǐ   How much, how many?

广   53

7. 庫 庫 k'ù ㄎㄨ A treasury or storehouse; a granary.

11. 廣 广 kǔang ㄍㄨㄤ Broad, extensive.

12. 廠 厂 ch'ǎng ㄔㄤ A mill, factory.

    廢 废 fèi ㄈㄟ To abolish.

    賡 賡 kēng ㄍㄥ To continue.

    廟 庙 mìao ㄇㄧㄠ A temple, monastery.

    廡 庑 wǔ ㄨ A covered path or walk; a porch.

13. 慶 庆 ch'ìng ㄑㄧㄥ To congratulate.

16. 廬 庐 lú ㄌㄨ A hut.

    龐 庞 p'áng ㄆㄤ A high house; confused.

22. 廳 厅 t'īng ㄊㄧㄥ Parlor, court.

弓   57

8. 張 张 chāng ㄓㄤ To draw a bow; to publish, open; classifier for sheet-like objects (e.g., paper).

11. 彆 别 pīeh ㄅㄧㄝ Difficult, contrary; awkward.

12. 彌 弥 mí ㄇㄧ To fill; full; long distant; used in transliterating.

    彈 弹 tàn ㄉㄢ A bullet, pellet, shot; a crossbow. To strum (an instrument); to snap the finger; to rebound; to press down.

13. 彎 弯 wān ㄨㄢ To bend; curved; to draw a bow.

6. 後 后 hòu ㄏㄡ After, behind; the back; to come after.

7. 徑 径 chìng ㄐㄧㄥ A short cut; diameter; direct, straight.

8. 徠 徕 lài ㄌㄞ To urge, encourage; to induce to come.

   從 从 ts'úng ㄘㄨㄥ From; to follow.

9. 復 复 fù ㄈㄨ To return to or recover; again.

12. 徹 彻 ch'è ㄔㄜ To penetrate; discerning, pure.

   徵 征 chēng ㄓㄥ To draft (for military service); to collect duty.

心 忄 忄 61

8. 悵 怅 ch'àng ㄔㄤ Disappointed, dissatisfied.

   悶 闷 mén ㄇㄣ Mournful, melancholy; depressed; to cover.

   惡 恶 ò ㄨ Evil, bad; to hate.

9. 愛 爱 aì ㄞ To love (to ....).

   惱 恼 nǎo ㄋㄠ To get angry; resentful.

   惻 恻 ts'è ㄘㄜ To pity, sympathize with.

10. 愴 怆 ch'ùang Sad.

   愾 忾 hsì ㄒㄧ To sigh, groan.

   愷 恺 k'ǎi ㄎㄞ Joyful, good, kind.

   憑 凭 p'íng ㄆㄧㄥ Proof, evidence; rely upon, according to.

   憑 凭 p'íng ㄆㄧㄥ According to, as.

態	态	t'ài ㄊㄞ	Attitude.
惲	恽	yǔn ㄩㄣ	To deliberate, consult.
11.愜	惬	ch'ieh ㄑㄧㄝ	Satisfied, contented; cheerful.
愨	悫	ch'ùeh	Guileless, upright; ingenuous.
慮	虑	lü ㄌㄩ	To plan, care for; anxious.
11.慪	怄	òu ㄡ	To excite, irritate.
		kōu ㄎㄡ	Stingy, petty.
愯	愯	sùng ㄙㄨㄥ	To alarm, alert.
		tsǔng ㄘㄨㄥ	(Variant).
慚	惭	ts'án ㄘㄢ	Grieved; sad; cruel.
慟	恸	t'ùng ㄊㄨㄥ	Grief; sadness.
憂	忧	yū ㄧㄡ	To be worried, anxious, sad.
12.慳	悭	ch'ien ㄑㄧㄢ	Penurious, stingy.
慣	惯	kùan ㄍㄨㄢ	Accustomed; experienced.
憒	愦	kùei ㄍㄨㄟ	Troubled, anxious, concerned; dazed, confused.
		k'ùei ㄎㄨㄟ	(Variant).
憫	悯	mǐn ㄇㄧㄣ	To sympathize with; to pity.
憚	惮	tàn ㄊㄢ	To shrink from; to dread.
憮	怃	wǔ ㄨ	Disappointed, disraught; to cherish.
		hsǚ ㄒㄩ	Arrogant; to fawn upon.
		hū ㄏㄨ	Great; arrogant.
13.憤	愤	fèn ㄈㄣ	Zeal, ardor.
憶	忆	i ˉ	To remember, bring to mind.
懌	怿	i ˋ	To rejoice, pleased

憊	惫	pèi ㄅㄟ		Exhausted, worn out, fatigued.
應	应	yīng ㄧ		Ought, must.
14. 懞	蒙	měng ㄇㄥ		Stupid, dull.
懇	恳	k'ěn ㄎㄣ		To request, beg; earnestly; honest.
懟	怼	tùi ㄉㄨㄟ		To dislike.
懨	恹	yèn ㄧㄢ		Sickly.
15. 懸	悬	hsüan ㄒㄩㄢ		To suspend; anxious; distant from; separated.
懑	懑	min ㄇㄣ		Mournful, melancholy; to stupify; to cover.
16. 懲	惩	ch'éng ㄔㄥ		To correct, punish; to warn.
懷	怀	húai ㄏㄨㄞ		The bosom; to carry; to be pregnant; to cherish.
懶	懒	lǎn ㄌㄢ		Lazy, indolent; reluctant.
		lài ㄌㄞ		Evil.
17. 懺	忏	ch'àn ㄔㄢ		To regret, repent; Buddhist and Taoist ritual.
18. 懾	慑	ché ㄓㄜ		Afraid, faint hearted.
		shè ㄕㄜ		To coerce.
懼	惧	chü ㄐㄩ		To fear.
19. 戀	恋	lüan ㄌㄩㄢ		To hanker after; to dote on, be fond of.
		lien ㄌㄧㄢ		(Variant).
23. 戇	戆	chùang ㄔㄨㄤ		Stupid, dull, moranic.

戈   62

戋	戈	chīen ㄐㄧㄢ		Small, narrow; prejudiced.

144

8. 戠 只 chīh ㄓ A sword; to gather.

饊 饯 ch'ùang ㄔㄨㄤ To create, make invent; to begin.

戰 战 chàn ㄔㄢ War; to fight, contest; to tremble.

戲 戏 hsì ㄒㄧ A play, drama; to play, jest.

手 扌 64

7. 挾 挟 hsíeh ㄒㄧㄝ To hold under the arm; to put in the bosom.

捆 困 k'ǔn ㄎㄨㄣ To tie together, bind; to plait.

8. 捲 卷 chǔan ㄐㄨㄢ To gather, grasp; to roll up, curly

掄 抡 lún ㄌㄨㄣ To choose, select; in turn; to wave, brandish, to swing.

         lūn ㄌㄨㄣ (Variant).

捫 扪 mén ㄇㄣ To feel, lay hands on; to hold; cover.

掃 扫 sǎo ㄙㄠ To sweep.

         sào A broom.

捨 舍 shě ㄕㄜ To give up, part with, relinquish.

掗 押 yǎ ㄧㄚ Snapping of twigs.

9. 揀 拣 chiěn ㄐㄧㄢ Select; to pick up.

揮 挥 hūi ㄏㄨㄟ To move, shake; direct.

搗 捣 tǎo ㄉㄠ To beat, pound; to attack.

揚 扬 yáng ㄧㄤ To scatter, spread; to publish abroad; to praise; to display.

10. 搶 抢 ch'iang ㄑㄧㄤ To take by force; to wrestle for; to rob, ravish.

         ch'iàng ㄑㄧㄤ Adverse.

145

		ch'ūang		To oppose, rush against.
撫	抚	fǔ	ㄈㄨ	To cherish; to rub.
損	损	sǔn	ㄙㄨㄣ	To injure, spoil; to destroy; disadvantage.
11. 摺	折	ché	ㄓㄜ	To fold.
		chě	ㄓㄜ	Pleats.
執	执	chíh	ㄓ	To hold, grip.
摰	挚	chìh	ㄓ	To grasp, grab; in advance; to break down.
摑	掴	kūo	ㄍㄨㄛ	To slap.
摳	抠	k'ōu	ㄎㄡ	To raise; to feel for; to scrape.
摟	搂	lǒu	ㄌㄡ	To drag, pull; to hug, embrace.
摻	掺	shān	ㄕㄢ	A delicate hand; tapering, beautiful.
摶	抟	t'úan	ㄊㄨㄢ	To roll in the hand; to model.
		chùan	ㄓㄨㄢ	To lead.
12. 擊	击	chī	ㄐㄧ	To hit, strike.
撟	挢	chǐao	ㄐㄧㄠ	To bend, twist.
撳	揿	chìn	ㄑㄧㄣ	To press down with the hand; to lean on.
撏	挦	hsíen	ㄒㄧㄢ	To take, select; to pull out hair.
		hsìen		Appearance of water.
撱	揞	kùan	ㄍㄨㄢ	To be familiar with; to take.
撈	捞	lāo	ㄌㄠ	To drag for, especially in the water; to fish for.
撓	挠	náo	ㄋㄠ	To scratch, vex; to disturb.
撥	拨	pō	ㄅㄛ	To distribute, disperse, allot; to transfer; to stir up, prod; to pluck (strings).

146

撲 扑	p'ū ㄆㄨ		To beat, strike, pound; to rush on; used in rendering sound.
撣 掸	tǎn ㄉㄢ		To grasp; to hit against.
13.擇 择	ché ㄔㄜ		To select, choose.
	tsé ㄗㄜ		(Variant).
撿 捡	chǐen ㄐㄧㄢ		To restrict, bind.
拙 擉	ch'ō ㄔㄛ		To pierce, penetrate.
搚 挞	chūa ㄔㄨㄚ		To beat or strike.
據 据	chǜ ㄐㄩ		To hold as base; to base; basis according to; to receive (a communication).
㧖 抌	k'ǔai ㄎㄨㄞ		To rub, scratch; to bear an ax on the arm.
擄 掳	lǔ ㄌㄨ		To take captive, to seize; a prisoner, slave.
擔 担	tān ㄉㄢ		To carry.
擋 挡	tǎng ㄉㄤ		To resist, ward off, oppose, pervert; to stop.
擁 拥	yūng ㄩㄥ		To push; to give (moral) support.
14.擠 挤	chǐ ㄐㄧ		To crawl, push; to squeeze.
擲 掷	chīh ㄓ		To throw, fling away.
擱 搁	kō ㄍㄜ		To place, put; to put down.
擴 扩	k'ùo ㄎㄨㄛ		To extend, enlarge, stretch; to escalate.
擬 拟	nǐ ㄋㄧ		To determine, intend; to compare; to resemble; to estimate, guess.
	ǐ ㄧ		(Variant).
擰 拧	níng ㄋㄧㄥ		To pull about; to create confusion; to twist.
15.擷 撷	hsíeh ㄒㄧㄝ		To collect, take up; a lapful.

147

擾	扰	jǎo	ㄐㄠ	To disturb, annoy; to give trouble; to bug.
攗	攈	měn	ㄇㄣ	To expel, drive out.
擺	摆	pǎi	ㄆㄞ	To arrange, displace; move back and forth, pendulum.
擯	摈	pìn	ㄆㄣ	To expel, reject; to set in order.
攄	摅	shū	ㄕ	To spread, unroll.
擻	擞	shǔ	ㄙㄡ	To shake.
16. 攬	揽	lǎn	ㄌㄢ	To seize, grasp; to monopolize.
攛	撺	ts'ūan	ㄘㄨㄢ	To stir up evil.
17. 攔	拦	lán	ㄌㄢ	To obstruct, impede.
攏	拢	lǔng	ㄌㄨㄥ	To collect; to grasp; to take action.
攖	撄	yīng	ㄧ	To oppose; to attack.
18. 攙	搀	ch'ān	ㄔㄢ	To sustain, support; assist; to mix.
攝	摄	shè	ㄕㄜ	To gather; to control, act for.
攤	㩳	sǔng	ㄙㄨㄥ	Frightened, terrified.
攞	捰	lǒ	ㄌㄨㄛ	To split; to choose; to rap, wipe.
19. 孿	孪	lǜan	ㄌㄩㄢ	To bend, warp; crooked, winding.
		lǘan		To bind, tie; to take hold of; to drag along.
攤	摊	t'ān	ㄊㄢ	To spread, apportion.
攢	攒	tsūan	ㄗㄨㄢ	To gather together, collect; to hold in the hand.
		ts'úan	ㄘㄨㄢ	(Variant).
20. 攪	搅	chiǎo	ㄐㄠ	To agitate or disturb; to cause trouble.

11. 數 数 shǔ ㄕㄨ To count, calculate, estimate.

敵 敌 tí ㄉㄧ Opponent, enemy.

13. 斂 敛 liěn ㄌㄧㄢ To gather, accumulate; to arrange, compose; to control oneself.

17. 爛 斕 lán ㄌㄢ Variegated, colored.

斤 69

8. 斷 断 tùan ㄉㄨㄢ To break, cut off.

日 72

昜 旸 yáng ㄧㄤ To expand; bright, glorious.

晝 昼 chòu ㄔㄡ Daytime.

時 时 shíh ㄕ Time; period, season.

暘 旸 yáng ㄧㄤ The rising sun.

暈 晕 yūn ㄩㄣ A mist, vapors; a halo; to be dizzy.

暢 畅 ch'àng ㄔㄤ Joyful, pleasant.

曄 晔 yèh ㄧㄝ Sparkling, said of a fire.

暫 暂 tsàn ㄗㄢ For a time, shortly, suddenly.

chàn ㄔㄢ (Variant).

曉 晓 hsiǎo ㄒㄧㄠ Dawn, light; to know, understand; apparent.

曆 历 lì ㄌㄧ Calendar.

曇 昙 t'án ㄊㄢ Dark clouds.

13. 曖 曖 ài ㄞ Obscure, vague.
14. 曠 旷 k'uàng ㄎㄨㄤ Wild; wasteland, desert, wilderness
曚 蒙 méng ㄇㄥ Sun below horizon; down.
17. 曨 昽 lúng ㄌㄨㄥ The rising sun obscured.
19. 曬 晒 shài ㄕㄞ To dry or air in the sun; to be affected by the sun, sunstroke.

日　73

6. 書 书 shū ㄕㄨ A book; to write.
9. 會 会 huǐ ㄏㄨㄟ A moment.
huì ㄏㄨㄟ To meet.

月　74

17. 朧 胧 lúng ㄌㄨㄥ The rising moon.

木　75

4. 東 东 tūng ㄉㄨㄥ East.
6. 條 条 t'iáo ㄊㄧㄠ (Classifier for long slender objects; roads, bridges, river, ribbons.)
7. 梘 枧 chǐen ㄐㄧㄢ A bamboo tube for carrying water.
欄 栏 lán ㄌㄢ A railing, rage.
8. 棧 栈 chàn ㄓㄢ A storehouse, shop.
根 根 ch'éng ㄔㄥ A prop, post.
極 板 chí ㄐ (Intensifying suffix); very.
棗 枣 tsǎo ㄗㄠ Jujube, "dates".

150

棟	栋	tùng	ㄉㄨㄥˋ	Ridge-pole; able man.
9. 楨	桢	chēn	ㄓㄣ	An evergreen shrub.
楓	枫	fēng	ㄈㄥ	Maple.
楊	杨	yáng	ㄧㄤˊ	Willow, popular, aspen.
業	业	yèh	ㄧㄝˋ	Profession, occupation.
10. 槍	枪	ch'iāng	ㄑㄧㄤ	A lance or spear.
		ch'éng	ㄔㄥˊ	A comet.
構	构	kòu	ㄍㄡˋ	To construct; finish; to join to-gether; to grasp, hook.
榮	荣	yúng	ㄩㄥˊ	Glory, honor; florishing, prosper-ing; beautiful; blood.
11. 槳	桨	chiǎng	ㄐㄧㄤˇ	An oar.
槧	椠	ch'ien	ㄑㄧㄢˋ	Wood blocks for printing; tablets for memorandum.
樁	桩	chūang	ㄓㄨㄤ	A stump , post.
樂	乐	lè	ㄌㄜˋ	Happy.
		yüeh	ㄩㄝˋ	Music.
樓	楼	lóu	ㄌㄡˊ	An upper-story or tower; a two-storied building.
標	标	pīao	ㄅㄧㄠ	Sign, signed, publish.
樞	枢	shū	ㄕㄨ	Pivot, axis, central point; indis-pensible, fundamental.
樅	枞	ts'ǔng	ㄘㄨㄥˇ	A species of oak (Quercus).
樣	样	yàng	ㄧㄤˋ	Shape, kind.
12. 橋	桥	ch'íao	ㄑㄧㄠˊ	A bridge.
樺	桦	húa	ㄏㄨㄚˊ	A birch (Betula sp.) found in Manchuria.
橈	桡	jáo	ㄖㄠˊ	An oar; to row.

橈	桡	náo	ㄋㄠ	Crooked; bent wood; unjust; weak, soft; to disperse, scatter.
樸	朴	p'ǒ	ㄆㄛ	Sincere, simple; the substance of things.
		p'ǔ	ㄆㄨ	(Variant).
		p'ú	ㄆㄨ	Simple, plain.
樹	树	shù	ㄕㄨ	A tree.
楕	楠	t'ǒ	ㄊㄨㄛ	Ellipse.

13. 欖 檻 chǐa ㄐㄚ A small evergreen shrub the leaves of which are used in a beverage.

櫛 栉 chíeh ㄐㄧㄝ A comb; to comb.

檉 柽 ch'ēng ㄔㄥ The tamarisk.

檢 检 chǐen ㄐㄧㄢ A label on a book; to arrange, collate.

檜 桧 kùei ㄍㄨㄟ The Chinese juniper.

櫃 柜 kùei ㄍㄨㄟ A chest, cupboard.

檔 档 tàng ㄉㄤ A cross-piece, as in a ladder chain.

14. 檸 柠 níng ㄋㄧㄥ A tree with bark of medicinal value; the lemon.

15. 櫧 槠 chū ㄓㄨ A species of live (evergreen) oak.

櫸 榉 chǔ ㄐㄩ A large tree used in making furniture; a kind of elm.

檻 槛 hsǐen ㄒㄧㄢ Bars, a railing; a cage.

櫟 栎 lì ㄌㄧ The chestnut-leaved oak, Quercus sinensis and Q. serrata.

櫓 橹 lǔ ㄌㄨ A turret on a city wall; a scull, sweep of an oar.

櫚 榈 lǘ ㄌㄩ A palm.

檳 槟 pìng ㄅㄧㄥ Areca nut, betel nut.

櫝 櫝	tú	ㄊㄨˊ	A casket; box.
16.櫬 槔	ch'èn	ㄔㄣˋ	A coffin; a kind of tree.
櫼 櫼	chǐen	ㄐㄧㄢ	Lower section of a tripartite door.
櫪 枥	lí	ㄌㄧˋ	A kind of oak; a stable.
櫞 櫞	yǔan	ㄩㄢˊ	Name of any of several kinds of trees.
17.欖 榄	lǎn	ㄌㄢˇ	Chinese olive tree.
櫳 栊	lúng	ㄌㄨㄥˊ	A cage or pen.
櫻 樱	yīng	ㄧㄥ	The cherry.
18.權 权	ch'ǔan	ㄑㄩㄢˊ	Power, authority.
19.欏 椤	ló	ㄌㄨㄛˊ	The horse-chestnut (<u>Aesculus</u> sp.).
欒 栾	lúan	ㄌㄨㄢˊ	A kind of small tree.
24.欞 棂	líng	ㄌㄧㄥˊ	A sill, lintel; lattice.

欠 76

11.歐欠 欧	ōu	ㄡ	To vomit, barf, puke.
13.歟欠 欤	yú	ㄩ	A final particle, indicating admiration, doubt, surprise.
18.歡 欢	hūan	ㄏㄨㄢ	Joyous; to be glad.

止 77

4.齒 齿	ch'ǐh	ㄔ	Tooth. This is radical 211.
12.歷 历	lì	ㄌㄧˋ	To pass through successive.
10.歲 岁	sùi	ㄙㄨㄟˋ	Year, age, harvest.
14.歸 归	kūei	ㄍㄨㄟ	Marriage of a woman; return; to restore; to send back.

153

8. 殘 残 ts'ái ㄘㄞ　To injure, appress.

10. 殞 殒 yǔn ㄩㄣ　To perish, die.

12. 殨 殨 hùi ㄏㄨㄟ　To open (a sore).

殫 殚 ān ㄢ　Quite, entirely.

13. 殮 殓 lièn ㄌㄧㄢ　To prepare a corpse for burial.

斃 毙 pì ㄅㄧ　To die a violent death; to kill, execute.

15. 殯 殡 pìn ㄅㄧㄣ　To carry to burial.

17. 殲 歼 chiēn ㄐㄧㄢ　To destroy.

6. 殺 杀 shā ㄕㄚ　To kill.

8. 殼 壳 k'ō ㄎㄨ　A skin or husk; egg shell; shed skin of reptiles or arthropods; shell of a mollusc.

11. 毆 殴 ōu ㄡ　To brawl, beat with sticks or fists.

11. 毿 毿 sàn ㄙㄢ　Hirsute, coarse hair.

13. 氈 毡 chān ㄓㄢ　Blanket.

6. 氣 气 ch'ì ㄑㄧ　Air.

氫 氢 ch'īng ㄑㄧㄥ Hydrogen.

水 氵 85

7. 浹 浃 chíeh ㄒㄧㄚ Dampness.

涇 泾 chīng ㄐㄧㄥ A large river in Kansuh; to flow straight through.

8. 淺 浅 ch'ĭen ㄑㄧㄢ Shallow, superficial, vulgar; easy to grasp.

灃 沣 fēng ㄈㄥ A stream in Shensi.

淶 涞 lái ㄌㄞ A brook, ripples.

淪 沦 lún ㄌㄨㄣ Ruined, lost; engulfed; eddies.

9. 渾 浑 hún ㄏㄨㄣ A turbid current; chaotic, confused.

溈 沩 kūei ㄍㄨㄟ Name of a river.

渦 涡 kūo ㄍㄨㄛ A river in Anwei.

        wō ㄨㄛ A whirlpool.

溮 浉 shìh ㄕ Name of a river.

湯 汤 t'āng ㄊㄤ Soup, gravy; to heat; hot water.

測 测 t'sè ㄘㄜ To fathom, measure.

淵 渊 yūan ㄩㄢ Abyss, deep gulf.

10. 準 准 chŭn ㄓㄨㄣ Exact, tone; to measure; to adjust, equalize; to allow.

溝 沟 kōu ㄍㄡ A ditch, drain; watercourse.

滄 沧 ts'āng ㄘㄤ Vast, cold.

11. 漲 涨 chàng ㄓㄤ To rise (water), inundate.

漸 渐 chìen ㄐㄧㄢ Gradually.

滯 滞 chìh ㄓ To impede; sluggish.

11. 漿 浆 chīang ㄐㄧㄤ To starch; thick fluid.

漢 汉 hàn ㄏㄢ The dynasty.

瀉 泻 hsìeh ㄒㄧㄝ To drain off; to leak. Diarrhea.

潯 浔 hsìn ㄒㄧㄣ Steep side of a gorge; a river near Kiukiang.

滸 浒 hŭ ㄏㄨ A riverbank.

滬 沪 hù ㄏㄨ To fish by trapping; or fish in a weir; Shanghai.

漣 涟 lían ㄌㄧㄢ Flowing water; River in Hunan.

漊 溇 lóu ㄌㄡ Name of a river.

滷 卤 lŭ ㄌㄨ Salt, alkaline soil; bitter.

澠 渑 mìen ㄇㄧㄢ River in Honan.

漚 沤 òu ㄡ To soak, steep.

　　 ōu Bubbles on water.

漬 渍 tzù ㄗ To soak, steep, soggy.

潁 颍 yìng ㄧ River in Shantung.

漁 渔 yú ㄩ To fish, seize.

12. 濟 济 chì ㄐㄧ To succor.

澆 浇 chīao ㄐㄧㄠ To wash with water; to pour over.

潔 洁 chíeh ㄐㄧㄝ Clean, clear, pure.

澗 涧 chìen ㄐㄧㄢ A swift mountain stream.

潧 浕 chìn ㄐㄧㄣ A rapid river.

潰 溃 hùi ㄏㄨㄟ A stream overflowing; dispersed, scattered.

　　 k'ùei ㄎㄨㄟ (Variant).

潤 润 jùn ㄖㄨㄣ To moisten, enrich, fatten; shining, sleep.

潦	涝	lào	ㄌㄠ	A torrent; great waves; to overflow, flood.
潷	滗	pì	ㄅㄧ	To decant.
潑	泼	p'ō	ㄆㄛ	To sprinkle, scatter; to dissipate, waste.
滲	渗	shèn	ㄕㄣ	To leak, soak through;
		shēn		Downy growing plumage.
澠	渑	shéng	ㄕㄥ	River in Shantung.
澾	迖	t'à	ㄊㄚ	Slippery.
濤	涛	t'áo	ㄊㄠ	Billows, large waves.

13. 澤 泽 ché ㄓㄜ A marsh, damp; to fertilize, enrich; glossy, smooth; to deprive of; to point out.

                    tsé ㄗㄜ (Variant)。

濁	浊	chó	ㄓㄨㄛ	Impure.
彙	汇	hùi	ㄏㄨㄟ	A class, series; to classify.
澒	鸿	húng	ㄏㄨㄥ	Vast, profound.
澮	浍	kùai	ㄎㄨㄞ	Water current; a drain.
		kùei	ㄎㄨㄟ	(Alternate).
濃	浓	núng	ㄋㄨㄥ	Thick (liquid); dark hue; dense.
澱	淀	tìen	ㄉㄧㄢ	Sediment, dregs. Note: This is not 淀 (tien) - Shallow water; a lake in Hopei.
澦	滪	yù	ㄩ	Tributary, in Yangtze River.

14. 滙 汇 hùi ㄏㄨㄟ To send money; bank draft; to converge, converging waters.

瀏	浏	líu	ㄌㄧㄡ	Clear deep water.
濛	蒙	méng	ㄇㄥ	Mist, drizzle.
瀰	㳽	mí	ㄇㄧ	A watery expanse.

157

		mǐ	ㄇ	Overflowing.
濘	泞	nìng	ㄋㄧㄥ	Mud.
		nèng	ㄋㄥ	(Variant).
澀	涩	sè	ㄙㄜ	Rough, harsh; uneven.
濕	湿	shīh	ㄕ	Wet.
濰	潍	wéi	ㄨㄟ	A river in Shantung.
15. 濺	溅	chīen	ㄐㄧㄢ	Rushing water.
		chìen		To splash.
澙	泻	hsìeh	ㄒㄧㄝ	To flow, drain; dysentery.
濫	滥	làn	ㄌㄢ	To overflow.
濼	泺	lò	ㄌㄜ	A river in Shantung.
濾	滤	lǜ	ㄌㄩ	To filter, strain.
濱	滨	pīn	ㄅㄧㄣ	A bank, shore.
		p'ín	ㄆㄧㄣ	(Variant).
瀆	渎	tú	ㄉㄨ	A ditch, drain.
16. 瀨	濑	lài	ㄌㄞ	Water flowing over shallows, ripples; name of a river in Kwangsi.
瀝	沥	lì	ㄌㄧ	A drop, to drip; detail, in detail.
瀘	泸	lú	ㄌㄨ	A hsien in Szechwan; river in Kiangsi, also in Szechwan.
瀋	沈	shěn	ㄕㄣ	To pour out water; to leak.
17. 瀟	潇	hsīao	ㄒㄧㄠ	Sound of beating rain and wind.
瀾	澜	lán	ㄌㄢ	Billows, waves.
瀲	潋	lían	ㄌㄧㄢ	Crystal clear.
瀧	泷	lúng	ㄌㄨㄥ	River in Kwangtung.

瀕 瀕	pīn	ㄆㄧㄣ	A bank, shore, beach.	
18. 灕 漓	lí	ㄌㄧ	Name of a river.	
灄 湐	shè	ㄕㄜ	Name of a river.	
19. 灑 洒	sǎ	ㄙㄚ	To scatter, sprinkle; free.	
	hsìn	ㄒㄧㄣ	To shiver; alarmed.	
	hsièn	ㄒㄧㄢ	Solemn, distinguished.	
	ts'ǔi	ㄘㄨㄟ	Lofty.	
灘 滩	t'ān	ㄊㄢ	Rapids, breakers.	
21. 灝 灏	hào	ㄏㄠ	Vast, boundless.	
灑 洒	sǎ	ㄙㄚ	To sprinkle, spill, scatter.	
22. 灣 湾	wān	ㄨㄢ	A bay, cove, bend of a river.	
23. 灤 滦	lúan	ㄌㄨㄢ	To drip.	
24. 灩 滟	yèn	ㄧㄢ	Elegant and beautiful, said of a woman.	

火 灬 86

5. 烏 乌	wū	ㄨ	A crow or raven; black.	
8. 無 无	wú	ㄨ	Without; non-, un-; negative.	
煢 茕	ch'íung	ㄑㄩㄥ	Alone, desolate.	
煩 烦	fán	ㄈㄢ	To trouble; to feel vexed.	
煉 炼	lìen	ㄌㄧㄢ	To refine, purify.	
煒 炜	wěi	ㄨㄟ	A raging, glowing.	
煬 炀	yáng	ㄧㄤ	To roast, sear; to fuse, smelt.	
熗 炝	ch'iàng	ㄑㄧㄤ	A species of cookery, using vinegar and vegetables.	
滅 灭	mìeh	ㄇㄧㄝ	To destroy, extinguish.	

燄	荧	yíng	ㄥˊ	Shining, sprinkling, sparkling.
11. 熱	热	jè	ㄖㄜˋ	Warm; hot; to heat.
燁	烨	yèh	ㄧㄝˋ	A blaze of fire; splendid, glorious.
12. 熾	炽	chìh	ㄓˋ	Blaze; splendid, illustrious; to burn.
燼	烬	chìn	ㄐㄧㄣˋ	Ashes, embers; remains, remnants.
燜	焖	mēn	ㄇㄣ	To steam food.
燒	烧	shāo	ㄕㄠ	To burn, heat; to raost or bake; fever.
燙	烫	t'àng	ㄊㄤˋ	To scald.
燈	灯	tēng	ㄉㄥ	A lamp.
13. 燭	烛	chú	ㄓㄨˊ	Candle, torch; to light.
燴	烩	hùi	ㄏㄨㄟˋ	To cook in a sauce of sesame oil and starch.
燦	灿	t'sàn	ㄘㄢˋ	Brilliant.
竈	灶	tsào	ㄗㄠˋ	Kitchen; furnace, stove.
營	营	yíng	ㄥˊ	A camp, barracks; a scheme or plan.
15. 爐	炉	lú	ㄌㄨˊ	Stove; to bake.
爍	烁	shùo	ㄕㄨㄛˋ	Bright, splendid.
爛	烂	làn	ㄌㄢˋ	Rotten, over ripe; ragged, broken; bright, glistening.

爪 87

8. 爲	为	wéi	ㄨㄟˊ	Is, as.
		wèi		For, because.

父　88

9. 爺 爷　yéh　ㄝ　Old man.

爻　89

10. 爾 尔　ěrh　ㄦ　You; just so.

片　91

15. 牘 牍　tú　ㄉㄨ　Writing tablets; registers.

牛 牛　93

7. 牽 牵　ch'ien ㄑㄧㄢ　To lead along, pull; to drag.
10. 犖 荦　lò　ㄌㄜ　A brindled ox; open, manifest.
15. 犢 犊　tú　ㄉㄨ　A sacrificial calf.
17. 犧 牺　si　ㄒ　Sacrificial victims; animals of uniform color.

犬 犭　94

3. 獨 独　tú　ㄉㄨ　Alone, single.
4. 狀 状　chùang ㄔㄨㄤ　Condition; appearance.
　獰 狞　níng　ㄋㄧㄥ　Fierce aspect; fur of dogs.
7. 狹 狭　hsía　ㄒㄧㄚ　Narrow; narrow-minded.
　狽 狈　pèi　ㄅㄟ　A mythical animal with short fore-legs, reputed to ride on the backs of wolves.

9. 猶 犹 yú ㄩ As if; still; like.

10. 猻 狲 sūn ㄙㄨㄣ A kind of monkey.

獅 狮 szū ㄙ A lion.

shīh ㄕ (Variant).

11. 獄 狱 yǔ ㄩ A prison; a court trial.

13. 獫 猃 hsien ㄒㄧㄢ Shoddy, sly, and crafty.

獪 狯 kùai ㄎㄨㄞ Sly, crafty; mischievous.

kùei ㄎㄨㄟ (Alternate).

14. 獲 获 hùo ㄏㄨㄛ To take in hunting; to bag (game); to obtain.

穫 To harvest a crop.

獷 犷 kǔang ㄎㄨㄤ Fierce, rude.

kùang (Variant).

15. 獵 猎 lieh ㄌㄧㄝ To hunt; hunting, field-sports.

獸 兽 shòu ㄕㄡ Animal, beast.

16. 獺 獭 t'à ㄊㄚ The otter.

17. 獻 献 hsien ㄒㄧㄢ To offer, present, report; to show.

獼 猕 mí ㄇㄧ A female monkey.

玉 王 96

7. 現 现 hsièn ㄒㄧㄢ Glitter of gems; to see, appear.

9. 琿 珲 hún ㄏㄨㄣ Fine jade; a precious gem.

瑋 玮 wěi ㄨㄟ A reddish jade; rare, precious.

10. 瑲 玱 ch'iang ㄑㄧㄤ Tinkling of gems.

瑪 玛 mǎ ㄇㄚ Agate; cornelian. Used in transliterating.

162

璅 璅 sǔo ㄙㄨ Fragments; petty, troublesome, annoying.

瑩 瑩 yíng ㄥ The sparkle of gems.

11.璉 璉 lǐan ㄌㄢ Royal ceremonial vessel to hold grain.

12.璣 玑 chī ㄐ An asymmetrical pearl (or woman).

璡 珒 chìn ㄣ A decorative article made of jade.

璽 玺 hsǐ ㄧ The great seal, imperial signet.

13.璦 瑷 ai ㄞ Beautiful jade.

瓊 琼 ch'iong ㄩㄥ A hsien on Hainan.

環 环 húan ㄏㄨㄢ A ring, to encircle.

16.瓊 琼 ch'iong ㄩㄥ A red stone; excellent, beautiful.

瓏 珑 lúng ㄌㄨㄥ A gem cut in the form of a dragon.

17.瓔 璎 yīng ㄥ A jewel, gem.

19.瓚 瓒 tsàn ㄗㄢ Beautiful jade.

瓦 98

11.甌 瓯 ōu ㄨ A bowl or cup.

甘 99

6.甚 什 shén ㄕㄣ What?

生 100

6.產 产 ch'ǎn ㄔㄢ To produce; reproduce (biol.).

163

4. 畝 亩 mǒu ㄇㄡ A measure of land; 6.6 mou equal one acre.

5. 畝 亩 mǔ ㄇㄨ A mou, a Chinese acre.

6. 畫 画 hùa ㄏㄨㄚ Picture, drawing; a mark, line.

畢 毕 pì ㄅㄧ To end, finish.

8. 當 当 tāng ㄉㄤ Just at; ought; suitable.

14. 疇 畴 ch'óu ㄔㄡ Arable land.

18. 疊 迭 tíeh ㄉㄧㄝ To fold; layer.

7. 痙 痉 chìng ㄐㄧㄥ Convulsions, fits.

9. 瘋 疯 fēng ㄈㄥ Insane, insanity; leprosy.

瘧 疟 yào ㄧㄠ Malaria.

nüeh ㄋㄩㄝ (Variant).

瘍 疡 yáng ㄧㄤ Ulcers, sores.

10. 瘡 疮 ch'ūang ㄔㄨㄤ A sore abscess.

瘞 瘗 ì — A secluded spot; to bury.

11. 瘻 瘘 lú ㄌㄨ A running sore, an ulcer.

12. 癇 痫 hsíen ㄒㄧㄢ Fits, convulsions.

癆 痨 láo ㄌㄠ Wasting away; consumption; injurious.

癘 疠 lì ㄌㄧ A sore, ulcer, esp. caused by "varnish poisoning".

療 疗 líao ㄌㄧㄠ To cure, heal.

癉 癉 tàn ㄊㄢ Weared, fatigued; distressed from overwork.

13. 癤 疖 chīeh ㄐㄧㄝ A small sore, pimple.

癢 痒 yǎng ㄧㄤ To itch.

14. 癟 瘪 pǐeh ㄅㄧㄝ Shrivelled, empty, flaccid, limp.

15. 癥 症 chēng ㄓㄥ Obstructions of the bowels.

癮 瘾 yǐn ㄧㄣ A rash; a yearning for drink or a drag.

16. 癩 癞 lài ㄌㄞ Skin blemishes; mange; leprosy.

癧 疬 lì ㄌㄧ Lump or swellings.

17. 癬 癣 hsüan ㄒㄩㄢ Ringworm, dermatitis.

癭 瘿 yǐng ㄧㄥ A goiter; a knob or a tree.

18. 癲 癫 tīen ㄉㄧㄢ Insane, mad; convulsions.

癰 痈 yūng ㄩㄥ A boil, abscess.

19. 癱 瘫 t'ān ㄊㄢ To be paralyzed.

癶 105

7. 發 发 fā ㄈㄚ To manifest, send out; to develop (an ailment).

白 106

10. 皚 皑 ái ㄞ Whiteness.

皮 107

9. 皸 皲 chūn ㄐㄩㄣ Chapped skin.

10. 皺 皱 chòu ㄔㄡ Facial wrinkles, or creases in clothes.

皿 108

8. 盞 盏 chǎn ㄓㄢ A shallow cup for oil; a wine cup. Classifier for oil-burning lamps.

蓋 盖 kài ㄍㄞ To cover, lid.

9. 盡 尽 chìn ㄐㄧㄣ Exhaustive(ly); all, entirely.

10. 盤 盘 pán ㄆㄢ A plate, dish, bathtub.

11. 監 监 chiēn ㄐㄧㄢ To supervise.

chìen Supervisor; eunuch; to examine.

19. 鹽 塩 yén ㄧㄢ Saline, salty.

目 皿 109

7. 眾 众 chùng ㄔㄨㄥ Great number, crowd; all, entirety.

睏 困 k'ùn ㄎㄨㄣ To sleep, nap; to nod.

8. 睪 睪 i ㄧ To spy.

睞 睐 lài ㄌㄞ To squint at.

瞘 眍 k'ōu ㄎㄡ Deeply-sunk eyes.

瞜 瞜 lóu ㄌㄡ Eye (archaic).

瞞 瞒 mán ㄇㄢ To deceive; to blind; eyes half-closed.

12. 瞭 了 líao ㄌㄧㄠ Clear, to understand; to clarify.

13. 瞼 睑 chiěn ㄐㄧㄢ Eye (archaic).

21. 矚 瞩 chǔ ㄓㄨ To gaze.

12. 矯 矫　chiǎo ㄐㄠˇ　To dissemble.

6. 硃 朱　chū ㄓㄨ　Vermillion; imperial.

7. 硤 硖　hsía ㄒㄧㄚˊ　Ancient town near Ichang (Hupeh).

　硯 砚　yèn ㄧㄢˋ　Stone on which ink is rubbed.

9. 碩 硕　shùo ㄕㄨㄛˋ　Great, large, full, ripe.

　　　shíh ㄕˊ　(Variant).

　碭 砀　tàng ㄉㄤˋ　A colored veined stone; to overflow, exceed.

10. 碼 码　mǎ ㄇㄚˇ　Weights for money; one yard (measure).

　磑 硙　wèi ㄨㄟˋ　A mill; to grind or pulverize.

11. 磧 碛　ch'í ㄑㄧˊ　Exposed rock on ocean shore.

　磚 砖　chūan ㄔㄨㄢ　A brick or slab; square tile; brick tea.

　確 确　ch'üeh ㄑㄩㄝˋ　Solid, as a rock; really, actually.

12. 磯 矶　chī ㄐㄧ　An obstruction in the water; a jetty.

　磽 硗　ch'īao ㄑㄧㄠ　Stony soil.

13. 礎 础　ch'ǔ ㄔㄨˇ　Clear; painful.

　礦 矿　k'ùang ㄎㄨㄤˋ　A mine, ore.

14. 礙 碍　ai ㄞˋ　To impede.

　礤 碜　ch'ěn ㄔㄣˇ　Sand, grit.

　礪 砺　lì ㄌㄧˋ　Sandstone, a coarse whetstone; to grind.

15. 礬 矾 fán ㄈㄢˊ Alum; sulphate.

    礫 砾 lì ㄌㄧˋ Small stones, rubble; broken pottery.

16. 礱 砻 lúng ㄌㄨㄥˊ To grind, sharpen; a mill.

示 礻 113

4. 祇 只 chǐh ㄓˇ To respect.

9. 禎 祯 chēn ㄓㄣ Lucky, auspicious.

    禍 祸 hùo ㄏㄨㄛˋ Calamity, misfortune; tough luck.

    禕 祎 ī ㄧ Rare, excellent, precious.

12. 禪 禅 ch'án ㄔㄢˊ Zen Buddhism.

            shán ㄕㄢˊ To meditate.

            shàn ㄕㄢˋ To clear and level land for an alter; to abdicate.

    禦 御 yǜ ㄩˋ To withstand, resist, hinder; an opponent.

13. 襖 袄 ǎo ㄠˇ A short jacket.

    禱 祷 tǎo ㄊㄠˇ To pray.

14. 禮 礼 lǐ ㄌㄧˇ Propriety; rite.

    禰 祢 ni ㄋㄧˇ A deceased father after his tablet has been placed in the ancestral temple.

禾 115

9. 稱 称 ch'ēng ㄔㄥ To address; call; a name, title; to praise.

    種 种 chǔng ㄓㄨㄥˇ A seed; kind, species.

168

種 种 chùng ㄓㄨㄥˋ To plant.

穀 谷 kǔ ㄍㄨˇ Grain, corn.

11. 積 积 chī ㄐㄧ To accumulate; to store (a supply or cache).

穌 稣 sū ㄙㄨ To revive, rise again.

穎 颖 yǐng ㄧㄥˇ A full, heavy head of grain; a writing brush.

13. 穡 穑 sè ㄙㄜˋ To harvest; husbandry.

14. 穢 秽 hùi ㄏㄨㄟˋ Dirty, dirty, foul; a growth of weeds.

     wèi ㄨㄟˋ (Variant).

穩 稳 wěn ㄨㄣˇ Firm, stable, secure.

宀 116

9. 窮 穷 ch'iung ㄑㄩㄥˊ Poor; thoroughly, the end.

窪 洼 wā ㄨㄚ Hollow, concavity.

窩 窝 wō ㄨㄛ A nest, hole, den; a depression.

11. 窶 窭 chü ㄐㄩˋ Rustic, unceremonious.

窺 窥 k'ūei ㄎㄨㄟ To pry into, to spy.

13. 竅 窍 ch'iao ㄑㄧㄠˋ A hole, cavity; the mind, intelligence.

竄 窜 ts'úan ㄘㄨㄢˊ To sneak away, escape.

15. 竇 窦 tòu ㄉㄡˋ A hole; a drain.

17. 竊 窃 ch'ieh ㄑㄧㄝˋ To steal; surreptitiously, furtively.

9. 竪　竖　shù ㄕㄨ To establish; upright, vertical, perpendicular; a perpendicular stroke.

15. 競　竞　chìng ㄐㄥ To compete; emulate; **to quarrel**.

6. 筆　笔　pǐ ㄅ A writing instrument.

8. 箋　笺　chīen ㄐㄢ A tablet or pad of paper; a document, note.

9. 篋　箧　ch'ieh ㄑㄧㄝ A trunk; a portfolio.

　 篤　笃　tǔ ㄉㄨ True, genuine; stable.

10. 築　筑　chú ㄓㄨ To beat down, tamp or ram earth; to build.

　 箆　箆　pì ㄅ A wooden comb.

　 篩　筛　shāi ㄕㄞ A sieve; to strain or sift.

11. 簍　篓　lǒu ㄌㄡ A hamper, basket.

　 簀　箦　tsé ㄗㄜ A mat, bed-mat.

12. 簡　简　chǐen ㄐㄢ A slip of bamboo for notes; documents.

　 簣　篑　k'ùei ㄎㄨㄟ A basket for carrying earth.

　 簞　箪　tān ㄉㄢ A small basket for cooked rice.

13. 籤　签　ch'īen ㄑㄧㄢ To sign; slips, lots.

　 簫　箫　hsīao ㄒㄧㄠ A panpipe; a flute of bamboo.

14. 籌　筹　ch'óu ㄔㄡ To calculate, devise.

15. 籃　篮　lán ㄌㄢ A basket.

籠	笼	lúng	ㄌㄨㄥˊ	A cage or basket, or similar ventilated container.
16. 籟	籁	lài	ㄌㄞˋ	A three-reed musical pipe.
籜	箨	t'ò	ㄊㄨㄛˋ	First leaves of bamboo shoots; the sheath enveloping emerging leaves.
17. 籤	签	ch'īen	ㄑㄧㄢ	A tally stick, bamboo slip.
籬	篱	lí	ㄌㄧˊ	A bamboo fence.
		lí		A fence.
18. 籪	簖	tùan	ㄉㄨㄢˋ	To stop; interrupt.
19. 籮	箩	ló	ㄌㄨㄛˊ	Deep open baskets; sieve; crate.
籩	笾	pīen	ㄅㄧㄢ	A woven basket, used for giving fruits in offering.

米　119

10. 糞	粪	fèn	ㄈㄣˋ	Manure, night-soil; worthless.
12. 糧	粮	liang	ㄌㄧㄤˋ	Provisions.
14. 糲	粝	lì	ㄌㄧˋ	Coarse (applied to grain).
糰	团	t'úan	ㄊㄨㄢˊ	Dumplings。
16. 糴	籴	tí	ㄉㄧˊ	To buy up grain.
19. 糶	粜	t'ìao	ㄊㄧㄠˋ	To sell grain.

糸　糸　纟　120

2. 糾	纠	chǐu	ㄐㄧㄡ	A confederacy; to collect.
3. 紀	纪	chǐ	ㄐㄧ	Records, chronicles.
紂	纣	chòu	ㄓㄡˋ	A crupper; traces.
紇	纥	hóu	ㄏㄡˊ	Tassels, end of a fringe.

紅	红	húng	ㄏㄨㄥ	Red; symbol of good luck.
紉	纫	jén	ㄖㄣ	To thread (as a needle), to string, to join together to sew, stitch.
紈	纨	wán	ㄨㄢ	White silk, white。
紆	纡	yū	ㄩ	To twist, distort.
約	约	yüeh	ㄩㄝ	A covenant, agreement; to bind, restrain.
4.紖	纼	ch'ĕn	ㄔㄣ	A lead for cattle, rope.
紙	纸	chĭh	ㄓ	Paper, stationery.
純	纯	ch'ún	ㄔㄨㄣ	Purely.
紡	纺	fǎng	ㄈㄤ	To spin, twist.
紛	纷	fēn	ㄈㄣ	Confused, mixed.
納	纳	nà	ㄋㄚ	To give or receive; to enter, be appointed; to insert.
紐	纽	nĭn	ㄋㄡ	A knot; to tie.
紕	纰	p'ī	ㄆㄧ	Spoiled silk.
		p'í		Tassel, silk fringe.
紗	纱	shā	ㄕㄚ	Gauge, thin silk; yarn; muslin.
紓	纾	shū	ㄕㄨ	Slow, remiss; little by little.
紋	纹	wén	ㄨㄣ	Stripes, line, figures; a crack.
紜	纭	yún	ㄩㄣ	Tangled, confused; numerous.
5.紬	绅	ch'óu	ㄔㄡ	A thread, clue; to investigate.
絀	绌	ch'ū	ㄔㄨ	Crimson silk; deficiency, impediment.
		chó	ㄓㄨㄛ	(Variant).
終	终	chūng	ㄓㄨㄥ	The end; the whole of; after all.
綍	绂	fú	ㄈㄨ	Rope for pulling a bier。

細 细 hsì ㄒㄧ Fine, minute, delicate; carefully.

緤 绁 hsieh ㄒㄧㄝ To tie with cords; a bridle.

絆 绊 pàn ㄅㄢ Obstacle; to trip.

紹 绍 shào ㄕㄠ To connect, join; to hand down, continue.

紳 绅 shēn ㄕㄣ A girdle, to bind; the gentry.

紿 绐 tài ㄊㄞ To fool, cheat; pretend.

組 组 tsǔ ㄗㄨ A silk band, girdle, fringe; group, section.

6. 給 给 chǐ ㄐㄧ To give to, grant; to issue.

      kěi ㄍㄟ (more common pronunciation)

絳 绛 chiàng ㄐㄧㄤ Deep red.

絞 绞 chiǎo ㄐㄧㄠ To bind, twist; to wrap.

結 结 chiéh ㄐㄧㄝ To incur an obligation; to contract; cohesion; to flourish, bear fruit.

絕 绝 chüéh ㄐㄩㄝ To interrupt, break off; extinct.

絎 绗 háng ㄏㄤ Printed fabric.

縣 县 hsièn ㄒㄧㄢ District, <u>hsien</u>, prefecture.

絢 绚 hsüàn ㄒㄩㄢ Silken pouch hung from the girdle; stylish; ornamental.

絨 绒 júng ㄖㄨㄥ Sponge, velvet, wool; nap, down.

紺 绀 kàn ㄍㄢ Violet or purple.

絝 绔 k'ù ㄎㄨ Trousers, pants, slacks.

絡 络 lò ㄌㄨㄛ Unreeled silk, hemp, cotton; to spin silk; continuous, to connect; blood vessels; a halter.

絲 丝 szū ㄙ Silk, wire, fiber; strings of musical instruments.

·絰 绖 tiéh ㄉㄧㄝ A white hemp cloth worn by mourners.

統	统	t'ŭng ㄊㄨㄥˇ	To govern, rule, control.
網	网	wǎng ㄨㄤˇ	A net; to fish (with a net).
7. 經	经	chīng ㄐㄧㄥ	Classic books; to plan, manage; constant, recurring; (indicator for past tense).
絹	绢	chüan ㄐㄩㄢˋ	Cheap silk; pongee.
綃	绡	hsīao ㄒㄧㄠ	Raw silk.
繡	绣	hsìu ㄒㄧㄡˋ	To embroider, embellish; variegated, illustrated.
綆	绠	kěng ㄍㄥˇ	A well-rope.
綁	绑	pǎng ㄅㄤˇ	To tie, bind.
綏	绥	sīu ㄙㄨㄟ	To comfort; to retreat.
綈	绨	t'í ㄊㄧˊ	Coarse dark pongee.
8. 綻	绽	chàn ㄓㄢˋ	A ripped seam; to split, rent.
綺	绮	chǐ ㄑㄧˇ	Open work silk fabric; beautiful, pretty.
緋	绯	fēi ㄈㄟ	Dark red.
綽	绰	ch'ò ㄔㄨㄛˋ	Spacious, ample; kind generous.
綢	绸	ch'óu ㄔㄡˊ	Thin silk; silk goods.
綴	缀	chùi ㄓㄨㄟˋ	To baste; to connect, continue; to mix, variegated.
		chò ㄔㄨㄛˋ	To stop, cease.
綫	线	hsìen ㄒㄧㄢˋ	Thread, wire; a line, clue, fuse.
緒	绪	hsǜ ㄒㄩˋ	The end of a ball of thread; a clue; to connect.
綱	纲	kāng ㄍㄤ	Large rope of a net; lanes, principles.
綑	绲	kŭn ㄍㄨㄣˇ	An embroidered sash; a cord; to sew.
綸	纶	kūan ㄍㄨㄢ	A silk handkerchief.

綸	纶	lún ㄌㄨㄣˊ	Silken threads, to twist silk.
綾	绫	líng ㄌㄧㄥˊ	Damask, thin silk.
綹	绺	liǔu ㄌㄧㄡˇ	A skein of silk; a pocket.
綠	绿	lǜ ㄌㄩˋ	Green; chlorine.
		lù ㄌㄨˋ	(Variant).
綿	绵	mién ㄇㄧㄢˊ	Soft, downy; prolonged, drawn out, continuous.
綳	绷	pèng ㄆㄥˋ	To bind, tape, or bandage.
綬	绶	shòu ㄕㄡˋ	To give to, confer; to transmit.
緇	缁	tzū ㄗ	Blade silk; a dark color.
綜	综	tsùng ㄗㄨㄥˋ	Arranging threads for weaving; to sum up, inquire into.
綰	绾	wǎn ㄨㄢˇ	To string together; to bind up, to put up (hair).
維	维	wéi ㄨㄟˊ	To tie, hold together; to hold fast.
縝	缜	chěn ㄓㄣˇ	Close-woven; to tie.
緝	缉	ch'i ㄑㄧ	To twist; to join, continue, to follow up; to arrest, catch.
緘	缄	chīen ㄐㄧㄢ	To bind, seal.
9.縑	缣	chīen ㄐㄧㄢ	A kind of waterproof silk fabric.
緊	紧	chǐn ㄐㄧㄣˇ	Urgent, important.
綣	绻	ch'üan ㄑㄩㄢˇ	Bound in a league; a parasite.
緗	缃	hsīang ㄒㄧㄤ	Light-yellow.
緩	缓	hǔan ㄏㄨㄢˇ	Slow, leisurely; gradually; to delay, retard.
緱	缑	kòu ㄍㄡ	Cord binding on the hilt of a sword.
練	练	lìen ㄌㄧㄢˋ	To practice, drill; to select, train.
緲	缈	mǐao ㄇㄧㄠˇ	Minute, infinitesimal; indistinct.

175

緬	缅	mǐen	ㄇㄧㄢ	To think of, to recall.
緡	缗	mín	ㄇㄧㄣ	A fishing line; a cord.
編	编	pīen	ㄅㄧㄢ	To compile, add; to weave manually.
緦	缌	szū	ㄙ	Coarse cotton cloth, used for mourning.
緹	缇	t'í	ㄊㄧ	A light red silk.
締	缔	t'í	ㄊㄧ	A knot, connection.
緞	缎	tùan	ㄉㄨㄢ	Satin.
緯	纬	wěi	ㄨㄟ	The wool of a web; parallels of latitude; tassels.
10.緻	致	chìh	ㄓ	To mend, patch; soft, delicate; secret.
縉	缙	chìn	ㄐㄧㄣ	Red silk.
縐	绉	chòu	ㄓㄡ	Wrinkled, shrunk; crepe.
縋	缒	chùi	ㄓㄨㄟ	A cord; to let down, lower; to suspend.
縛	缚	fú	ㄈㄨ	To tie.
縊	缢	ì	ㄧ	To strangle oneself.
縟	缛	jù	ㄖㄨ	Adorned, beautiful; gay, elegant.
縞	缟	kǎo	ㄍㄠ	Plain white silk.
縭	缡	lí	ㄌㄧ	A bridal ornament.
繩	绳	shéng	ㄕㄥ	Rope, cord, a marking line; to measure; to restrain.
縧	绦	t'āo	ㄊㄠ	A sash cord.
縗	缞	ts'ūi	ㄘㄨㄟ	A part of a mourning garment.
縈	萦	yúng	ㄩㄥ	To wind about, reel, coil.
緣	缘	yǔan	ㄩㄢ	Destiny; connection, cause, reason; to follow, climb; the hem of a garment.

縕 縕	yǜn	ㄩㄣ	Ravelled silk.	
	yūn	ㄩㄣ	Vague, confused.	
	wěn	ㄨㄣ	Orange color.	
11.績 绩	chī	ㄐ	To spin or join threads.	
縴 纤	ch'ien	ㄑㄧㄢ	A top-rope; to pull, lead; to bring together.	
縶 絷	chíh	ㄓ	To tie up, connect, fetter.	
縫 缝	féng	ㄈㄥ	To sew, stitch.	
縲 缧	léi	ㄌㄟ	To bind with ropes; a bond.	
縷 缕	lǚ	ㄌㄩ	Hempen or silky threads; to state in detail.	
縵 缦	mán	ㄇㄢ	Silk thread; thin silk, unpatterned.	
繆 缪	mìu	ㄇㄧㄡ	Error; in error; to mislead.	
	móu	ㄇㄡ	To wind around.	
	chīu	ㄐㄧㄡ	To tie, bind.	
縹 缥	p'ǐao	ㄆㄧㄠ	Clear, bright, misty, indistinct.	
繅 缫	sāo	ㄙㄠ	To reel silk from cocoons.	
	tsǎo	ㄗㄠ	Elegant, of paintings.	
縮 缩	shū	ㄕㄨ	To draw in, shrink; to bind fast; straight, upright.	
	sō	ㄙㄨ	(Variant).	
總 总	tsǔng	ㄗㄨㄥ	General, always, ever.	
縱 纵	tsùng	ㄗㄨㄥ	To permit, relax, loosen; to let go, be indulgent.	
	tsūng		Perpendicular, vertical	
12.纚 纥	chì	ㄐ	Used for transliteration.	

177

織	织	chīh 业		To weave.
繞	绕	jǎo 玄		To surround, to coil; to wind round; to make a detour.
繚	缭	líao 玄		To bind, wrap; fetters; lines for a sail.
繕	缮	shàn 弓		To write out, copy.
繒	缯	tsēng ㄗ		Silken fabrics.
13. 繫	系	chì ㄐ		To tie.
繮	缰	chīang ㄐㄤ		A bridle, reins.
繳	缴	chǐao ㄐㄠ		To bind, wind about; to involve.
繯	缳	húan ㄏㄨㄢ		Fine silk; to bind, tie.
繪	绘	hùi ㄏㄟ		To draw, sketch; to paint.
繹	绎	ì —		To unravel silk, to get the clue; to explain; continuous.
繰	缲	sāo 玄		To reel silk from cocoons.
		tsǎo 玄		Crimson silk.
14. 纏	缠	ch'án ㄔㄢ		To bind up, wrap; to involve.
繼	继	chì ㄐ		To follow, continue; to adapt; to inherit.
繾	缱	ch'ǐen ㄑㄢ		Involved with, loving.
纊	纩	k'ùang ㄎㄨㄤ		Fine floss silk.
辮	辫	pìen ㄅㄢ		Pigtail.
15. 纈	缬	hsíeh ㄒㄝ		To tie silk into skeins; a knot.
續	续	hsǜ ㄒㄩ		To connect, join, add; continuous.
纍	累	léi ㄌㄟ		To join, bind; to cling to; to creep.
繽	缤	pīn ㄅㄣ		A colorful (object).
17. 纖	纤	hsīen ㄒㄢ		Small, fine, delicate.

纜 缆 làn ㄌㄢˋ A hawser, cable, rope, line.

纓 缨 yǐng ㄧㄥ A neck or chin band on a hat; a tassel or fringe.

18.纔 才 ts'ái ㄘㄞˊ Then, just.

19.纘 缵 tsǔan ㄗㄨㄢˇ To carry on, continue; to imitate.

缶 121

14.罌 罂 yǐng ㄧㄥ An earthenware jar with a small mouth and two or four ears; a pitcher.

16.罈 坛 t'án ㄊㄢˊ Earthenware jar.

网 罒 122

9.罰 罚 fá ㄈㄚˊ To punish.

罷 罢 pà ㄅㄚˋ To desist, quit; indicating suggestion (at the end of a clause).

14.羅 罗 ló ㄌㄛˊ Gauze, netting; a surname. A net for birds; to arrange; for transliterating.

羆 罴 p'í ㄆㄧˊ A kind of bear.

20.羈 羁 chī ㄐㄧ A halter; to restrain; to block.

羊 123

7.羥 羟 ch'īang ㄑㄧㄤ A wild goat.

義 义 ì - Right (correct), meaning; - ism.

179

羽　124

5.	習	习	hsí ㄒㄧ	To practice; habit.
9.	翬	翚	hūi ㄏㄨㄟ	Variegated. A kind of pheasant.
12.	翹	翘	ch'íao ㄑㄧㄠ	Long curved tail feathers; to elevate, raise the head; warped women's head ornaments.

耒　127

11.	耬	耧	lóu ㄌㄡ	A drill for sowing seed.
12.	耢	耢	lăo ㄌㄠ	A wooden seive.
15.	耙	耰	pá ㄆㄚ	A rake; to rake.

耳　128

7.	聖	圣	shèng ㄕㄥ	Holy, sacred; wise.
8.	聞	闻	wén ㄨㄣ	To hear; smell; perceive.
11.	聯	联	lien ㄌㄧㄢ	To unite; joined, associated, united.
	聲	声	shēng ㄕㄥ	Voice, noise.
	慫	篞	sŭng ㄙㄨㄥ	To excite, provoke; to agitate, stire up.
	聰	聪	t'sūng ㄘㄨㄥ	Astute; acute (hearing); clever.
12.	職	职	chīh ㄓ	To govern, supervise, direct; only, particularly; numerous.
	聵	聩	k'ùei ㄎㄨㄟ	Deaf; born deaf.
			hùi ㄏㄨㄟ	(Variant).
	聶	聂	nìeh ㄋㄧㄝ	To whisper; to pick up one's skirts.

聶	聂	chè	ㄓㄜ	To slice meat into **strips**; to close up.
14. 聹	聍	níng	ㄋㄧㄥ	(An intensifying auxiliary werb, used with advice.).
16. 聾	聋	lúng	ㄌㄨㄥ	A deaf person.
聽	听	t'īng	ㄊㄧㄥ	To hear, listen; to understand.

聿 129

9. 肅	肃	sù	ㄙㄨ	Stern, respectful; to write; Kansu.

肉 月 130

6. 脅	胁	hsíeh	ㄒㄧㄝ	The ribs, flank; to coerce; to be forced.
7. 脛	胫	chìng	ㄐㄧㄥ	The shinbone.
		hsìng	ㄒㄧㄥ	(Alternate).
8. 脹	胀	chàng	ㄓㄤ	Swollen abdomen; inflated, bloated.
勝	胜	shēng	ㄕㄥ	To endure, be able to endure; deserving.
		shèng		To win.
9. 腸	肠	ch'áng	ㄔㄤ	The bowels; feelings, affections.
腫	肿	chŭng	ㄓㄨㄥ	Swollen, bloated; to swell.
腦	脑	năo	ㄋㄠ	Brain.
腎	肾	shèn	ㄕㄣ	Kidneys, testes.
11. 膠	胶	chíao	ㄐㄧㄠ	Glue; sticky.
膞	䏝	chúan	ㄓㄨㄢ	A part of a muscle.
膚	肤	fū	ㄈㄨ	The skin, flesh; superficial.

12.膩	腻	nì	ㄋㄧ	Grease, fat; oily; glossy.
13.膾	脍	kùai	ㄎㄨㄞ	Minced meat or fish.
臉	脸	liěn	ㄌㄧㄢ	The face.
膿	脓	núng	ㄋㄨㄥ	Pus.
膽	胆	tǎn	ㄉㄢ	The gall bladder; bravery, courage.
15.臘	腊	là	ㄌㄚ	To sacrifice, a year; the twelfth lunar month; dried meat.
臏	膑	pìn	ㄅㄧㄣ	To expell, reject.
16.臚	胪	lú	ㄌㄨ	The skin; abdomen.
騰	腾	t'èng	ㄊㄥ	To mount, ascend; to move, to turn out.
17.螣	螣	t'éng	ㄊㄥ	A kind of fish.
19.臠	脔	lŭan	ㄌㄨㄢ	Sliced meat.
臢	臜	tsān	ㄗㄢ	A hair-lip; dirty.
		tsāng	ㄗㄤ	(Variant).

臣　　131

2.臤	収	chīen	ㄐㄧㄢ	Firm, strong.
11.臨	临	lín	ㄌㄧㄣ	To approach, draw near; just before, about to, provisional.

至　　133

8.臺	台	t'ái	ㄊㄞ	Terrace, stage, platform.

182

7. 擧 举 chǔ ㄐㄩ　To lift, raise; to elect.

與 与 yǔ ㄩ　To give; and.

　　　 yù ㄩ　To participate.

8. 興 兴 hsīng ㄒㄧㄥ　To flourish.

　　　 hsìng ㄒㄧㄥ　Interest.

18. 舊 旧 chìu ㄐㄧㄡ　Old.

舟　137

10. 艙 舱 ts'āng ㄘㄤ　The hold of a ship.

16. 艦 舰 chìen ㄐㄧㄢ　A warship.

艫 舻 lú ㄌㄨ　The stem or prow of a ship.

艮　138

11. 艱 艰 chīen ㄐㄧㄢ)　Hardship; difficult.

色　139

18. 艷 艳 yèn ㄧㄢ　Beautiful, glamorous; wanton.

屮屮 屮丨　140

4. 芻 刍 ch'ú ㄔㄨ　To cut grass; hay, straw.

6. 滎 荥 yúng ㄩㄥ　Dashing of waves; streams of water; brooks.

7. 莢	荚	chīeh ㄐㄧㄝ	Seeds of legumes.
節	节	chíeh ㄗㄧㄝ	Verse; festival, a fair.
		chǐeh	Knot (in wood).
莊	庄	chūang ㄓㄨㄤ	Dignified; a farm village, shop.
莖	茎	hsìng ㄒㄧㄥ	A stem or stalk; the hilt of a sword.
		chīng ㄐㄧㄥ	(Alternate).
8. 華	华	húa ㄏㄨㄚ	Flowery, elegant; glory, splendor.
萊	莱	lái ㄌㄞ	Goosefoot (Chenopodium sp.); wild herbs; fallow fields.
萬	万	wàn ㄨㄢ	Ten thousand.
9. 範	范	fàn ㄈㄢ	Normal; mean; a law, a surname.
葷	荤	hūn ㄏㄨㄣ	A meat (non-vegetarian) diet.
苙	苙	k'úng ㄎㄨㄥ	A red-leaved vegetable.
蒼	苍	ts'āng ㄘㄤ	Green; old.
葦	苇	wěi ㄨㄟ	A reed.
萵	莴	wō ㄨㄛ	Plants similar to lettuce.
葉	叶	yèh ㄧㄝ	Leaf.
10. 蒓	莼	ch'ún ㄔㄨㄣ	A water plant (Brasenia purpurea).
蓮	莲	líen ㄌㄧㄢ	Water lily.
蔦	茑	nǐao ㄋㄧㄠ	A morning glory; a parasitic plant such as mistletoe.
萆	萆	pì ㄅㄧ	Plant in hemp family.
蒔	莳	shíh ㄕ	To plant, erect.
蓀	荪	sūn ㄙㄨㄣ	The iris (flower).
11. 蔣	蒋	chīang ㄐㄧㄤ	An edible aquatic grass.
蔞	蒌	lóu ㄌㄡ	A species of Artemisia.

蔔	卜	pei	ㄅㄟ	Carrot, turnips, or radish.
		po	ㄅㄛ	(Variant).
葓	茒	ts'úng	ㄘㄥ	A small edible plant, like water cress.
蔭	荫	yìn	ㄣ	Shade, shady; to shelter, protect.
12. 蔵	蕆	ch'ǎn	ㄔㄢ	To prepare; complete command.
薑	姜	chīang	ㄐㄤ	Ginger.
薌	芗	hsīang	ㄒㄧㄤ	An aromatic plant.
蕘	荛	jáo	ㄖㄠ	Grass, rushes, stubble, fuel.
蕢	蒉	k'ùei	ㄎㄨㄟ	A straw basket.
蕁	荨	t'án	ㄊㄢ	Nettle.
蕩	荡	tàng	ㄉㄤ	Large, vast, magnificent.
蕪	芜	wú	ㄨ	A dense stand of weeds; neglected, waste lands.
蕕	莸	yú	ㄧㄡ	A foul-smelling aquatic plant.
蕓	芸	yún	ㄩㄣ	Rue; used for girls name.
13. 薊	蓟	chì.	ㄐ	A thistle.
薺	荠	chì	ㄗ	The shepherd's purse (Capsella sp.).
薔	蔷	ch'iang	ㄑㄧㄤ	A red rose.
薦	荐	chìen	ㄐㄧㄢ	To recommend (a person).
薈	荟	hui	ㄏㄨㄟ	To flourish, as in plants.
襝	裣	lìen	ㄌㄧㄢ	Front part of an old-fashioned jacket.
14. 藹	蔼	ai	ㄞ	Kind, gentle, friendly.
蕎	荞	ch'íao	ㄑㄧㄠ	Buckwheat.
藉	借	chìeh	ㄐㄧㄝ	By means of, to borrow.
藎	荩	chìn	ㄐㄧㄣ	A plant whose root produce a yellow dye; loyal.

蕭	萧	hsīao ㄒㄧㄠ	A kind of <u>Artemesia</u>; sighing of wind, mournful; annoying, troublesome; reverent.
薩	萨	sā ㄙㄚ	Pusa; (used in transliterating.)
15. 繭	茧	chǐen ㄐㄧㄢ	Cocoon.
藭	劳	ch'iung ㄑㄩㄥ	Poor, impoverished; exhausted; to investigate thoroughly, sift out.
藝	艺	ì ㄧ	Skill, art.
藍	蓝	lán ㄌㄢ	Blue, indigo.
藪	薮	sǒu ㄙㄡ	A marshy wildlife preserve.
		shǔ ㄕㄨ	A pad for the head.
藥	药	yào ㄧㄠ	Drug, medicine; to prescribe medicine.
16. 蘄	蕲	ch'i ㄑㄧ	To beg, beseech.
藶	苈	lǐ ㄌㄧ	A plant with hooks on the seed.
藺	蔺	lìn ㄌㄧㄣ	Kind of rush used for mats.
蘢	茏	lúng ㄌㄨㄥ	A kind of waterweed, or duckweed, <u>Polygonum</u>.
蘆	芦	lú ㄌㄨ	Reed, rushes.
蘀	萚	t'ò ㄊㄨㄛ	Fallen leaves and bark.
蘊	蕴	yùn ㄩㄣ	To collect, bring together.
		wèn ㄨㄣ	(Variant)
17. 蘚	藓	hsǐen ㄒㄧㄢ	Moss on damp walls.
蘭	兰	lán ㄌㄢ	Orchid.
蘞	蔹	lìen ㄌㄧㄢ	A wild grape (<u>Vitis pentaphylla</u>).
蘋	苹	p'íng ㄆㄧㄥ	Apple; duckweed.
蘇	苏	sū ㄙㄨ	To relieve; surname; thyme.
18. 勸	劝	ch'üan ㄑㄩㄢ	To urge, persuade.

19. 蘿蔔 ló ㄌㄛˊ Creeping plants.

虍 141

5. 處 处 ch'ù ㄔㄨˋ A place.
6. 號 号 hào ㄏㄠˋ A mark, sign; (ordinal suffix).
   盧 虜 lú ㄌㄨˊ Rice vessel, surname.
10. 盧 卢 lú ㄌㄨˊ Rice vessel.
11. 虧 亏 k'ūei ㄎㄨㄟ Deficiency, loss.

虫 142

7. 蛺 蛱 chiéh ㄐㄧㄝ A butterfly.
   蜆 蚬 hsǐen ㄒㄧㄢˇ Small smooth clams.
8. 雖 虽 súi ㄙㄨㄟˊ Although, even if.
9. 蝦 虾 hsīa ㄒㄧㄚ A shrimp, prawn.
   蝸 蜗 wō ㄨㄛ A snail.
   　　 kūa ㄎㄨㄚ (Variant).
10. 螞 蚂 mǎ ㄇㄚˇ A leech; locust; ant.
    螄 蛳 szū ㄙ A spiral shell.
    　　 shīh ㄕ (Variant).
11. 蟄 蛰 chíh ㄓ To hibernate, become torpid.
    蟈 蝈 kūo ㄍㄨㄛ A small green frog; a cicada.
    螻 蝼 lóu ㄌㄡˊ The mole-cricket.
    螢 萤 yíng ㄧㄥˊ A glow-worm, firefly.
12. 蠆 虿 ch'ài ㄔㄞˋ Scorpion-like insect. Dragon.

蟬 蝉 ch'án ㄔㄢˊ Cicada

蟣 虮 chī ㄐㄧ A louse (Anoplura).

蟲 虫 ch'úng ㄔㄨㄥˊ Insect, reptile, small crawling animal, worm.

蟯 蛲 jáo ㄖㄠˊ Intestinal worms.

蠅 蝇 yíng ㄧㄥˊ Flies.

13.蟶 蛏 ch'ēng ㄔㄥ Mussels, bivalve.

蟻 蚁 ǐ ㄧˇ An ant; used for the first person in petitions.

14.蠐 蛴 ch'í ㄑㄧˊ A large maggot.

蠑 蝾 yúng ㄩㄥˊ A kind of lizard.

15.蠟 蜡 là ㄌㄚˋ A candle; wax, waxy, glazed.

蠣 蛎 lì ㄌㄧˋ Rock-oysters.

17.蟏 蟏 hsiāo ㄒㄧㄠ A small, long-legged spider.

蠱 蛊 kǔ ㄍㄨˇ Internal worms; insanity; poison.

19.蠻 蛮 mán ㄇㄢˊ Aboriginal tribes south of China; fierce, uncivilized.

21.蠶 蚕 ts'án ㄘㄢˊ Silkworm.

血   143

11.衊 衊 mieh ㄇㄧㄝ Defiled with blood; to calumniate.

行   144

5.術 术 shù ㄕㄨˋ A trick; skill.

9.衝 冲 ch'ūng ㄔㄨㄥ To rush to; to collide.

　　　ch'ùng Facing.

衞 卫 wèi ㄨㄟˋ To protect; to escort.

7. 裝 装 chuāng ㄓㄨㄤ Attire, dress; to fill up, pack.

裏 里 lǐ ㄌㄧˇ Inside, interior.

補 补 pǔ ㄅㄨˇ To mend, patch, repair; billion.

8. 製 制 chìh ㄓˋ To cut and make clothes; to construct, build.

喪 丧 sàng ㄙㄤˋ To lose, die; to destroy.

sāng To mourn for parents.

9. 複 复 fù ㄈㄨˋ Complex, double; a double garment.

10. 劊 刽 kāi ㄎㄞ To sharpen a knife; carefully; to influence.

褲 裤 k'ù ㄎㄨˋ Trousers, pants, slacks. See 绔.

褳 裢 lien ㄌㄧㄢˊ A pouch, pocket.

褻 亵 hsìeh ㄒㄧㄝˋ Vile, irreverant; to revile.

褸 褛 lǔ ㄌㄩˇ Lapel of a coat; soiled, ragged.

裊 袅 nǐao ㄋㄧㄠˇ To curl, as smoke.

12. 襉 裥 chǐen ㄐㄧㄢˇ **Part** of a garment.

13. 襖 袄 ǎo ㄠˇ Heavy padded coat; overcoat.

襠 裆 tāng ㄊㄤ Breeches, trousers.

15. 襤 褴 lán ㄌㄢˊ Ragged clothes.

襪 袜 wà ㄨㄚˋ Stockings, socks, hose.

16. 襯 衬 ch'èn ㄔㄣˋ To be lined with; underclothing; to assist.

襲 袭 hsí ㄒㄧˊ Garment lining; (classifier for clothing); to wear; to inherit; to invade.

189

12. 覆 复 fú ㄈㄨ To reply, answer, to repeat.

見 见 147

見 见 chìen ㄐㄧㄢ To see, meet.

4. 規 规 kūei ㄍㄨㄟ Compasses; circle; a rule, regulation.

覓 觅 mì ㄇㄧ To search for; to look after.

視 视 shìh ㄕ To look at, inspect; to regard.

5. 覘 觇 chān ㄔㄢ To spy, keep under close observation.

7. 覡 觋 hsì ㄒㄧ A wizard.

8. 靚 靓 chìng ㄐㄧㄥ To decorate; to paint the face.

9. 親 亲 ch'ìn ㄑㄧㄣ Related to, near to; parent; intimate, to love, to kiss.

覦 觎 yú ㄩ To long for, covet; to spy upon.

10. 覬 觊 chì ㄐㄧ To covet, desire.

覯 觏 kòu ㄍㄡ To meet suddenly; unforeseen.

覽 览 lǎn ㄌㄢ To look at; inspect.

11. 覲 觐 chìn ㄐㄧㄣ To be granted an appointment or audience.

覷 觑 ch'ǜ ㄑㄩ To spy, watch for.

12. 覺 觉 chüeh ㄐㄩㄝ To feel.

chìao ㄐㄧㄠ To wake up; to sleep.

14. 覿 觌 tí ㄊㄧ Face to face; to be granted an audience.

18. 觀 观 kūan ㄍㄨㄢ Behold, observe.

角 148

11.	觴 觞	shāng	ㄕㄤ	A goblet, feast.
		ch'áng	ㄔㄤ	(Variant).
13.	觸 触	ch'ù	ㄔㄨ	To butt, gore, knock against.

言 讠 149

	言 讠	yén	ㄧㄢ	Speech, language.
2.	計 计	chì	ㄐㄧ	A plan, scheme, device; to calculate.
	訃 讣	fù	ㄈㄨ	Parent's obituary.
	訂 订	tìng	ㄉㄧㄥ	To arrange, settle; to edit.
3.	記 记	chì	ㄐㄧ	To remember; to record.
	訖 讫	ch'ē	ㄑㄧ	To stop, finish; to settle, complete; until.
	訐 讦	chíeh	ㄐㄧㄝ	To accuse, charge.
	訓 训	hsùn	ㄒㄩㄣ	To advise, counsel, instruct.
	訌 讧	húng	ㄏㄨㄥ	To slander; discord, revolution.
	訒 讱	jèn	ㄖㄣ	Slow or cautious in speech.
	訕 讪	shān	ㄕㄢ	To abuse, revile.
	討 讨	t'ǎo	ㄊㄠ	To beg, demand; to punish, put to death.
4.	訣 诀	chǘeh	ㄐㄩㄝ	Mystery, secret; esoteric.
	訪 访	fǎng	ㄈㄤ	To inquire about.
	訢 䜣	hsīn	ㄒㄧㄣ	Joy and pleasure.
		hsī	ㄒㄧ	Vapor-rising from the ground.

訢	䜣	yín	ㄣ	Respectful.
訩	讻	hsīung	ㄒㄩㄥ	To brawl, sold.
許	许	hsǔ	ㄒㄩ	To promise, allow; perhaps; excess, very; final particle.
訥	讷	nà	ㄋㄚ	To raise the voice.
		nò	ㄋㄜ	To speak cautiously.
訛	讹	ó	ㄜ	To cheat, deceive; false.
設	设	shè	ㄕㄜ	To establish, found; to arrange devise; supposing (interrogative).
訟	讼	sùng	ㄙㄨㄥ	Litigation, dispute.
訝	讶	yà	ㄧㄚ	Exclamation of surprise.
5. 詐	诈	chà	ㄓㄚ	To deceive; bogus.
詔	诏	chào	ㄓㄠ	To proclaim, as a king, to appeal to.
診	诊	chěn	ㄓㄣ	To examine (medically); to give treatment (medically).
詎	讵	chǜ	ㄐㄩ	How? (to indicate surprise).
詘	诎	ch'ū	ㄑㄩ	To squat, bend down; to stammer.
訶	诃	hó	ㄏㄜ	To blame.
詗	诇	hsìung	ㄒㄩㄥ	To dispense information; to gossip to spy; clever, shrewd.
詒	诒	í	—	To bequeath, send.
		t'ài	ㄊㄞ	To deceive; to ridicule.
詁	诂	kǔ	ㄍㄨ	To comment, explain.
評	评	p'íng	ㄆㄧㄥ	To arrange, criticize; to comment on, a commentary.
訴	诉	sù	ㄙㄨ	To tell, inform, to slander, complain.
詆	诋	tǐ	ㄉㄧ	To slander, defame.

詛	诅	tsŭ	ㄗ	To curse.
詞	词	tz'ú	ㄘ	Phrase(s), word; stories.
6.詫	诧	ch'à	ㄔ	To wonder at.
諍	诤	chēng	ㄓㄥ	To remonstrate (with), to caution.
誠	诚	ch'éng	ㄔㄥ	Sincere, honest; certainly.
詰	诘	chíeh	ㄐㄧㄝ	To investigate; to preserve order; to punish.
誅	诛	chū	ㄓ	To punish, execute; to extirpate.
詮	诠	ch'ūan	ㄔㄩㄢ	To explain, comment, illustrate; to enforce.
詳	详	hsiang	ㄒㄧㄤ	In detail; to examine with care, to judge; carefully; to report to a superior; to roam.
詡	诩	hsŭ	ㄒㄩ	To boast; to make known; harmony; bold, vigorous; to flatter.
話	话	hùa	ㄏㄨㄚ	Words, speech.
詼	诙	hūi	ㄏㄨㄟ	To ridicule; to banter.
詣	诣	ì	ㄧ	To arrive, attain.
該	该	kāi	ㄍㄞ	Ought, should; obligation.
詬	诟	kòu	ㄍㄡ	Shame; to abuse.
詿	诖	kùa	ㄍㄨㄚ	To impose upon; to disturb.
誇	诤	k'ūa	ㄎㄨㄚ	To boast.
誆	诓	k'ūang	ㄎㄨㄤ	To swindle; deceive.
詭	诡	kŭei	ㄍㄨㄟ	To feign, cheat.
誄	诔	lĕi	ㄌㄟ	To praise the dead; a eulogy.
詩	诗	shīh	ㄕ	Poetry, a poem, ode.
試	试	shìh	ㄕ	To test, try; to examine; trained, disciplined.

語 语	yǔ	ㄩ	To speak; words, language, conversation; soft speech.
	yù		To tell to.
諂 谄	ch'ăn ㄔㄢ		To flatter, distinguish.
誡 诫	chìai ㄐㄧㄞ		A warning, admonishment; command; to distinguish.
誚 诮	ch'iao ㄑㄧㄠ		To blame, scold; to ridicule.
誒 诶	è ㄜ		(An interjection).
認 认	jèn ㄖㄣ		To recognize, know; to confess, acknowledge.
誥 诰	kào ㄍㄠ		A title (of nobility); a patent.
誑 诳	k'úang ㄎㄨㄤ		Lies; to deceive.
說 说	shúo ㄕㄨㄛ		To say, speak, talk.
誦 诵	sùng ㄙㄨㄥ		To hum, recite, chant; a song.
誤 误	wù ㄨ		To obstruct, impede; to be mistaken.
誘 诱	yǔ ㄧㄡ		To induce, entice; to lead on.
8. 請 请	ch'ĭng ㄑㄧㄥ		To invite, request; please.
諄 谆	chūn ㄓㄨㄣ		To reiterate, repeatedly; to impress upon.
誹 诽	fěi ㄈㄟ		To slander.
誼 谊	ì ㄧ		Suitable, proper; related, connected, friendships.
課 课	k'ò ㄎㄜ		A lessen, assignment.
諒 谅	liang ㄌㄧㄤ		To excuse; to consider.
論 论	lùn ㄌㄨㄣ		To discuss, speak; to argue. An essay, thesis.
諗 谂	shěn ㄕㄣ		To consult, to seek counsel; to announce.
誰 谁	shúi ㄕㄨㄟ		Who, which?
	shéi		(Alternate).

194

誶 诶	sùi ㄙㄨㄟˋ	To vilify; to scold, abuse, acuse; to question.
誕 诞	tàn ㄉㄢˋ	A birthday; to have children.
談 谈	t'án ㄊㄢˊ	To chat.
調 调	t'íao ㄊㄧㄠˊ	To stir up, mix, blend, harmonize; to train.
諏 诹	tsōu ㄗㄡ	To plan, consult, deliberate.
諉 诿	wěi ㄨㄟˇ	To excuse oneself; to decline; to lay blame on others.
諛 谀	yú ㄩ	To flatter.
9. 諳 谙	ān ㄢ	To have knowledge of.
諶 谌	ch'én ㄔㄣˊ	Sincere, faithful.
諫 谏	chìen ㄐㄧㄢˋ	To admonish, to plead with.
諸 诸	chū ㄓㄨ	All, every.
諷 讽	fěng ㄈㄥˇ	To chant, recite; to ridicule.
諧 谐	hsíeh ㄒㄧㄝˊ	To harmonize, accord with; to agree.
諝 谞	hsǔ ㄒㄩˇ	Knowledge, discrimination; prudence.
諱 讳	hùi ㄏㄨㄟˋ	To conceal; to shun, avoid the use of.
諢 诨	hùn ㄏㄨㄣˋ	Obscene jibes; off-color banter; a unisexual joke, usually concerning illicit sexual relations, or excretion.
諼 谖	hsūan ㄒㄩㄢ	False, deceptive; to forget.
諾 诺	nò ㄋㄛˋ	To respond, answer; to promise; used in transliterating.
謔 谑	nüeh ㄋㄩㄝˋ	To jest, mock.
	hsüeh ㄒㄩㄝˋ	(Variant).

195

論	㑂	p'ien	ㄆㄧㄢ	To boast.
諦	谛	ti	ㄉㄧ	To judge, examine; to discriminate.
諜	谍	tíeh	ㄉㄧㄝ	To spy.
諮	谘	tzǔ	ㄗ	To consult, plan; a dispatch.
謂	谓	wèi	ㄨㄟ	To speak about; to be called.
謁	谒	yèh	ㄧㄝ	A visit.
諺	谚	yèn	ㄧㄢ	A proverb.
諭	谕	yù	ㄩ	To proclaim; an official order.
10. 講	讲	chiǎng	ㄐㄧㄤ	To speak; to argue, discuss.
謙	谦	ch'ien	ㄑㄧㄢ	Retiring, modest, self-effacing; humility.
謝	谢	hsièh	ㄒㄧㄝ	To thank; be grateful; to decline; to confess; to hand over.
謊	谎	huǎng	ㄏㄨㄤ	To misstate, lie; falsehood.
謎	谜	mú	ㄇㄨ	A riddle, puzzle.
謐	谧	mì	ㄇㄧ	To whisper; quiet, inattentive.
謗	谤	pàng	ㄅㄤ	To slander.
謚	谥	shìh	ㄕ	A posthumous title for royalty.
謖	谡	shù	ㄕㄨ	To raise; to rise.
		sù	ㄙㄨ	(Variant).
謄	誊	t'éng	ㄊㄥ	To copy, transcribe.
諏	诹	tsōu	ㄗㄡ	To jest; to bawl.
謠	谣	yáo	ㄧㄠ	To sing; rumor.
11. 謫	谪	ché	ㄓㄜ	To blame, to find fault, to disgrace an official.
譾	谫	chiěn	ㄐㄧㄢ	Stupid, shallow.
謹	谨	chǐn	ㄐㄧㄣ	Attentive; carefully, judiciously.

謾	谩	mán ㄇㄢ		To deceive, insult.
謬	谬	mìu ㄇㄡ		Falsehood, error, exaggeration.
謨	谟	mò ㄇㄛ		A plan, course of action; to imitate, false.
		mù ㄇㄨ		(Variant).

12. 證 证 chèng ㄓ　Proof, evidence, to give evidence.

譏 讥 chī ㄐ　To ridicule; to inspect.

譙 谯 ch'íao ㄑㄠ　A lookout, tower.

　　　ch'ìao　To blame, ridicule.

譎 谲 chúeh ㄐㄩㄝ　To pretend, deceive.

繺 亦 lúan ㄌㄨㄢ　To tie together.

謳 讴 ōu ㄡ　To sing ballads; songs, ballads.

譜 谱 p'ǔ ㄆㄨ　A register, family register; a treatise.

識 识 shìh ㄕ　To know, be acquanted with; to recognize, distinguish.

　　　chìh ㄓ　To remember, record.

譚 谭 t'án ㄊㄢ　To boast.

13. 譧 谵 chān ㄓㄢ　Loquacious.

議 议 ì ˉ　To discuss, talk over, consult; to criticize; an agreement.

譯 译 ì ˉ　To explain, interpret; to translate.

譽 誉 yíi ㄩ　To flatter, praise.

14. 譴 谴 ch'ìen ㄑㄢ　To reprimand, scold.

護 护 hù ㄏㄨ　To guard, protect; to escort, shelter.

辯 辩 pìen ㄅㄢ　To argue, debate; to discuss.

讞	变	shěn	ㄕㄣˇ	To cross examine, interrogate.
16. 讎	讐	ch'óu	ㄔㄡˊ	An enemy, rival; to hate; to compare; a mate or class.
讞	谳	yèn	ㄧㄢˋ	To decide judicially, negotiate.
17. 讒	谗	ch'án	ㄔㄢˊ	To slander.
讖	谶	ch'èn	ㄔㄣˋ	To verify; an omen.
讕	谰	lán	ㄌㄢˊ	To make a false charge.
讓	让	jàng	ㄖㄤˋ	To let, allow, permit; polite, yielding.
20. 讌	讌	yèn	ㄧㄢˋ	A feast; to entertain; to rest, quiet.

豆　151

3. 豈	岂	ch'ǐ	ㄑㄧˇ	How (can it be)? (Interrogatory particle).
		k'ǎi	ㄎㄞˇ	Delighted.
11. 豐	丰	fēng	ㄈㄥ	Rich, abundant.

豕　152

13. 豶	豮	fén	ㄈㄣˊ	To geld a pig.

貝 贝　154

貝	贝	pèi	ㄆㄟˋ	Shell, clamshell; precious.
2. 貞	贞	chēn	ㄓㄣ	Chaste.
負	负	fù	ㄈㄨˋ	To bear, to support on the shoulders.

3. 貢　貢　kùng　ㄍㄨㄥˋ　Tribute.

財　財　ts'ái　ㄘㄞˊ　Wealth; bribe.

4. 販　販　fàn　ㄈㄢˋ　To traffic in; to deal in.

貨　貨　hùo　ㄏㄨㄛˋ　Goods, commodities, produce.

敗　敗　pài　ㄅㄞˋ　To defeat.

貧　貧　p'ˊ　ㄆㄣˊ　Poor, impoverished.

貪　貪　t'ān　ㄊㄢ　To covet, want; avaricious.

責　責　tsé　ㄗㄜˊ　To upbraid; to ask of; to punish.

　　　chái　ㄔㄞˊ　(Variant).

5. 貯　貯　chǔ　ㄓㄨˇ　To hoard, store.

貳　貳　èrh　ㄦˋ　Double; chargeable.

費　費　fèi　ㄈㄟˋ　To waste, spend; expenditure, expensis.

賀　賀　hò　ㄏㄜˋ　To congratulate; to send a gift of congratulations.

貽　貽　í　ㄧ　To give to, hand down; to leave to.

貫　貫　kùan　ㄍㄨㄢˋ　To pierce, to string on a thread.

貺　貺　k'ùang　ㄎㄨㄤˋ　To give, grant; to confer.

　　　hùang　ㄏㄨㄤˋ　(Variant).

貴　貴　kùei　ㄍㄨㄟˋ　Honorable; expensive, valuable.

買　买　mǎi　ㄇㄞˇ　To buy.

賁　贲　pì　ㄆㄧˋ　A military emblem, or symbol, or banner。

貶　贬　pìen　ㄅㄧㄢˋ　To exile.

賒　赊　shìh　ㄕ　To buy on credit; to borrow; to let or hire.

貸　贷　tài　ㄉㄞˋ　To loan for interest; to borrow.

199

貼 貼	t'iēh	To paste, attach.
6. 價 價	chǐa	Price.
	kǔ	To trade; a merchant.
質 质	chíh	Disposition; matter, substance, elements; to confront, call as a witness.
	chìh	A pledge, pawn.
賄 賄	hùi	Riches, wealth.
賅 賅	kāi	To give.
賃 賃	lín	To rent, lease.
	jēn	(Variant).
賊 賊	tséi	A thief, rebel; to hurt, plunder; a term of abuse.
	tsé	(Variant).
資 資	tzū	Wealth, property; to aid; to rely upon; disposition.
7. 賑 賑	chèn	Liberal; to aid the needy or distressed.
賒 賒	shē	To buy or sell on credit; distant; to shirk, put off.
8. 賬 賬	chàng	An account, bill, check.
	chī	To grasp and offer, subserviently.
賤 賤	chien	Mean, worthless; to hold lightly.
	chien	Mean, cheap, worthless.
賙 賙	chōu	To give alms.
賚 賚	lài	To confer; to reward, bestow (on an inferior).
賣 卖	mài	To sell.

賠 賠	p'éi ㄆㄟ	To restore, indemnify; to apologize.
賞 賞	shǎng ㄕㄤ	To reward, grant; an award, praise; to enjoy, appreciate.
賭 賭	tǔ ㄉㄨ	To gamble, risk.
9. 賦 賦	fù ㄈㄨ	To spread, diffuse.
賢 賢	hsíen ㄒㄧㄢ	Virtuous, good, worthy; used in transliterating.
賴 賴	lài ㄌㄞ	To rely upon, to trust.
賜 賜	tz'ù ㄘ	To give.
10. 賺 賺	chùan ㄔㄨㄢ	To earn, profit; to cheat.
賻 賻	fù ㄈㄨ	Funeral gifts.
購 购	kòu ㄍㄡ	To buy, hire.
賽 賽	sài ㄙㄞ	To compete; to contend, rival; to emulate.
11. 贄 贄	chìh ㄓ	A gift to a superior, or offering.
贅 贅	chùi ㄓㄨㄟ	To repeat; tautology; irrelevants useless, parasitic.
12. 賻 賻	chìn ㄐㄧㄣ	Farewell or parting gifts.
贊 贊	tsàn ㄗㄢ	To assist; to second; to praise admire; to inform; to bring to light.
贈 贈	tsèng ㄗㄥ	To bestow, confer, give (a gift).
贗 贗	yèn ㄧㄢ	False, counterfeit; spurious; fake.
13. 贍 贍	shàn ㄕㄢ	To give, aid, supply; to be sufficient for.
贏 贏	yíng ㄧㄥ	Full, replete; to produce; profit, gain.
15 贖 贖	shú ㄕㄨ	To redeem, ransom; to atone for.
17 贛 贛	kàn ㄍㄢ	Region south of Po-yang Lake, Kiangsi Province.

18. 臟贓　tsāng ㄗㄤ　Plunder, stolen goods; bribes, corruption.

赤　155

9. 頳赪　ch'ēng ㄔㄥ　Deep red; to blush.

走　156

7. 趙赵　chào ㄔㄠ　To hasten to; to visit; surname.

趕赶　kǎn ㄍㄢ　To hurry.

10. 趨趋　ch'ú ㄔㄨ　Yeast; mother of vinegar.

19. 趲趱　tsǎn ㄗㄢ　To hasten, hurry.

足 足　157

7. 踊踊　yǔng ㄩㄥ　To leap, jump; exult, enthusiastic; to have one's toes cut off as punishment.

8. 踐践　chièn ㄐㄧㄢ　To trample upon.

10. 蹌跄　ch'īang ㄑㄧㄤ　To walk rapidly.

蹕跸　pì ㄅㄧ　To clear the way for the emperor; imperial stopping place.

11. 蹣蹒　mán ㄇㄢ　To jump over.

12. 蹺跷　ch'īao ㄑㄧㄠ　To raise or cross the legs when sitting.

蹮跹　hsīen ㄒㄧㄢ　To walk aimlessly, meander.

13. 躓踬　chíh ㄓ　To walk with a limp.

蠹𨀝　tǔn ㄊㄨㄣ　To store.

14. 蹜 跮 chī ㄕ To increase, augment.

躊 踌 ch'óu ㄔㄡ Embarrassed.

躍 跃 yùeh ㄩㄝ To jump.

15. 躑 踯 chìh ㄓ Embarrassed; bewildered.

17. 躦 躜 tsúan ㄗㄨㄢ To jump.

ts'úan ㄘㄨㄢ (Variant)

躥 蹿 ts'ùan ㄘㄨㄢ To leap; spurt out, eject.

18. 躡 蹑 nìeh ㄋㄧㄝ To tread, step; to ascend.

21. 躪 躏 lìn ㄌㄧㄣ A cart-rut; to run over, trample.

身　158

12. 軀 躯 ch'ū ㄑㄩ The human body; oneself.

車 车　159

車 车 ch'ē ㄔㄜ A vehicle.

1. 軋 轧 yà ㄧㄚ To crush.

chà ㄔㄚ To crowd about; a creaking sound.

2. 軌 轨 kǔei ㄍㄨㄟ A rut or track; axel of a wheel; a law.

軍 军 chūn ㄐㄩㄣ Military.

3. 軒 轩 hsǖan ㄒㄩㄢ A porch, balcony, side room; merry, jovial; a surname.

軔 轫 jèn ㄖㄣ To skid, to stop; a catch, an impediment; hard, firm, tough.

4. 斬 斩 chǎn ㄓㄢ To behead, bisect.

軟 软 jǔan ㄖㄨㄢ Soft, yielding; weak.

203

軛 軛	ò	ㄜ	A yoke, collar; to restrain.
載 载	tsài	ㄗㄞ	To load, contain; to carry in a vehicle; to enter in a register; to go to work.
5. 軫 轸	chěn	ㄓㄣ	Distressed, distraught, upset, saddened.
軸 轴	chú	ㄓㄨ	An axel; a dowel on which maps or scrolls are rolled.
軼 轶	ì	ㄧ	To overtake (in a vehicle); to rush out; to surpass; exceeding.
軻 轲	k'ō	ㄎㄜ	A pair of wheels.
軲 轱	kū	ㄍㄨ	A wheel; to revolve.
6. 較 较	chǐao	ㄐㄠ	To test; than; relatively.
	chǐao		To compare.
軽 轻	chìh	ㄓ	A kind of chariot.
輅 辂	lù	ㄌㄨ	A carriage, chariot.
軾 轼	shìh	ㄕ	A stretcher in a palanquin.
7. 輒 辄	ch'è	ㄔㄜ	Sides of a chariot; at once, abruptly.
輕 轻	ch'īng	ㄑㄥ	Light (eight).
輔 辅	fǔ	ㄈㄨ	Auxiliary; props.
輥 辊	kǔn	ㄍㄨㄣ	To revolve; a stone roller.
8. 輟 辍	ch'ò	ㄔㄨㄛ	To mend.
輝 辉	hūi	ㄏㄨㄟ	Brightness, shining; glory.
輛 辆	lìang	ㄌㄧㄤ	A pair of wheels; classifier for vehicles.
輪 轮	lún	ㄌㄨㄣ	To turn; a turn, revolution.
輦 辇	nǐen	ㄋㄧㄢ	A chair used as a hand carriage the emperor's carriage; the royal court.

輩 輩	pèi ㄆㄟ		Generation.
輜 輜	tzū ㄗ		A baggage wagon; baggage.
輞 辋	wǎng ㄨㄤ		Rim or tire of a wheel; felloe, felly.
9.輯 辑	chì ㄐㄧ		To collate, edit.
輻 辐	fú ㄈㄨ		Spokes or blades in a wheel.
輸 输	shū ㄕㄨ		To pay (as tribute); an offering; to transport, introduce; to loses to submit; to report to a super-ior; to overturn.
輳 輳	ts'òu ㄘㄡ		The hub of a wheel.
10.輾 辗	chǎn ㄓㄢ		To turn half over; to roll over.
轄 辖	hsía ㄒㄧㄚ		Linch - pin of a wheel; to govern or control.
轂 轂	kǔ ㄍㄨ		Hub of a wheel.
輿 輿	yú ㄩ		The bottom of a carriage; to con-tain, hold; earth, people, public.
轅 辕	yǔan ㄩㄢ		The shafts of a horsedrawn vehicle.
11.轉 转	chǔan ㄓㄨㄢ		To change direction, alter course, a revolution, to turn around, revolve; to cause to turn; to transfer, transmit.
轆 辘	lù ㄌㄨ		A pulley, windless, block.
12.轍 辙	ch'è ㄔㄜ		The track of a wheel; a precedent.
轎 轿	chìao ㄐㄧㄠ		A sedan-chair, palanquin.
轔 辚	lín ㄌㄧㄣ		Rumbling of vehicles; a threshold.
轡 辔	p'èi ㄆㄟ		Reins, a bridle. Also written 辔
14.轟 轰	hūng ㄏㄨㄥ		To rumble, roar; to blow up, ex-plode.
15.轢 轢	lì ㄌㄧ		A wheel-rut.

9. 辦 办 pàn ㄅㄢ To manage, do, transact.

12. 辭 辞 tz'ú ㄘ Words, speech; instructions; to shirk, make excuses; to resign.

6. 農 农 néng ㄋㄨㄥ To cultivate; agriculture.

6. 迴 回 húi ㄏㄨㄟ To revolve, circle, return.

7. 這 这 chè ㄓㄜ This (thing), this, these.

連 连 lían ㄌㄧㄢ To connect, join; including, together with; even; a company of soldiers.

8. 進 进 chìn ㄐㄧㄣ To enter, advance.

9. 遜 逊 hsǔn ㄒㄩㄣ To yield; humble, modest.

過 过 kùo ㄍㄨㄛ To pass through; to experience.

達 达 tá ㄉㄚ To open; inform; to reach; attain.

違 违 wéi ㄨㄟ To object, oppose, disobey; to avoid.

運 运 yǔn ㄩㄣ To move about, transport.

10. 遞 递 tì ㄉㄧ To hand over; transmit.

遠 远 yǔan ㄩㄢ Far (away).

11. 遲 迟 ch'íh ㄔ Slow, late.

適 适 shìh ㄕ To go to; to reach; a bride's moving to husband's house; to marry (of women); to suit, succeed; pleasure; amusements; suddenly, just now.

#				
12.	遷 迁	ch'ien ㄑㄧㄢ		To move, remove.
	選 选	hsüan ㄒㄩㄢ		To select.
	遺 遗	í ㄧ		To hand down, bequeath; to lose, neglect, abandon; to forget.
	遼 辽	liao ㄌㄧㄠ		Liao Dynasty.
	邁 迈	mài ㄇㄞ		To take a trip; to surpass.
13.	還 还	húan ㄏㄨㄢ		Yet, still.
		hái ㄏㄞ		Yet, still.
	邊 边	piēn ㄅㄧㄢ		Side.
14.	邇 迩	ěrh ㄦ		Near, close.
19.	邐 逦	lǐ ㄌㄧ		To walk in crowds.
	邏 逻	ló ㄌㄛ		To patrol, make a circuit; to watch.

邑 阝 163

#				
6.	郟 郏	chīa ㄐㄧㄚ		A district in Honan.
8.	郵 邮	yú ㄧㄡ		Mail, post.
9.	鄉 乡	hsīang ㄒㄧㄤ		Rural, rustic.
	鄔 邬	wū ㄨ		A place name.
	鄆 郓	yǔn ㄩㄣ		An ancient city in Lu.
10.	鄒 邹	tsōu ㄗㄡ		Ancient state, in present Shantung (where Mencius was born).
12.	鄭 郑	chèng ㄓㄥ		Surname.
	鄰 邻	lín ㄌㄧㄣ		A neighbor.
	鄲 郸	tān ㄉㄢ		A place name.
	鄧 邓	tèng ㄉㄥ		District in Honan; surname.

13.	鄶 郐	kùai	ㄎㄨㄞ	A small feudal state in area of present day Honan.
	鄴 邺	yèh	ㄧㄝ	Place name, north of Honan.
14.	鄺 邝	kŭang	ㄎㄨㄤ	A surname.
19.	酈 郦	lì	ㄌㄧ	Place-name in State of Lu.

酉 164

9.	醞 酝	yùn	ㄩㄣ	To brew, ferment.
10.	醜 丑	ch'ŏu	ㄔㄡ	Ugly.
11.	醬 酱	chìang	ㄐㄧㄤ	Jam, soy-sauce.
	醫 医	ī	ㄧ	Medicine.
15.	釀 酿	nìang	ㄋㄧㄤ	To brew (by fermentation).
19.	釁 衅	hsìn	ㄒㄧㄣ	To offer a blood sacrifice; to annoint before worship; to embalm; a quarrel, a wrong.
	釅 酽	yèn	ㄧㄢ	Strong, rich (as applied to fluids).

釆 165

13.	釋 释	shìh	ㄕ	To release, open out; to explain; used in transliterating.

金 钅 167

1.	釔 钇	ĭ	ㄧ	The element yttrium (Y).
	釓 钆	ká	ㄍㄚ	The element gadolinium (Gd).
2.	釗 钊	cháo	ㄓㄠ	An ancient weapon.
	針 针	chēn	ㄓㄣ	A needle, pin, probe; a sting, a stitch.

釕 釕	líao ㄌㄧㄠˇ	The element ruthenium (Ru).
釙 钋	p'ò ㄆㄛˋ	The element polonium (Po).
釘 钉	tīng ㄉㄧㄥ	A nail, spike.
3. 釵 钗	ch'āi ㄔㄞ	A hairpin; womankind.
釧 钏	ch'ùan ㄔㄨㄢˋ	Bracelet.
釩 钒	fán ㄈㄢˊ	The element vanadium (V).
釬 钎	hàn ㄏㄢˋ	Solder.
釹 钕	nǚ ㄋㄩˇ	The element neodymium (Nd).
釙 钚	pu ㄅㄨ	The element plutonium (Pu).
釤 钐	sān ㄙㄢ	The element samarium (Sm).
釣 钓	tìao ㄉㄧㄠˋ	To fish with a hook and line
釷 钍	t'ù ㄊㄨˋ	The element thorium (Th).
4. 鈔 钞	ch'ǎo ㄔㄠˇ	A money order; paper money; taxes.
鈐 钤	ch'íen ㄑㄧㄢˊ	A stamp, seal.
欽 钦	ch'in ㄑㄧㄣ	Respectful; to command respect; to hope for.
鈞 钧	chūn ㄐㄩㄣ	A unit of weight (30 catties).
鈁 钫	fáng ㄈㄤˊ	The element francium (Fr).
鈃 钘	hsíng ㄒㄧㄥˊ	A sacrificial caldron.
鈥 钬	hǔo ㄏㄨㄛˇ	The element holmium (Ho).
鈣 钙	kài ㄍㄞˋ	The element calcium (Ca).
鈧 钪	k'àng ㄎㄤˋ	The element scandium (Sc).
鈎 钩	kōu ㄍㄡ	A hook, barb; to connect.
鉚 铆	mǎo ㄇㄠˇ	A spike, large nail.
鈉 钠	nà ㄋㄚˋ	To sharpen wood; to hammer metal to a point; the element sodium (Na).

鈕	钮	nǐu ㄋㄧㄡˇ		A knob, button.
鈀	钯	pà ㄆㄚˋ		The element palladium (Pd).
鈦	钛	t'ài ㄊㄞˋ		The element titanium (Ti).
鈄	钭	tǒu ㄉㄡˇ		Wine flask.
鈍	钝	tùn ㄊㄨㄣˋ		Blunt, obtuse; dull-witted.
5. 鉦	钲	chēng ㄔㄥ		A gong.
鉀	钾	chǐa ㄐㄧㄚˇ		The element potassium (K).
鉗	钳	ch'íen ㄑㄧㄢˊ		Forceps, pincers, pliers; manacles.
鉛	铅	ch'īen ㄑㄧㄢ		The element lead (Pb).
鉉	铉	hsǔan ㄒㄩㄢˇ		Rings on a tripod; a decorated pole for carrying a tripod.
鈳	钶	k'ō ㄎㄛ		The element columbium (Cb); also written .
鈷	钴	kǔ ㄍㄨˇ		A flat-iron; the element cobalt (Co).
鈴	铃	líng ㄌㄧㄥˊ		Small bells.
鉬	钼	mù ㄇㄨˋ		The element molybdenum (Mo).
鈮	铌	ní ㄋㄧˊ		The element niobium (Nb), (syn. columbium).
鉍	铋	pì ㄅㄧˋ		The element bismuth (Bi).
鈹	铍	p'í ㄆㄧˊ		The element beryllium (Be).
鉑	铂	pó ㄅㄛˊ		The element platinum (Pt).
鉅	钜	p'á ㄆㄚˊ		The element promethium (Pm), See 鉅 .
鈰	铈	shíh ㄕ		The element cerium (Ce).
鉭	钽	t'àn ㄊㄢˋ		The element tantalium (Ta).
鈿	钿	t'íen ㄊㄧㄢˊ		Silver or gold filagree hairpin.
		tíen ㄉㄧㄢˊ		(Variant).

鉈 鉈	t'ó ㄊㄛ	A stone roller, a weight.
鈾 铀	yú ㄨ	The element uranium (U).
鈺 钰	yǔ ㄩ	(A given name.)
6. 鉞 钺	yüeh ㄩㄝ	A battle-axe.
錚 铮	chēng ㄔㄥ	A small gong; clang of metals.
鉿 铪	chīa ㄐㄚ	A sound of creaking.
鉸 铰	chiǎo ㄐㄠ	A hinge.
鋏 铗	chīeh ㄐㄝ	Tongs; a sword.
銖 铢	chū ㄓㄨ	Ancient silver coin.
	shú ㄕㄨ	(Variant).
銃 铳	ch'ùng ㄔㄨㄥ	A kind of firearm.
銓 铨	ch'ūan ㄔㄨㄢ	To estimate quality or quantity; to select.
鉺 铒	ér ㄦ	The element erbium (Er).
銜 衔	hsíen ㄒㄧㄢ	A bit; to hold in the mouth; to gag, control.
銑 铣	hsǐen ㄒㄧㄢ	A small chisel; burnished, bright.
鉶 铏	hsíng ㄒㄧㄥ	A sacrificial cauldron; also written .
銦 铟	ī ㄧ	The element indium (In).
銥 铱	ī ㄧ	The element iridium (Ir).
銣 铷	jú ㄖㄨ	The element rubidium (Rb).
鎧 铠	k'ǎi ㄎㄞ	Armor (on a person).
銬 铐	k'ào ㄎㄠ	Handcuffs; manacles.
銘 铬	kò ㄍㄜ	The element chromium (Cr).
銠 铑	láo ㄌㄠ	The element rhenium (Rh).
銘 铭	míng ㄇㄧㄥ	To engrave, carve.

鉕 鉕	p'ō	The element promethium (Pm). Sometimes written 鉕.
銫 銫	sè	The element cesium (Cs).
銚 銚	t'íao	A spear.
	tìao	A pan with a long handle.
	yáo	A weeding impliment; a surname.
銩 銩	tīu	The element thulium (Tm).
銅 铜	t'úng	Brass, bronze; the element copper (Cu).
銪 銪	yǔ	The element europium (Eu).
7. 鐵 鐵	ch'īen	To engrave.
鋤 鋤	ch'ú	A hoe.
鋦 鋦	chǚ	The element curium (Cm).

鋒 鋒	fēng	A sharp tip of spear or lance.
銹 銹	hsìu	Rust; to corrode.
銷 销	hsīao	To melt, fuse.
鋅 鋅	hsīn	The element zinc (Zn).
	tzǔ	Hard.
銳 锐	jùi	A sharp-pointed weapon; acute, zealous, valiant.
鋯 鋯	kào	The element zirconium (Zr).
銀 银	láng	An ornament.
鋰 鋰	lí	The element lithium (Li).
鋁 铝	lǚ	The element aluminum (Al).
鋩 鋩	máng	A sharp point.
鋨 铖	óu	The element osmium (Os).

鋇	钡	pèi ㄆㄟ	The element barium (Ba).
鋪	铺	p'ū ㄆㄨ	To spread out, arrange.
鋱	铽	t'è ㄊㄜ	The element terbium (Tb).
銻	锑	t'ī ㄊㄧ	The element antimony (Sb).
鋌	铤	t'ǐng ㄊㄧㄥ	Iron or copper ore; to ingots or bars.
銼	锉	ts'ò ㄘㄛ	A file; iron pan.
銀	银	yín ㄧㄣ	Riches, wealth, treasure; the element silver (Ag).

8.
錒	锕	ā ㄚ	The element actinium (Ac).
鑹	镩	ch'á ㄔㄚ	A spade.
鍺	锗	ché	The element germanium (Ge).
錢	钱	ch'íen ㄑㄧㄢ	Money, wealth.
錦	锦	chǐn ㄐㄧㄣ	Delicate brocade; elegant.
錘	锤	chūi ㄔㄨㄟ	Ancient Chinese weight, 12 ounces.
鋸	锯	chǔ ㄐㄩ	A saw; to saw; serrate.
錫	锡	hsī ㄙ	Tin, pewter; the element tin (Sn). See 锡 .
鋼	钢	kāng ㄍㄤ	Hard, strong; steel.
錁	锞	k'ò ㄎㄜ	A grease-pot; small ingots.
錮	锢	kù ㄍㄨ	To pour molten metal into cracks; to close, stop.
錸	铼	lái ㄌㄞ	The element rhenium (Rh).
鏈	链	líen ㄌㄧㄢ	A chain or cable.
錄	录	lù ㄌㄨ	To record.
鍆	钔	mén ㄇㄣ	The element mendelevium (Md).
錳	锰	měng ㄇㄥ	The element manganese (Mn).

213

錶 錶	piǎo ㄅㄧㄠˇ	A watch, clock; to manifest.
錇 锫	p'éi ㄆㄟˊ	The element berkelium (Bk).
鎝 锝	té ㄊㄜˊ	The element technetium (Tc).
錠 锭	tìng ㄊㄧㄥˋ	An ingot.
錯 错	ts'ò ㄘㄛˋ	Fault; error; to be confused; alternately.
錙 锱	tzū ㄗ	An ancient measure of weight, equal to one <u>chu</u> 銖 .

9. 鎄 锿 | āi ㄞ | The element einsteinium (Es). |
鍘 铡	chā ㄓㄚ	A knife for cutting chaff.
鎮 镇	chèn ㄓㄣˋ	To repress, hold down; to guard; to keep off evil; a market; a regiment.
鍬 锹	ch'īao ㄑㄧㄠ	A hoe.
鍥 锲	ch'ìeh ㄑㄧㄝˋ	A sickle; to cut, oppress.
鍵 键	chìen ㄐㄧㄢˋ	A door bolt; piano key.
鍾 钟	chūng ㄓㄨㄥ	An ancient measure, equalling four <u>tou</u> 斗 or about a peck; a cup or goblet; to bring together.
鐶 镮	húan ㄏㄨㄢˊ	A metal ring; a weight of more than six taels (archaic).
鍋 锅	kūo ㄍㄨㄛ	A cooking pot, saucepan.
鎦 镏	líu ㄌㄧㄡˊ	The element lutetium (Lu).
鏤 镂	lòu ㄌㄡˋ	To engrave, carve.
錨 锚	máo ㄇㄠˊ	An anchlor.
鎇 镅	méi ㄇㄟˊ	The element americium (Am).
鎂 镁	měi ㄇㄟˇ	The element magnesium (Mg).
鍩 锘	nù ㄋㄨˋ	The element nobelium (No).
鍍 镀	tù ㄊㄨˋ	To plate, gild.

214

鍛	锻	tùan	ㄊㄨㄢˋ	To forage metal.
鎡	镃	tzū	ㄗ	A hoe or mattock.
鎢	钨	wū	ㄨ	The element tungsten (W).
10.鎵	镓	chīa	ㄐㄧㄚ	The element gallium (Ga).
鎰	镒	ì	ㄧˋ	A piece of gold weighing 20 taels; wealth.
鎬	镐	kǎo	ㄍㄠˇ	A tool.
鎘	镉	kè	ㄎㄜˋ	The element cadmium (Cd).
鎿	镎	nà	ㄋㄚˋ	The element neptunium (Np).
鎳	镍	nieh	ㄋㄧㄝˋ	The element nickel (Ni).
鎊	镑	pàng	ㄆㄤˋ	A pound (measure).
鎵	镼	shàn	ㄕㄢ	A metal fan.
鎖	锁	shǔ	ㄕㄨˇ	A lock, chains; to lock.
11.鏟	铲	ch'ǎn	ㄔㄢˇ	A shovel, spade; to cut, pare.
鏘	锵	ch'īang	ㄑㄧㄤ	Tinkling of small bells.
鏡	镜	chìng	ㄐㄧㄥˋ	A mirror, speculum.
鐘	钟	chūng	ㄓㄨㄥ	Gong; clock.
鐫	镌	chūan	ㄓㄨㄢ	To engrave.
鏇	镟	hsùan	ㄒㄩㄢˋ	A pewter flask for keeping spirits warm; a lathe.
鏵	铧	húa	ㄏㄨㄚˊ	A spade or shovel.
鏝	镘	mán	ㄇㄢˊ	A trowel.
鏢	镖	pīao	ㄆㄧㄠ	A metal dart.
鎪	锼	sōu	ㄙㄡ	To engrave on metal or wood.
鏜	镗	t'āng	ㄊㄤ	Roll or boom of drums.
鏑	镝	tí	ㄉㄧˊ	The point of an arrow or spear.

鏨 鏨	tsàn ㄗㄢˋ	A cold chisel; to engrave, cut out.	
鏃 鏃	tsù ㄗㄨˋ	Head of an arrow or spear.	
	ts'ù ㄘㄨˋ	(Variant).	
鏞 鏞	yūng ㄩㄥ	A large bell.	
12. 錢 錢	chǐang ㄐㄧㄤˇ	Money, coins.	
	ch'ǐang ㄑㄧㄤˇ	(Variant).	
鍘 鍘	chīen ㄐㄧㄢ	A knife used in execution.	
鐝 鐝	chǘeh ㄐㄩㄝˊ	A pick, hoe.	
鐨 鐨	fèi ㄈㄟˋ	The element fermium (Fm).	
鐦 鐦	k'āi ㄎㄞ	The element californium (Cf).	
鏗 鏗	k'ēng ㄎㄥ	Tinkling or jingling of metals.	
鐒 鐒	láo ㄌㄠˊ	The element lawrencium (Lw).	
鐐 鐐	liao ㄌㄧㄠ	Manacles, fetters; furnace.	
鐃 鐃	náo ㄋㄠˊ	Bells, cymbals.	
鏷 鏷	p'ǔ ㄆㄨˇ	The element protactinium (Pa).	
鐠 鐠	p'ǔ ㄆㄨˇ	The element praseodymium (Pr).	
饊 饊	sǎn ㄙㄢˇ	Fried round cakes of wheat flour.	
鐙 鐙	tèng ㄉㄥˋ	A stirrup.	
鐵 鐵	t'ǐeh ㄊㄧㄝˇ	Firmness; firm, decided; the element iron (Fe).	
鐓 鐓	tūn ㄊㄨㄣ	Anvil.	
13. 鐺 鐺	ch'ēng ㄔㄥ	A griddle.	
鑕 鑕	chǐh ㄓˇ	A metallic substance.	
鐲 鐲	chó ㄓㄨㄛˊ	A small bell; bracelets, bangles.	
鐶 鐶	húan ㄏㄨㄢˊ	A metal ring; a weight of more than six taels (archaic).	

鐿	镜	ì 一		The element ytterbium (Yb).
鐳	镭	lèi ㄌㄟ		A pot; small copper coin; element radium (Ra).
鐮	镰	lien ㄌㄢ		A nickle, sythe.
鐺	铛	tāng ㄊㄤ		A small gong used by peddlers.
鐸	铎	tó ㄊㄛ		A bell with a clapper.
14. 鑄	铸	chù ㄓㄨ		To cast metals; to coin.
鑊	镬	hùo ㄏㄨㄛ		A boiler, cauldron; a skillet.
15. 鑑	鉴	chìen ㄐㄢ		A metal mirror; to view.
鑞	镴	là ㄌㄚ		Tin, copper, pewter. See 锡 and 錫 .
鑣	镳	pīao ㄅㄠ		A metal dart.
鑠	铄	shùo ㄕㄨㄛ		To melt, to polish; shinning.
鑿	凿	tsò ㄘㄨㄛ		A chisel; to chisel.
17. 鑲	镶	hsīang ㄒㄤ		To inlay, esp. with jewels.
鑭	镧	lán ㄌㄢ		The element lanthanum (La).
鑰	钥	yò ㄩㄛ		A key; lock.
		yǎo ㄧㄠ		(Variant).
鑷	镊	nieh ㄋㄧㄝ		Tweezers, forceps; to pull out.
鑽	镩	ts'ùan ㄘㄨㄢ		A temper (a metal).
鑼	锣	ló ㄌㄨㄛ		A gong.
鑾	銮	lúan ㄌㄨㄢ		Bells on a royal chariot; imperial, a term of respect.
鑽	钻	tsūan ㄗㄨㄢ		To drill into, bore, pierce; to enter deeply, penetrate.
		tsān ㄗㄢ		(Variant).
钁	镢	kùo ㄎㄨㄛ		A mattock.

鏜 鎲 t'ăng ㄊㄤ An ancient weapon.

長長长 168

長 长 ch'áng ㄔㄤ Long, good; excelling.

門门 169

門 门 mén ㄇㄣ Entrance.

1. 閂 闩 shūan ㄕㄨㄢ A bolt used to bar a door.

2. 閃 闪 shǎn ㄕㄢ To flash, as lightning.

3. 閉 闭 pì ㄅㄧ To close.

4. 間 间 chīen ㄐㄧㄢ In, among, on.

               chìen To divide, separate.

  閑 闲 hsíen ㄒㄧㄢ A bar, fence, corral; to defend; trained.

  閏 闰 jùn ㄖㄨㄣ Extra; inserted between others, intercalate.

  開 开 k'āi ㄎㄞ To open, to explain; to operate.

  閔 闵 mǐn ㄇㄧㄣ To mourn, weep; to encourage.

5. 閘 闸 chá ㄓㄚ A flood-gate, a lock (in a canal), a barrier.

  鬧 闹 nào ㄋㄠ A disturbance; to make a disturbance; noise.

  閡 阂 ài ㄞ To shut others out; obstructed.

             hè ㄏㄜ (Variant).

6. 閥 阀 fá ㄈㄚ Ranking, classification.

  閤 合 hó ㄏㄜ A small side door.

218

閣	阁	kó ㄍㄜ	A pavilion; vestibule; bookcase.
閨	闺	kūei ㄍㄨㄟ	Women's apartment; lady-like, feminine.
閩	闽	mǐn ㄇㄧㄣ	A kind of snake; Fukien Province.
7. 閫	阃	k'ǔn ㄎㄨㄣ	A threshold; entrance to women's apartments.
閬	阆	lǎng ㄌㄤ	A high door.
閭	闾	lǘ ㄌㄩ	A gate of a village.
閱	阅	yüeh ㄩㄝ	To examine, inspect, review; to pass through.
8. 閶	阊	ch'āng ㄔㄤ	The gates of heaven; west wing.
闃	阒	ch'ü ㄑㄩ	To live alone; still, quiet.
鬩	阋	hsì ㄒㄧ	To quarrel; animosity, resentment.
閽	阍	hūn ㄏㄨㄣ	A door-keeper, an entrance.
閼	阏	ò ㄜ	To close, obstruct; to conceal.
閺	阌	wén ㄨㄣ	To look at closely.
閹	阉	yēn ㄧㄢ	To castrate, emasculate.
閻	阎	yén ·ㄧㄢ	Gate to a village; a hamlet.
		nién ㄊㄧㄢ	(Variant).
閾	阈	yù ㄩ	A door-sill, threshold.
9. 闋	阕	ch'üeh ㄑㄩㄝ	To close a door; to close, rest.
闊	阔	k'ùo ㄎㄨㄛ	Broad, ample; affluent.
闌	阑	lán ㄌㄢ	A door screen; to cut off.
闆	板	pǎn ㄅㄢ	Board; shop-owner.
闈	闱	wéi ㄨㄟ	Doors leading to women's quarters.
10. 闖	闯	ch'ǔang ㄔㄨㄤ	To rush in; suddenly.
闕	阙	ch'üeh ㄑㄩㄝ	A look-out tower at a city gate. An imperial city.

閜 阖 hó ㄏㄜˊ Leaf of a door.

闓 闿 k'ăi ㄎㄞˇ To loosen or open.

闐 阗 t'íen ㄊㄧㄢˊ To fill up; rumbling sounds.

tìen ㄊㄧㄢˋ A place name.

11. 闞 阚 k'àn ㄎㄢˋ To peep; a pavilion.

關 关 kūan ㄍㄨㄢ A mountain pass, entry; custom-house.

12. 闡 阐 ch'ăn ㄔㄢˇ To open; explain.

闥 闼 t'à ㄊㄚˋ The door of an inner room.

13. 闢 辟 p'ì ㄆㄧˋ To cleave, split open; to develop.

阜 阝 170

7. 陣 阵 chèn ㄓㄣˋ A group of soldiers; a battle; a time, occasion.

陘 陉 hsíng ㄒㄧㄥˊ A gorge, pass; niche near a stove.

陝 陕 shăn ㄕㄢˇ Mountain passes; the Province of Shensi.

8. 陳 陈 ch'én ㄔㄣˊ Stale; to arrange, spread out.

陸 陆 lù ㄌㄨˋ Land; six.

陰 阴 yīn ㄧㄣ Female principle; cloudy, shady, dark.

9. 隊 队 tùi ㄉㄨㄟˋ A regiment or group of men, air-planes, warships.

陽 阳 yáng ㄧㄤˊ Male principle; sun.

際 际 chì ㄐㄧˋ Interval; limit; border.

隕 陨 yŭ ㄩㄣˇ To fall.

階 阶 chīeh ㄐㄧㄝ Steps, degrees.

隱 隐 yǐn ㄧㄣ To avoid, conceal; retired, hidden; small, minute; painful, sore; grieved.

yèn ㄧㄢ To lean on.

隨 随 súi ㄙㄨㄟ To follow.

險 险 hsǐen ㄒㄧㄢ A narrow pass; danger, dangerous, risk.

隴 陇 lúng ㄌㄨㄥ A dike or bank.

隶　171

9. 隸 隶 lì ㄌㄧ Attached to, belonging to; to control, to rule.

隹　172

2. 隻 只 chīh ㄓ A classifier for objects of a pair (e.g., arms, legs, etc.)

10. 雛 雏 ch'ú ㄔㄨ A chick, fledgling; to brood.

離 离 ·lí ㄌㄧ Distant from.

雙 双 shūang ㄕㄨㄤ A pair (of), a couple.

雜 杂 tsá ㄗㄚ Mixed; confused.

11. 難 难 nán ㄋㄢ Difficult, hard.

雨　173

4. 雲 云 yǔn ㄩㄣ Cloud.

5. 電 电 tìen ㄉㄧㄢ Electricity; electric.

10. 霧 雾 wù ㄨ Fog, mist, vapor.

221

12. 霽 霁 chì ㄓ A clearing sky.

15. 靆 靆 tài ㄉㄞˋ Cloudy sky.

16. 靈 灵 líng ㄌㄧㄥˊ Spirit; spiritual, divine; supernatural; intelligent, ingenious; a coffin with a corpse.

17. 靉 靉 ài ㄞˋ Cloudy, obscure, nebulous.

面 176

14. 靨 厌 yèh ㄧㄝ The jaws, cheeks.

革 177

6. 鞏 巩 kŭng ㄍㄨㄥˇ Secure, solid.

9. 鞦 秋 ch'īu ㄑㄧㄡ A swing; a crupper.

13. 韃 鞑 tá ㄊㄚˊ A nomadic tribe, formerly of northwest China.

16. 韆 千 ch'īen ㄑㄧㄢ A swing.

17. 韉 鞯 chīen ㄐㄧㄢ A saddle-cloth.

韋 韦 178

韋 韦 wéi ㄨㄟˊ Leather, hide.

3. 韌 韧 jèn ㄖㄣˋ Pliable but strong, leather like.

5. 韍 韍 fú ㄈㄨˊ A leather knee-pad; a leather strap for a seal.

8. 韓 韩 hàn ㄏㄢˋ A fence, a surname; old name for Korea.

9. 韙 韪 wěi ㄨㄟˇ Right; that which is right, correct, proper.

10. 韜 韬　t'āo ㄊㄠ　A bow-case, sheath; just, liberal.

韞 韫　yùn ㄩㄣ　An orange color.

頁 页 181

頁 页　yèh ㄜ　A page, leaf.

2. 頃 顷　ch'ǐng ㄑㄧㄥ　An instant, a short time; one hundred <u>mou</u>, 畝 , ca 15 acres.

頂 顶　tǐng ㄉㄧㄥ　The top; extremely, utmost, very.

3. 頇 顸　hān ㄏㄢ　A large face.

項 项　hsiàng ㄒㄧㄤ　The nape; an item, kind; a term, as in algebra.

須 须　hsū ㄒㄩ　Necessary, must; a moment, to wait.

順 顺　shùn ㄕㄨㄣ　Favorable, prosperous; to obey, agree; in accordance with; to allow, indulge; to persist in.

4. 頊 顼　hsū ㄒㄩ　Anxious, worried.

顧 顾　kù ㄍㄨ　To care for, look after.

頏 颃　háng ㄏㄤ　To fly down.

頌 颂　sùng ㄙㄨㄥ　To praise, commend; hymns, odes.

頓 顿　tùn ㄉㄨㄣ　A time, turn; to injure; suddenly; classifier for times.

頑 顽　wán ㄨㄢ　Obstinate, wayward; stupid; corrupt; bigoted.

預 预　yü ㄩ　To prepare, before hand; to be at ease, pleased, comfortable.

5. 領 领　lǐng ㄌㄧㄥ　The throat; collar; to lead, guide or direct; to receive.

頗 颇　p'ō ㄆㄛ　Inclined to one side, leaning; somewhat, rather.

頋	頔	p'ū ㄆㄨ		(Variant).
6. 頦	頦	hái ㄏㄞ		The chin.
頜	頜	hó ㄏㄛ		The jowels.
		kó ㄍㄛ		(A variant).
頡	頡	hsíeh ㄒㄧㄝ		To soar, ascend in flight.
7. 頰	頰	chía ㄐㄧㄚ		The jaw, cheeks.
頸	颈	chǐng ㄐㄧㄥ		The neck, throat.
頤	颐	í -		The chin, jaws; to nurish, to rear.
頻	频	p'ín ㄆㄧㄣ		Urgent, hurried; imminent; a shore, a band.
頭	头	t'óu ㄊㄡ		Head.
頹	颓	t'úi ㄊㄨㄟ		To fall, descend; ruin.
8. 頷	颔	hàn ㄏㄢ		The chin, jaws.
顆	颗	k'ō ㄎㄛ		A kernel; classifier for small objects.
9. 顓	颛	chūan ㄓㄨㄢ		Good, sedate, simple.
類	类	lèi ㄌㄟ		Class, species, genus.
額	额	ó ㄜ		Forehead; amount, a fixed number.
題	题	t'í ㄊㄧ		The forehead; a heading, item, subject.
顛	颠	tīen ㄉㄧㄢ		To jolt.
顏	颜	yén ㄧㄢ		Color; to dye.
10. 顙	颡	sǎng ㄙㄤ		The forehead.
願	愿	yüan ㄩㄢ		Willing; wish.
顢	颟	mān ㄇㄢ		A large face; dawdling.
12. 顥	颢	hào ㄏㄠ		Luminous, bright; hoary, white.

髟頁	须	hsü ㄒㄩ	Mustache, beard.
顧	顾	kù ㄍㄨ	To care for.
13. 顫	顫	chàn ㄓㄢ	A cocked head; shaking, unsteady.
		ch'àn ㄔㄢ	(Variant).
14. 㬎頁	显	hsǐen ㄒㄧㄢ	Comspicuous; make plain.
需頁	颥	jú ㄐㄨ	The temporal bone.
15. 步頁	步頁	p'ín ㄆㄧㄣ	To knit the brows; to look disraught.
16. 盧頁	顱	lú ㄌㄨ	The skull, forehead.
18. 雚頁	顴	ch'ǘan ㄑㄩㄢ	The cheek-bones.
聶頁	聶頁	nìeh ㄋㄧㄝ	The temporal bones.

風 凤 182

風	风	fēng ㄈㄥ	Wind.
5. 颯	飒	sà ㄙㄚ	The sound of wind; a gust suddenly.
颱	台	t'āi ㄊㄞ	Strong wind; typhoon.
6. 颳	刮	kūa ㄍㄨㄚ	To blow (wind); to be blown.
7. 颶	飓	chǜ ㄐㄩ	Hurricane, typhoon.
9. 飀	飗	líu ㄌㄧㄡ	Sighing of the wind.
11. 飄	飘	p'ǐao ㄆㄧㄠ	To whirl (like wind); floaring, graceful.
颼	飕	sōu ㄙㄡ	A chilling wind; a whizzing sound.
12. 飆	飙	pīao ㄅㄧㄠ	Whirlwind.

飛 飞 183

飛	飞	fēi ㄈㄟ	To fly. (This is radical 183).

食 𠂊		shíh ㄕ	To eat.
4.飭 饬		ch'íh ㄔ	To direct; to prepare.
飯 饭		fàn ㄈㄢ	Cooked rice; food; a meal.
飪 饪		jěn ㄖㄣ	To cook thoroughly.
飲 饮		yǐn ㄧㄣ	To drink, swallow.
飫 饫		yù ㄩ	To overeat.
5.飽 饱		pǎo ㄠ	Satiated, replete.
˙飾 饰		shìh ㄕ	To adorn; to set off; to deceive; ornaments.
飼 饲		szù ㄙ	To feed, nurish; provision, food.
6.餃 饺		chiǎo ㄐㄠ	A meat dumpling.
餌 饵		ěrh ㄦ	Cakes; dumplings.
餉 饷		hsiǎng ㄒㄧㄤ	Rations or pay for troops; revenue; gifts of provisions.
餅 饼		pǐng ㄅㄥ	Cake, biscuit.
蝕 蚀		shíh ㄕ	To eat, consume slowly; an eclipse.
7.餒 馁		něi ㄋㄟ	To be hungry, famished; feeble.
餓 饿		ò ㄜ	Hungry.
餘 余		yú ㄩ	The rest, remainder.
8.餞 饯		chièn ㄐㄧㄢ	A bye-bye gift or party.
饉 馑		chìn ㄐㄧㄣ	A death; famine.
餡 馅		hsièn ㄒㄧㄢ	Fruit, meat, sugar, etc., as stuffing in pastry; a secret.
餛 馄		hún ㄏㄨㄣ	Dumpling.
餜 馃		kǔo ㄍㄨㄛ	Cakes or biscuits.

館 馆	kǔan ㄍㄨㄢ	A place to lodge; a tavern; a public office.
養 养	yǎng ㄧㄤ	To give birth to; to rear, care for, support.
10. 餼 饩	hsì ㄒㄧ	A sacrificial victim; to give a ration of grain.
餾 馏	lìu ㄌㄧㄡ	To steam food.
11. 饈 馐	hsīu ㄒㄧㄡ	Delicacies.
饅 馒	mán ㄇㄢ	Steamed bread.
餿 馊	sou ㄙㄡ	Rancid, sour.
12. 饑 饥	chi ㄐㄧ	Hunger, famine; scarcity.
饗 飨	hsiǎng ㄒㄧㄤ	To offer in sacrifice or at a feast.
饒 饶	jáo ㄖㄠ	To forgive, spare, overlook; to be liberal, indulgent.
饋 馈	k'ùei ㄎㄨㄟ	Provisions, food; to offer a gift, esp. of food.
14. 饜 厌	yèn ㄧㄢ	To eat to repletion; to be replete.
18. 饞 馋	ch'án ㄔㄢ	Gluttonous.

馬 马 187

馬 马	mǎ ㄇㄚ	A horse; at once; used in trans- literating.
2. 馮 冯	féng ㄈㄥ	A surname; a horse running.
	p'íng ㄆㄥ	To ford a stream.
馭 驭	yǔ ㄩ	To drive (a chariot); to manage; to wait on, set before; an attend- and; imperial.
	yà ㄧㄚ	To invoke; to meet.
3. 馳 驰	ch'íh ㄔ	To go quickly.

馬川	马川	hsún ㄒㄩㄣ	Tame; docile, well-bred.
馬大	马大	t'ó ㄊㄛ	To carry on the back; to bear.
4. 駁	马犮	pó ㄅㄛ	To refute.
5. 駕	驾	chìa ㄐㄚ	To ride; to yoke, control.
馬主	马主	chù ㄓㄨ	To halt; to reside temporarily.
馬句	马句	chū ㄐㄩ	A colt; strong.
馬付	马付	fù ㄈㄨ	An extra harnessed by the side of a team.
駑	驽	nú ㄋㄨ	Worn-out old horses; referring to a man in the intellectual menopause.
駛	马史	shǐh ㄕ	To ride in; to be driven; to proceed to.
馬四	马四	szù ㄙ	A team of four horses.
駘	马台	t'ái ㄊㄞ	A worn-out horse, a nag.
駝	驼	t'ó ㄊㄛ	The camel.
駔	马且	tsăng ㄗㄤ	A powerful horse; a broken, inferior, coarse.
		tsŭ ㄗㄨ	A cord attached to a badge.
6. 駭	马亥	hài ㄏㄞ	To terrify; startled.
駱	马各	lò ㄌㄛ	Camel.
駢	马并	p'íen ㄆㄧㄢ	A pair of horses; to associate, join together.
		p'īn ㄆㄧㄣ	(Variant).
7. 騁	马甹	ch'ěng ㄔㄥ	To gallop, hasten.
駸	马寻	ch'īn ㄑㄧㄣ	A fleet horse.
駿	马夋	chün ㄐㄩㄢ	A spirited, vigorous horse; swift; lofty.
8. 騏	马其	ch'í ㄑㄧ	A piebald horse; spotted.

騎	骑	ch'í ⤶	To mount, ride.
騅	骓	chūi ㄓㄨㄟ	A piebald horse.
騍	骒	k'ò ㄎㄜ	A mare.
9. 鶖	鹙	ch'īu ㄑㄧㄡ	A long-legged wading bird.
騮	骝	líu ㄌㄧㄡ	A bay horse with a black mane.
騙	骗	p'ìen ㄆㄧㄢ	To cheat, swindle.
騷	骚	sāo ㄙㄠ	To annoy; sad, grieved; moved; lascivious; poetic.
10. 騫	骞	ch'īen ㄑㄧㄢ	Defective, ailing; to raise the head.
騭	骘	chìh ㄓ	A stallion; to promote; to determine.
騸	骟	shàn ㄕㄢ	To geld a horse or ass.
騶	驺	tsōu ㄗㄡ	To go; a mythical animal.
11. 驅	驱	ch'ū ㄑㄩ	To expel, to drive.
驊	骅	hūa ㄏㄨㄚ	A chestnut horse.
騾	骡	ló ㄌㄨㄛ	A mule.
驃	骠	p'ìao ㄆㄧㄠ	A charger; fleet, rapid.
驄	骢	ts'ūng ㄘㄨㄥ	A piebald horse.
12. 驕	骄	chīao ㄐㄧㄠ	A high spirited horse; proud, haughty.
驍	骁	hsīao ㄒㄧㄠ	A good horse; brave, strong skillful.
驂	骖	ts'ān ㄘㄢ	The two outside horses of a team of four abreast.
13. 驚	惊	chīng ㄐㄧㄥ	Alarm.
驗	验	yèn ㄧㄢ	To verify, fulfill; to examine.
14. 驛	驿	ì ㄧ	A government post.

驟	骤	tsòu ㄗㄡ	A fast horse; sudden and violent; long continued.
15. 驢	驴	lú ㄌㄨ	An ass, donkey.
16. 驥	骥	chì ㄐㄧ	A thoroughbred.
17. 驤	骧	hsīang ㄒㄧㄤ	To prance, like a spirited horse.
19. 驪	骊	lí ㄌㄧ	A fine horse, black horse.

骨   188

4. 骯	肮	āng ㄤ	Dirty, soiled.
11. 髏	髅	lóu ㄌㄡ	Skull.
13. 體	体	t'ǐ ㄊㄧ	Body, form, substance.
髒	脏	tsāng ㄗㄤ	Dirty; fat, obese.
		tsàng	The viscera, entrails.

髟   190

5. 髮	发	fǎ ㄈㄚ	Hair on human head.
8. 鬆	松	sūng ㄙㄨㄥ	Loose; to loosen.
9. 鬍	胡	hú ㄏㄨ	Beard, mustache.
12. 鬢	鬓	pìn ㄅㄧㄣ	Hair on the temples.

鬥   191

鬥	斗	tòu ㄉㄡ	To fight, wrangle.
16. 鬮	阄	chīu ㄐㄧㄡ	A ticker or lot (of chance); to draw lots.

16. 鬱郁　yù ㄩ　Anxious, sullen, surname.

鬼 194

8. 鬿魖　hăng ㄏㄤˇ　A fairy, sprite.
14. 魘魘　yĕn ㄧㄢˇ　Nightmare.

魚鱼 195

2. 魛魛　tāo ㄊㄠ　The mullet (Family Mugilidae).
4. 魴魴　fáng ㄈㄤˊ　A kind of bream.
　　鮔鮔　hù ㄏㄨˋ　The shad (Family Clupeidae).
　　魯鲁　lŭ ㄌㄨˇ　Stupid; common, vulgar; Shantung.
　　鮍鲅　pān ㄆㄢ　A flounder or sole (Heterosomata).
　　魠鲀　t'ún ㄊㄨㄣˊ　A fresh water porpoise, the "white-flag" dolphin, Lipotes vexillifer.
　　魷鱿　yú ㄩˊ　A kind of squid.
　　魭魭　yŭan ㄩㄢˇ　A sea turtle.
5. 鮓鮓　chă ㄓㄚˇ　Sweets made from fish concentrate; preserved fish.
　　鮒鲋　fù ㄈㄨˋ　A perch-like fish.
　　鮎鲇　nién ㄋㄧㄢˊ　The sheat-fish.
　　魾魾　pá ㄆㄚˊ　A species of threadfin, (Family Polynemidae); 马 魾.
　　鮑鲍　pào ㄆㄠˋ　Salted, pickled or dried fish; abalone.
　　鮃鲆　p'íng ㄆㄧㄥˊ　A flatfish or sole (Family Soleidae or Cynoglossidae).

231

鮐 鲐	t'ái ㄊㄞ	A puffer (Tetraodontidae).
鮀 鉈	t'ó ㄊㄛ	A snakefish (Family Ophichthyidae).
鮣 鮣	yìn ㄧㄣ	The shark-sucker (Family Echeneidae).
鮋 鮋	yíu ㄧㄡ	Rockfish or scorpionfish (Family Scorpaenidae).
6. 鮫 鲛	chīao ㄐㄧㄠ	A shark, or other elasmobranch.
鮰 鮰	húi ㄏㄨㄟ	A kind of catfish (Family Amblycepidae); sometimes a sturgeon (Family Acipenseridae).
鯗 鯗	hsǐang ㄒㄧㄤ	Dried, salted fish.
鮮 鲜	hsīen ㄒㄧㄢ	Fresh (pert. to fruit, flowers, meat, fish); delicious.
鱘 鲟	hsín ㄒㄧㄣ	A sturgeon (Family Acipenseridae).
	hsǔn ㄒㄩㄣ	(Variant).
鮭 鮭	kúei ㄍㄨㄟ	Fresh-water porpoise (Lipotes sinensis); also a species of salmon (Family Salmonidae).
鮦 鮦	t'úng ㄊㄨㄥ	A snakefish (Family Ophichthyidae).
鮠 鮠	wéi ㄨㄟ	A kind of shad (Family Clupeidae).
鮪 鮪	wěi ㄨㄟ	A shovel-nosed sturgeon; a tuna (Family Thunnidae).
7. 鯁 鲠	kěng ㄍㄥ	Fish bones, things that stick in the throat. Unyielding, blunt of speech.
鮌 鮌	kǔei ㄍㄨㄟ	A large fish.
鯉 鲤	lǐ ㄌㄧ	The carp; also a small fish (topminnow) Cyprinodontidae.
鯆 鯆	p'ù ㄆㄨ	A ray or skate; an elasmobranch fish.
8. 鲫 鲫	chì ㄐㄧ	A large carp-like fish (Family Cyprinidae).

鯕 鯕	ch'í ㄧˊ	Dolphin, written 鱀 鰍.
鯖 鯖	ch'īng ㄑㄥ	Mackerel, mullet.
	chīng ㄐㄥ	To fry.
鯨 鯨	ch'ǐng ㄑㄥ	A whale; gigantic.
	chīng ㄐㄥ	(Alternate).
鯡 鯡	féi ㄈㄟ	A herring (Family Clupeidae).
鯤 鯤	k'ūn ㄎㄨㄣ	A sea monster; fry of fish.
鯪 鯪	líng ㄌㄥ	A dace, a small cyprinid fish.
鯢 鯢	ní ㄋㄧ	The giant salamander, <u>Megalo-bactrachus</u> <u>davidianus</u>; the young of fish.
鯰 鯰	nien ㄋㄧㄢ	A sturgeon (Acipenseridae); or sheathfish (Siluridae).
鯛 鯛	tǐao ㄉㄧㄠ	Generic word for perch; more specifically a fish called the
	t'ǐao ㄊㄧㄠ	John Dory (Family Zeidae), or the seabreams (Family Sparidae).
鯫 鯫	tsōu ㄗㄡ	A small fish.
	tsòu ㄘㄡ	A petty person.
鯔 鯔	tzù ㄗ	A mullet (Family Mugilidae).
鯽 鯽	chǐ ㄐ	The bastard carp.
鰍 鰍	ch'īu ㄑㄡ	The loach (Family Cobitidae). See
鰌 鰌	ch'iu ㄑㄡ	The loach (Family Cobitidae).
鰆 鰆	ch'ǔn ㄔㄨㄣ	A fish of the family Cybiidae.
鰉 鰉	húang ㄏㄨㄤ	A sturgeon (Family Acipenseridae).
鯶 鯶	hùn ㄏㄨㄣ	A kind of tench (Family Cyprinidae).
鰐 鰐	ò ㄜ	Crocodile.
鯿 鯿	pǐen ㄅㄧㄢ	A kind of bream.

鰓 鰓	sāi	ㄙㄞ	Gills of a fish.
鰈 鰈	tìeh	ㄊㄧㄝ	A flatfish, sole (Heterosomata).
鰂 鰂	tsé	ㄗㄜ	A cuttlefish, squid.
鰮 鰮	wèn	ㄨㄣ	A round-herring (Family Dussumieri-idae); also a sardine (Clupeidae).

10. 鰭 鰭 ch'í ㄑㄧ — Fin (of a fish).

鰥 鰥 kūan ㄍㄨㄢ — A large fish in the Yellow River; a widower; solitary.

鰣 鰣 shíh ㄕ — An anadromous fish, a shad (Family Clupeidae).

鰨 鰨 t'à ㄊㄚ — A flat fish (Heterosomata); sole, flounder, etc.

鰷 鰷 t'íao ㄊㄧㄠ — A slender fish.

鯧 鯧 ts'āng ㄘㄤ — The pomfret (Family Stromateidae) or man-of war fish (Family Nomeidae).

ch'āng — (Variant).

鰩 鰩 yáo ㄧㄠ — A flying fish (Family Exocoetidae); a skate or ray.

歔 歔 yǘ ㄩ — To fish, seize.

鰲 鰲 aó ㄠ — A sea monster.

11. 鱈 鱈 hsüeh ㄒㄩㄝ — The codfish (Family Gadidae).

hsìeh — (Variant).

鰳 鰳 lè ㄌㄜ — A kind of shad.

鰱 鰱 líen ㄌㄧㄢ — A tarpon (Family Elopidae); a species of bream.

鰻 鰻 mán ㄇㄢ — An eel; also a kind of catfish (Plotosidae or Ariidae). See 鲡

鰵 鰵 mǐn ㄇㄧㄣ — A kind of perch or cod.

鰾 鳔	piao	ㄠㄆㄠ	The air-bladder or swim-bladder of a fish.
鱅 鳙	yúng	ㄩㄥ	A kind of tench.
鱏 鲟	hsún	ㄒㄩㄣ	A sturgeon (Family Acipenseridae) or a trout (Family Salmonidae).
12. 鱟 鲎	hòu	ㄏㄡ	The king crab.
鱖 鳜	kùei	ㄍㄨㄟ	A kind of large-mouth striped perch.
鱗 鳞	lín	ㄌㄧㄣ	Fish scales; scaly, imbricate.
鱓 鳝	shàn	ㄕㄢ	A rice-field eel (Family Symbranchiidae).
13. 鱣 鳣	chán	ㄓㄢ	A sturgeon (Family Acipenseridae).
鱠 鲙	kùai	ㄎㄨㄞ	Minced meat or fish.
鱧 鳢	lǐ	ㄌㄧ	The snakefish, snakehead (Family Ophiocephalidae).
14. 鱨 鲿	ch'áng	ㄔㄤ	A kind of flying fish (Family Exocoetidae) yellow in color.
16. 鱸 鲈	lú	ㄌㄨ	A sea-perch, or seabass (Serranidae); a generic term for bass-like fish.
19. 鱺 鲡	lì	ㄌㄧ	An eel, 鰻 鲡 , (Family Anguillidae).

鳥 鸟 196

2. 鳩 鸠	chīu	ㄐㄧㄡ	A pigeon, dove (Streptopelia sp. or Oenopopelia sp.)
鳳 凤	fèng	ㄈㄥ	Phoenix, symbol of joy.
鳧 凫	fú	ㄈㄨ	Wild ducks; the shelldrake.
3. 梟 枭	hsīao	ㄒㄧㄠ	An owl, said to eat its mother; an unfilial son; brave and unscrupulous; highest throw in dice.

235

鳲 鸤	shīh ㄕ	A turtle dove (<u>Streptopelia</u>) (Family Columbidae).
鳶 鸢	yüan ㄩㄢ	A hawk, kite.
4.鴆 鸩	chèn ㄔㄣ	A predator bird; deadly.
	tān ㄊㄢ	Addicted to.
鴟 鸱	ch'īh ㄔ	An owl.
鴂 鴂	chǖeh ㄐㄩㄝ	A cuckoo (Cuculidae).
鴇 鸨	pǎo ㄅㄠ	A goose-like bird; a bustard; a procuress.
鳾 鸤	shìh ㄕ	A nuthatch (<u>Sitta</u>), of the family Sittidae.
鴉 鸦	yā ㄚ	A crow, rook, raven (Family Corvidae).
5.鴝 鸲	ch'ǘ ㄑㄩ	A species of mynah; a species of ruby-throat (<u>Luscenia</u>, Turdidae).
鴞 鸮	hsīao ㄒㄧㄠ	An owl, said to eat its mother, but leaving the head (Family Strigidae).
鴣 鸪	kū ㄍㄨ	A partridge.
鴒 鸰	líng ㄌㄧㄥ	A wagtail (<u>Motacilla</u> sp.). See 鶺
鴠 鴠	tān ㄊㄢ	A species of nightingale.
鴕 鸵	t'ó ㄊㄛ	The ostrich, emu.
鴨 鸭	yā ㄚ	A duck.
鴦 鸯	yāng ㄤ	Female mandarin duck.
鴥 鴥	yù ㄩ	Eagles flying fast; to swoop.
鴛 鸳	yūan ㄩㄢ	The drake of the mandarin duck.
6.鴂 鸡	chīao ㄐㄧㄠ	A species of crane or heron, with a red crest.
鴴 鸻	hèng ㄏㄥ	A species of pratincole (a wading bird) (Family Glareolidae); or a plover, (Family Charadriidae).

236

鵂鵂	hsīu	ㄒㄧㄡ	An owl, esp. a horned owl; bird of ill omen.
鴿鴿	kō	ㄍㄛ	A dove, pigeon. (Columba sp.);
鴰鴰	kūa	ㄍㄨㄚ	A crane-like wader.
鴷鴷	lìeh	ㄌㄧㄝ	A wryneck (Jynx torquilla) or a woodpecker (Family Picidae).
7. 鵑鵑	chūan	ㄐㄩㄢ	A cuckoo (Family Cuculidae).
鵝鵝	ó	ㄜ	The domestic goose; a swan (Cygnus sp.).
鵓鵓	pó	ㄅㄛ	Wood pigeon.
鵜鵜	t'é	ㄊㄜ	A pelican, 鵜鶘, (Family Pelicanidae).
鵒鵒	yù	ㄩ	The mynah.
8. 鵪鵪	ān	ㄢ	The quail (Coturnix sp.).
鵮鵮	ch'īen	ㄑㄧㄢ	To peck.
鶉鶉	ch'ún	ㄔㄨㄣ	The quail, partridge.
鵻鵻	chúi	ㄓㄨㄟ	Turtledove.
鵲鵲	ch'üeh	ㄑㄩㄝ	The magpie; small corvid birds.
	ch'ìao	ㄑㄧㄠ	(Variant).
鶊鶊	kēng	ㄍㄥ	The oriole.
鵬鵬	p'éng	ㄆㄥ	A large mythical bird, the roc.
鵰鵰	tíao	ㄉㄧㄠ	A large raptorial bird.
鶇鶇	tùng	ㄉㄨㄥ	A species of thrush (Turdus or Monticola) of the Family Turdidae.
鵡鵡	wǔ	ㄨ	A cockatoo (Psittacula sp.) or parrot.
9. 鵩鵩	fú	ㄈㄨ	A small owl.
鶡鶡	hó	ㄏㄛ	A kind of long-tailed pheasant; an emblem of courage; the crossbill (Loxia curvirostra).

鶘鶘	hú	ㄏㄨ	The pelican (Family Pelicanidae).
鶥鶥	mēi	ㄇㄟ	A species of thrush (Moupinia, Babax, or Garrulax) of the family Turdidae.
鶩鶩	mù	ㄇㄨ	Ducks.
	wù	ㄨ	(Variant).
鶚鶚	ò	ㄜˋ	Osprey (Family Pandionidae). See 鶂.
鷀鷀	tz'u	ㄘ	A cormorant (Family Phalacrocoracidae), esp. trained for fishing.
10. 鶺鶺	chī	ㄐ	A wagtail (Motacilla sp.), 鶺鶺 See 鴒.
鶼鶼	chīen	ㄐㄢ	A mythical bird with one eye and one wing.
鶻鶻	kù	ㄍㄨˊ	A falcon.
	hù	ㄏㄨ	(Variant).
鷉鷉	t'ī	ㄊ	A species of grebe (Family Colymbidae).
鶬鶬	ts'āng	ㄘㄤ	A species of crane.
鷀鷀	ts'ú	ㄘㄨˊ	A cormorant (Family Phalacrocoraiidae). See 鷀.
鷂鷂	yaò	ㄧㄠ	A generic term for diurnal raptors: sparrow-hawk (Accipiter sp.), Kite (Milvus sp.), etc.
鶯鶯	yīng	ㄧ	A species of willow-warbler (Cettia, Phylloscopus, Regulus, etc.), (Family Sylviidae).
11. 鷓鷓	chè	ㄓㄜˋ	A partridge.
鷙鷙	chìh	ㄓ	Predatory birds; violent, rapacious.
鶴鶴	hó	ㄏㄜˊ	A crane (Family Gruidae), symbol of longevity.
鷖鷖	ī	一	The widgeon; sometimes the phoenix.

鷚鷚 鷚	lìao	ㄌㄠˋ	A species of pipit (Anthidae) or hedge-sparrow (Prunellidae).
鷗鷗 鸥	ōu	ㄡ	Gulls, terns (Family Laridae).
12. 鷦鷦 鹪	chāo	ㄓㄠ	A species of wren - warbler (<u>Prinia</u>) (Family Sylviidae); or 鷦 鶌 , a true wren (Family Troglodytidae).
	chīao	ㄗㄠ	(Variant).
鷮鷮 鹬	chǐao	ㄐㄠˊ	A long-tailed pheasant.
鷲鷲 鹫	ch	ㄔㄡ	A condor, vulture; a buzzard (Family Accipitridae).
	chìu	ㄐㄡ	Rapacious.
鸒鸒 鸒	hsíao	ㄒㄠ	A kind of magpie (Family Corvidae).
鷴鷴 鹇 鷳鷳 鹇	nsíen	ㄒㄢ ㄒㄢ	The silver pheasant; once a badge of civil officials 5th grade.
鷯鷯 鹩	líao	ㄌㄠˊ	Small, dull-colored passerine birds: wrens, tits, etc.
鷥鷥 鸶	szū	ㄙ	An egret.
鷸鷸 鹬	yǜ	‧ㄩ	A snipe or sandpiper (Scolopacidae); turquoise fing fisher.
13. 鸇鸇 鹯	chān	ㄓㄢ	A sparrow-hawk (<u>Accipiter</u> sp.); swift in flight.
鷺鷺 鹭	lū	ㄌㄨ	A species of the heron family (Ardeidae).
鸊鸊 䴙	p'ì	ㄆㄧˋ	A species of grebe (Family Colymbidae).
16. 鸕鸕 鸬	lú	ㄌㄨˊ	A cormorant used for fishing.
17. 鸚鸚 鹦	yíng	ㄧㄥ	A parrot, cockatoo, etc.
18. 鵠鵠 鹄	kǔ	ㄏㄨ	The snow-goose (<u>Chen hyperborea</u>); a swan; hoary, white-haired.

鸛 鹳	kùan	ㄍㄨㄢ	A species of the crane family (Gruidae), or stork (Ciconiidae).

19. 鸝 鹂 lí ㄌㄧ   An oriole (<u>Oriolus</u> sp.), (Family Oriolidae).

鸞 鸾 lúan ㄌㄨㄢ   A mythical bird; bells whose sound is like the voice of this bird.

21. 鷹 鹰 yīng ㄧㄥ   A hawk, eagle, falcon; a falconer 鷹師.

鹵 卤 197

鹵 卤 lǔ ㄌㄨ   Salt, alkaline soil.

9. 鹹 咸 hsien ㄒㄧㄢ   Salty.

10. 鹺 鹾 ts'ó ㄘㄛ   Brine, salt.

13. 鹼 碱 chǐen ㄐㄧㄢ   Soda, alkali.

鹿 198

10. 麗 丽 lí ㄌㄧ   <u>Hsien</u> and river in Yunnan.

丽丽 lì ㄌㄧ   Beautiful, elegant.

麥 麦 199

4. 麩 麸 fū ㄈㄨ   Bran.

麥 麦 mái ㄇㄞ   Wheat. Used in transliterating.

6. 麴 曲 ch'ǘ ㄑㄩ   Yeast.

9. 麵 面 mìen ㄇㄧㄢ   Flour. (This is not radical 176.)

麻 200

麼 么 ma ㄇㄜ Interrogatory suffix.

黄 201

12. 黌 黉 húng ㄏㄨㄥ A school.

黑 203

5. 點 点 tiěn ㄉㄧㄢ✓ A spot; to spot or dot.

8. 黨 党 tǎng ㄊㄤ Party; group.

11. 黴 霉 méi ㄇㄟ✓ Moldy and black; bacteria; lichens; to rot. Sometimes written 霉 .

14. 黶 黡 yěn ㄧㄢ Black spots on body; moles.

15. 黷 黩 tú ㄊㄨ To blacken, soil; to insult.

黽 黾 205

黽 黾 mǐn ㄇㄧㄣ A toad, tree-frog; to put forth effort.

4. 黿 鼋 yǘan ㄩㄢ A marine turtle.

12. 鼉 鼍 t'ó ㄊㄛ An iguana; monitor lizard (Varanus sp.)

鼓 207

3. 鼕 冬 t'ūng ㄊㄨㄥ The noise of drums.

齊 齐 210

齊 齐 ch'í ㄑㄧˊ — Even, equal, uniform; to arrange.

3. 齋 斋 chāi ㄓㄞ — A fast; to abstain; a studio, shop; pure, refined; a study, library.

齒 齿 211

2. 齔 齓 ch'èn ㄔㄣˋ — Time of loss of milk teeth; i.e. young.

5. 齡 龄 líng ㄌㄧㄥˊ — The front teeth; (human) age.

齠 齠 t'íao ㄊㄧㄠˊ — To shed milk teeth, exuviate.

齟 齟 tsǔ ㄗㄨˇ — Unevenly fitting teeth; irregular; malocclusion.

6. 齦 龈 k'ěn ㄎㄣˇ — To knaw; to girdle a tree.

yén ㄧㄢˊ — The gums.

齜 齜 tzū ㄗ — Projecting teeth.

7. 齬 龉 yǔ ㄩˇ — Irregular teeth.

齪 龊 ch'ō ㄔㄛˊ — To grate one's teeth.

9. 齲 龋 ch'ǘ ㄑㄩˊ — Tooth decay.

齷 龌 wò ㄨㄛˋ — Small, petty, dirty.

龍 龙 212

龍 龙 lúng ㄌㄨㄥˊ — A dragon; a surname.

6. 龕 龛 k'ān ㄎㄢ — A shrine or recess for an idol; to contain.

龔 龚 kūng ㄍㄨㄥ — To give; to present to; decorous.

龜 龟 213

龜 龟 kūei ㄎㄨㄟ　Tortoise.

Appendix A

Table of Simplified Characters Identical to
Previously Existing Standard Forms

Stroke		Standard	Page	Simplified
2	几	Table	16	Very nearly.
				How much?
	了	Finished.	7	Clear; to understand.
	卜	To divine.	15	Carrot, turnip.
3	干	To concern.	28	Dry.
4	丑	2nd Earth's branch	11	To do, manage.
	斗	A Chinese peck.	42	To fight, wrangle.
	无	A negative.	38	Not, lacking; without.
5	只	Only, merely.	16	A sword; to gather.
			17	Classifier for objects of a pair.
	出	To depart.	12	A stanza, couple, classifier for plays (drama).
	台	Your (honorific).	17	Strong wind.
				Terrace, stage.
				Desk, table.
6	合	To join; suitable.	17	A small side door.
	后	Queen, empress.	17	After, behind.
	划	To pole or punt a small boat.	12	To designate, mark off.
	伙	Utensils, goods furniture.	8	Band, a group of companions.

	向	Toward, facing	17	Opposite; to guide.
	回	To return.	19	To revolve.
	冲	To dash against.	12	Facing.
	曲	Bent, twisted.	39	Yeast.
7	谷	Valley.	83	Grain, millet.
	余	I (1st person)	9	The rest, remainder.
	折	To reduce.	34	To fold; pleats.
	系	A system.	59	To tie.
	里	A Chinese mile.	93	Inside, interior.
	别	Other, different.	13	Difficult, awkward.
	隶	To reach (Rad. 171)	105	Attached to.
8	征	To attack	30	To draft (military service).
	制	System, institution.	13	To cut, construct.
	帘	Flag, sign.	28	A curtain.
	板	A board.	40	A shop owner.
	表	To express; a table, list.	74	A watch or clock; to manifest.
	舍	Residence.	9	To give up, relinquish.
	松	Pine.	40	Loose, to loosen.
9	姜	A surname.	24	Ginger.
	秋	Autumn.	56	A swing, crupper.
	面	Face, surface.	106	Flour.
	郁	Elegant.	92	Anxious, sullen.
10	症	Disease, ailment.	52	Obstruction of the bowels.

245

家	Family; residence.	25	Tools, furniture.
致	To cause, transmit.	69	To mend; delicate.
范	A surname.	70	Normal, mean.
造	To hasten, quickly.	91	To reach; to suit; just now.
11 旋	To revolve.	38	A pewter flask for spirits.
淀	Shallow water.	47	Sediment, dregs.
12 象	Elephant.	83	Appearance, resemblance.
須	Must, necessarily.	107	Beard, mustache.
漓	Water dripping.	30	To withstand, resist.
御	Imperial.	47	Name of a river.
13 辟	To punish.	90	To cleave, split open.
14 霉	Damp, moldy.	106	Moldy and black.
蒙	To hoodwink	83	Mist, drizzle; sun below, horizon.

Appendix B
Characters with Obscure Radicals

Listed under total number of strokes (Roman numerals). Numbers to the right are radical and residual strokes.

II

了	6	1
讠	149	

III

与	1	2
义	4	2
彡	4	2
亏	7	1
个	9	1
习	15	2
万	19	1
卫	26	1
么	28	1
于	51	
才	64	
纟	120	
门	169	
飞	183	
乞	184	
马	187	

IV

书	2	3
丰	2	3
韦	2	3
收	4	3
专	7	2
开	7	2
习	15	2
风	16	2
为	19	2
云	28	2
巾	50	1
丑	58	
无	71	
见	147	
贝	154	
车	159	
风	186	
乌	1	3

V

业	1	4

IV (continued)

归	4	4
专	7	2
兰	7	3
万	19	2
发	29	3
只	30	2
号	30	2
冬	36	2
头	37	2
击	46	2
帅	50	2
戋	62	1
旧	72	1
电	72	1
术	75	1
东	75	2
金	167	
长	168	
龙	212	

VI

長	1	5
亚	7	4
产	8	4
赤	8	4
伙	9	4
尧	10	4
关	37	3
师	50	3
页	181	
齐	210	

VII

克	10	5
肃	13	5
严	27 ·	5
县	28	5
枣	75	3
隶	181	
卤	197	

VIII

丽	13	6

凭	16	6
衰	32	5

IX

临	4	8
亲	8	7
举	12	7
尝	28	7
嗓	30	6
复	35	6
娄	38	6
姜	38	6
昼	72	5

X

离	8	8
党	30	7

XI

槛	43	9
毙	78	6
龚	212	6

Simplified Radicals

Simplified	Standard	Number	Pronunciation	Page
纟	糸	120	mǐ	59
见	見	147	chìen	75
讠	言	149	yén	76
贝	貝	154	pẹi	84
车	車	159	ch'ē	88
钅	金	167	chīn	93
长	長	168	ch'áng	102
门	門	169	mén	102
韦	韋	178	wéi	106
页	頁	181	yèh	106
风	風	182	fēng	109
飞	飛	183	fēi	109
饣	食	184	shíh	109
马	馬	187	mǎ	111
鱼	魚	195	yǜ	114
鸟	鳥	196	nǐao	118
卤	鹵	197	lǔ	123
麦	麥	199	mai	123
黾	黽	205	mǐn	123
齐	齊	210	ch'í	124
齿	齒	211	ch'ǐh	124
龙	龍	212	lúng	124
龟	龜	213	kuēi	125

Appendix D

Table of Radicals,

Arranged According to Number of Strokes

Radical		Page	Radical		Page
One stroke			15	⺀	11
1	一	6	16	几	12
2	丨	6	17	凵	12
3	丶	6	18	刀	12
4	丿	6	18	刂	12
5	乙	7	19	力	13
6	亅	7	20	勹	14
Two strokes			21	ヒ	--
7	二	7	21	七	--
8	亠	7	22	匚	14
9	人	8	23	匸	14
9	亻	8	24	十	15
9	𠆢	8	24	十	15
10	儿	10	24	艹	15
11	入		25	卜	15
11	入		26	卩	15
12	八	10	26	㔾	15
13	冂	11	27	厂	15
14	冖	11	28	厶	16

251

253

References

Anon. 1964. Jianhuazi zonbiao jianzi (简化字总表检字). Publ. Wenzi Gaige Chubanshe (文字改革出版社). Peking. 64 pp.

Anon. 1965. Jianhuazi zongbiao (简化字总表. 2nd ed. Zhongguo Wenzi Gaige Weiyuan. Huibian (中国文字改革委员会编). Peking. 32 pp.

Chennault, Anna. 1962. Dictionary of new simplified Chinese characters. Georgetown University. Washington, D. C. 88 pp.

Hsia, Tao-tai. 1956. China's language reforms. Mirror Series A. The Institute of Far Eastern Languages. Yale University. New Haven, Connecticut. 200 pp.

Yi, Hsi-wu (Ed.). 1955. Jianti Ziyuan (簡體字原、). Zhonghua Shuju Chuban 中華書局出版). Peking. 54 pp.